THE RADICAL KING

THE RADICAL KING

MARTIN LUTHER KING, JR.
Edited and introduced by CORNEL WEST

Beacon Press, Boston

Beacon Press
Boston, Massachusetts
www.beacon.org

Beacon Press books are published under the auspices of the Unitarian Universalist Association of Congregations. Beacon Press gratefully acknowledges the Unitarian Universalist Veatch Program at Shelter Rock for its generous support of the King Legacy series.

A portion of Cornel West's introduction "The Radical King We Don't Know" previously appeared in *We Have Not Been Moved: Resisting Racism and Militarism in 21st Century America*, Elizabeth Betita Martínez, Mandy Carter, and Matt Meyer, eds. (Oakland, CA: PM Press, 2012); www.pmpress.org. Reprinted here with permission.

Photo credits: Pages 2 and 220, courtesy Bettmann/Corbis. Page 72, Johnson Publishing Company, LLC; all rights reserved. Page 124, Charles Moore, courtesy Black Star Publishing Co., Inc.

"The King Legacy" is a federally registered trademark of the Unitarian Universalist Association Corporation.

Obvious typographical errors in transcriptions of spoken-word materials were corrected to aid in ease of reading. All other errors or stylistic inconsistencies have been retained in their original form.

Printed in the United States of America

18 17 16 15   8 7 6 5 4 3

This book is printed on acid-free paper that meets the uncoated paper ANSI/NISO specifications for permanence as revised in 1992.

Text design by Wilsted & Taylor Publishing Services

Library of Congress Cataloging-in-Publication data can be found on page 302.

"As I have moved to break the betrayal of my own silences and to speak from the burnings of my own heart . . . many persons have questioned me about the wisdom of my path. At the heart of their concerns this query has often loomed large and loud: Why are *you* speaking about the war, Dr. King? Why are *you* joining the voices of dissent? Peace and civil rights don't mix, they say. Aren't you hurting the cause of your people, they ask? And when I hear them, though I often understand the sources of their concern, I am nevertheless greatly saddened, for such questions mean that the inquirers have not really known me, my commitment or my calling."

—Dr. Martin Luther King, Jr., remarks delivered at Riverside Church, New York, April 4, 1967

CONTENTS

THE RADICAL KING WE DON'T KNOW

The FBI transcript of a June 27, 1964, phone conversation reveals Malcolm X receiving a message from Martin Luther King, Jr. This message supported the idea of getting the human rights declaration of the United Nations to expose the unfair, vicious treatment of black people in America. Malcolm X replied that he was eager to meet Martin Luther King, Jr.—as soon as the next afternoon. If they had met that day and worked together, the radical King would be well known.

In a speech to staff in 1966, King explained: "There must be a better distribution of wealth and maybe America must move toward a democratic socialism."[1] If he had lived and pursued this project, the radical King would be well known.

On April 4, 1968, in Memphis—the last day of his life—Martin Luther King, Jr., phoned Ebenezer Baptist Church in Atlanta with the title of his Sunday sermon: "Why America May Go to Hell." If he had preached this sermon, the radical King would be well known.

Yet in Dr. King's own time, he would say repeatedly, "I am nevertheless greatly saddened . . . that the inquirers have not really known me, my commitment, or my calling."[2] It is no accident that just prior to King's death, 72 percent of whites and 55 percent of blacks disapproved of his opposition to the Vietnam War and his efforts to eradicate poverty in America.[3] When much of the black leadership attacked or shunned him, King replied, "What you're saying may get you a foundation grant but it won't get you into the kingdom of truth."[4]

In short, Martin Luther King, Jr., refused to sell his soul for a mess of pottage. He refused to silence his voice in his quest for unarmed truth and unconditional love. For King, the condition of truth was to allow suffering to speak; for him, justice was what love looks like in public. In King's eyes, too many black leaders sacrificed the truth for access to power or reduced sacrificial love and service to selfish expediency and personal gain. This spiritual blackout among black leaders resulted in their use and abuse by the white political and economic establishment that constituted a kind of "conspiracy against the poor." This spiritual blackout—this lack of integrity and courage—primarily revealed a deep fear, failure of nerve, and spinelessness on behalf of black leaders. They too often were sycophants, cheerleaders, or bootlickers for big monied interests, even as the boots were crushing poor and working people. In stark contrast to this cowardice, King stated to his staff, "I'd rather be dead than afraid."[5]

Although much of America did not know the radical King—and too few know today—the FBI and US government did. They called him "the most dangerous man in America." They knew Reverend King was a revolutionary Christian, sincere in his commitment and serious in his calling. They knew he was a product of a black prophetic tradition, full of fire in his bones, love in his heart, light in his mind, and courage in his soul. Martin Luther King, Jr., was the major threat to the US government and the American establishment because he dared to organize and mobilize black rage over past and present crimes against humanity targeting black folk and other oppressed people.

Any such black awakening can either yield hatred and revenge or love and justice. This is why the prophetic words of Rabbi Abraham Joshua Heschel still haunt us: "The whole future of America will depend upon the impact and influence of Dr. King."[6] The fundamental question is: Does America have the capacity to hear and heed the radical King or must America sanitize King in order to evade and avoid his challenge?

King indeed had a dream. But it was not the American dream. King's dream was rooted in the American Dream—it was what the quest for life, liberty, and the pursuit of happiness looked like for people enslaved and Jim Crowed, terrorized, traumatized, and stigmatized by American laws and American citizens. The litmus test for realizing King's dream was neither a black face in the White House nor a black presence on Wall Street. Rather, the fulfillment of his dream was for all poor and working people to live lives of decency and dignity.

King's dream of a more free and democratic America and world had morphed into, in his words, "a nightmare," owing to the persistence of "racism, poverty, militarism, and materialism." He called America a "sick society." At one point, King cried out in despair, "I have found out that all that I have been doing in trying to correct this system in America has been in vain. I am trying to get at the roots of it to see just what ought to be done. The whole thing will have to be done away with."[7] He said to his dear brother Harry Belafonte days before his, King's, death, "Are we integrating into a burning house?"[8] He was weary of pervasive economic injustice, cultural decay, and political paralysis. He was not an American Gibbon chronicling the decline and fall of the American empire but a courageous and visionary Christian blues man, fighting with style and love in the face of the four catastrophes he identified, which are still with us today.

Militarism is an imperial catastrophe that has produced a military-industrial complex and national security state and warped the country's priorities and stature (as with the immoral drones dropping bombs on innocent civilians). Materialism is a spiritual catastrophe, promoted by a corporate-media multiplex and a culture industry that has hardened the hearts of hard-core consumers and coarsened the consciences of would-be citizens. Clever gimmicks of mass distraction yield a cheap soulcraft of addicted and self-medicated narcissists.

Racism is a moral catastrophe, most graphically seen in the prison-industrial complex and targeted police surveillance in black and brown ghettos rendered invisible in public discourse. Arbitrary uses of the law in the name of the "war" on drugs have produced, in legal scholar Michelle Alexander's well-known phrase, a new Jim Crow of mass incarceration. And poverty is an economic catastrophe, inseparable from the power of greedy oligarchs and avaricious plutocrats indifferent to the misery of poor children, elderly and disabled citizens, and working people.

The radical King was a warrior for peace on the domestic and global battlefields. He was a staunch anti-colonial and anti-imperial thinker and fighter. His revolutionary commitment to nonviolent resistance in America and abroad tried to put a brake on the escalating militarism running amok across the globe. As a decade-long victim of the vicious and vindictive FBI, King was a radical libertarian as well as having closeted democratic socialist leanings. His commitment to the precious rights and liberties for all was profound.

For King, dissent did not mean disloyalty—in fact, dissent was a high form of patriotism. When he said that the US government was "the greatest purveyor of violence in the world today,"[9] he was not trashing America. He was telling the painful truth about a country he loved. King was never anti-American; he was always anti-injustice in America and anywhere else. Love of truth and love of country could go hand-in-hand. Needless to say, under the policies of the National Security Agency and Obama administration, King could have been subject to detention without trial and assassination by executive decree (owing to his links to "terrorists" of his day, such as Nelson Mandela).

The radical King was a spiritual giant who tried to shatter the callousness and indifference of his fellow citizens. Following his dear friend and comrade Rabbi Abraham Joshua Heschel, King believed that indifference to evil is more evil than evil itself. And materialism, with its attendants hedonism and egotism, produces sleepwalkers bereft of compassion and zombies deficient in love. This spiritual crisis is not reducible to politics or economics. It is rooted in the relative decline of integrity, honesty, decency, and virtue, due in large part to the role of big money in American life. This coldhearted obsession with manipulation and domination drives our ecological catastrophe-in-the-making and our possible military Armageddon.

The radical King was a moral titan with profound allegiance to his roots—the black prophetic tradition and black freedom struggle. His genuine commitment to the dignity of whites, as well as to peoples of all hues, never overshadowed or downplayed his deep commitment to black people. For King, the struggle against the legacy of white supremacy was never a strategic move or tactical afterthought; rather, it was a profound existential and moral matter of great urgency. King knew that white supremacy, in various forms, was a global phenomenon. It remains shot through our hearts and minds, institutions and structures, smart phones and unwise politicians. The modes of racist domination—from barbaric slavery to bestial Jim Crow, Sr., to cruel Jim Crow, Jr.—are never reducible to individual prejudice or personal bias. Empire, white supremacy, capitalism, patriarchy, and homophobia are linked in complex ways, and our struggles against them require moral consistency and systemic analyses.

The radical King was a democratic socialist who sided with poor and working people in the class struggle taking place in capitalist societies. This class struggle may be visible or invisible, manifest or latent. But it rages on in a fight over resources, power, and space. In the past thirty years we have witnessed a top-down, one-sided class war against poor and working people in the name of a morally bankrupt policy of deregulating markets, lowering taxes, and cutting spending for those who are already socially neglected and economically abandoned. America's two main political parties, each beholden to big money, offer merely alternative versions of oligarchic rule. The radical King was neither Marxist nor communist, but he did understand the role of class analysis in his focus on poor and working people. He always had a healthy suspicion of all politicians—of any color—owing to his critique of legalized bribery and normalized corruption in money-saturated American politics. He noted, "I have come to think of my role as one which operates outside the realm of partisan politics. . . . I feel I should serve as a conscience of all the parties and all of the people."[10] This critical attitude toward politicians was deepened when he worked to register thousands of people to elect the first black mayor in modern times, Carl Stokes, in Cleveland in 1967, yet was uninvited to join the stage for the victory celebration.

Needless to say, the rich legacy of the radical King in the age of Obama celebrates the symbolic breakthrough of a black president and keeps track of the right-wing backlash against him. Yet the bailout for banks, record profits for Wall Street, and giant budget cuts on the backs of the vulnerable rather than mortgage relief for homeowners, jobs with a living wage, and investment in education, infrastructure, and housing reveal the plutocratic domination of the Obama administration. The dream of the radical King for the first black president surely was not a Wall Street presidency, drone presidency, and surveillance presidency with a vanishing black middle class, devastated black working class, and desperate black poor people clinging to fleeting symbols and empty rhetoric.

I shall never forget the first question I asked Barack Obama when he called to solicit my support: "What is the relation of your presidential policies to the legacy of Martin Luther King, Jr.?" He replied —in hours of dialogue—that the relation was strong. And I agreed to lend critical support. After sixty-five events, from Iowa to Ohio, in 2008, I knew that most of his advisers were not part of the King legacy. And Obama's betrayal of what the radical King stands for became undeniable.

Sadly, the damage done by Obama apologists—often for money, access, and status—is immeasurable and nearly unforgivable. For the first time in American history, black citizens are the most pro-war in American society. Black churches are among the weakest in prison ministry—even given the disproportionately high percentage of black prisoners. Black schools are under attack from profiteering enterprises. Forty percent of black children live in poverty.[11] Aside from a few exceptions, black musicians are more and more marginal in popular culture. Black deaths, especially among young people, are out of control. In other words, the Obama apologists who hide and conceal Wall Street crimes, imperial crimes, new Jim Crow crimes, and surveillance lies in order to protect the first black president have much to account for. And a health-care bill—a bonanza for big insurance and drug companies alongside access to new consumers—falls far short of the mark.

The response of the radical King to our catastrophic moment can be put in one word: revolution—a revolution in our priorities, a reevaluation of our values, a reinvigoration of our public life, and a fundamental transformation of our way of thinking and living that promotes a transfer of power from oligarchs and plutocrats to everyday people and ordinary citizens.

The radical King was first and foremost a revolutionary Christian —a black Baptist minister and pastor whose intellectual genius and rhetorical power was deployed in the name of the Gospel of Jesus Christ. King understood this good news to be primarily radical love in freedom and radical freedom in love, a fallible enactment of the Beloved Community or finite embodiment of the Kingdom of God.

King's radical love can be heard in John Coltrane's "A Love Supreme" or the Isley Brothers' "Caravan of Love." This radical love of an intensely hated people is both liberating and contagious, just as this radical freedom of a thoroughly unfree people is both emancipating and infectious.

The radical King was the most significant and effective organic intellectual in the latter half of the twentieth century whose fundamental motif was radical love. King's radical love was Christocentric in content and black in character. Like the Christocentric language of the Black Church that produced the radical King—Jesus as the Bright and Morning Star against the backdrop of the pitch darkness of the night, as water in dry places, a companion in loneliness, a doctor to the sick, a rock in a wearied land—his Christocentrism exemplifies the intimate and dependent relationship between God and person and between God and a world-forsaken people. The black character of King's radical love was its roots in the indescribable terror and inimitable trauma of being black in white supremacist America, during slavery, Jim Crow, Sr., or Jim Crow, Jr.

King's work and witness is a kind of prophetic pneumatology in motion—a kinetic orality, passionate physicality, and combative spirituality that wedded mind to movement, soul to sustenance, and body to empowerment. Like his most worthy theological precursor, Howard Thurman, King pulled from the rich insights of Western thinkers, yet he elevated the lived experiences of wounded, scarred, and bruised bodies of enslaved and Jim-Crowed black peoples to enact radical love.

King's radical love put a premium on artistic performance and existential praxis. His sermons were performances that authorized an alternative reality to the way the world is. His living radiated a radical tenderness, subversive sweetness, and militant gentleness. He found great joy in serving others.

Like his great contemporary Dorothy Day, the Catholic saint who looked at the world through the lens of her heart, Dr. King understood radical love as a form of death—a relentless self-examination in which a fearful, hateful, egoistic self dies daily to be reborn into a courageous, loving, and sacrificial self. For both Day and King, this radical love flows from an imitation of Christ, a response to an invitation of self-surrender in order to emerge fully equipped to fight for justice in a cold and cruel world of domination and exploitation. The scandal of the Cross is precisely the unstoppable and unsuffocatable love that keeps moving in a blood-soaked history, even in our catastrophic times. There is no radical King without his commitment to radical love.

This book unearths a radical King that we can no longer sanitize. His revolutionary witness—embodied in anti-imperial, anti-colonial, anti-racist, and democratic socialist sentiments—was grounded in his courage to think, his courage to love, and his courage to die. Could it be that we know so little of the radical King because such courage defies our market-driven world?

PART ONE
RADICAL LOVE

Dr. Martin Luther King, Jr., pulls up a cross that was burned on the front lawn of his home on April 26, 1960. To his left stands his son Martin Luther King III, aged two.

RADICAL LOVE sits at the center of the radical King. All the individual success, professional achievement, sharp analysis, and strategic calculation are but sounding brass and tinkling symbol without radical love. For King, radical love emerges from catastrophe, perseveres through crisis, and yields an indomitable spiritual center—a radical humility and radical integrity.

In this collection's first essay, "The Violence of Desperate Men," we see the source of King's radical love: his spiritual mountaintop experience in his kitchen in Montgomery, Alabama, just as he assumes leadership of the Montgomery Improvement Association. Following the pioneering work of David Garrow, James Cone, and Vincent Harding, I understand the radical King as a spiritual warrior equipped with Christian armor willing to love, serve, and die for his people. Radical love requires the cowardly self to die in order for the courageous self to live—daily. This death-in-life conversion sustains the self in the face of terror and trauma. King's kitchen experience is a kind of 9/11 moment—he and his precious family are unsafe, unprotected, subject to random violence, and hated for who he and they are. These 9/11 moments are integral to being black in America. King's loving parents, Martin and Alberta King, and supportive church and school, Ebenezer Baptist Church and Morehouse College, laid his strong foundations. But the love he received from them was radicalized—dipped in the dark pit of catastrophe and tested in the fierce fire of crisis—in Montgomery. His spiritual call for help came in the form of God's radical love for him.

The major intellectual and practical challenge to King's radical love came from the critiques of religion put forward by Karl Marx and Friedrich Nietzsche. King spent much time wrestling with these figures in his studies and in his life. Marx's claim was that religion was the opiate of the people—the instrument of those who rule in that it disinvests people of their own powers by investing God with all power and thereby rendering them submissive and deferential toward the status quo.

Nietzsche's view of Christian love as a form of resentment and revenge of the powerless and impotent toward the powerful and the strong led King briefly to "despair of the power of love in solving social problems."[1] Prophetic religion could empower people to fight against oppression and struggle for freedom—so Marx was only partly right. But could the love ethic of Jesus Christ be applied to groups, nations, or classes as well as to individuals? The Gandhian method of love-motivated (agapic) nonviolent resistance provided the radical King with a response to Marx and an answer to Nietzsche. Radical love was a moral and practical method—a way of life and a way of struggle in which oppressed people could fight for freedom without inflicting violence on the oppressor, humiliating the opponent, and hence, possibly transforming the moral disposition of one's adversary.

King's radical love—following Gandhi's great breakthrough—is often celebrated for his love of white oppressors. This misses the point. King's radical love of an often unloved people—black people—is the basis of his much-heralded love of white people. His radical love is inseparable from the radical freedom he wants for an unfree people—and for all others. A fuller discussion of King's radical love requires a comparative analysis of Malcolm X's radical love or Ella Baker's radical love—just as Gandhi's radical love should be contrasted with Ambedkar's radical love.

King's two sermons "Palm Sunday Sermon on Mohandas K. Gandhi" and "Loving Your Enemies," as well as his autobiographical "Pilgrimage to Nonviolence," lay bare his profound and poignant hammering out the idea and practice of radical love.

King was deeply concerned with bequeathing the rich tradition of radical love to the younger generation. He understood the deep insights of the Black Nationalist heritage, represented by giants such as Marcus Garvey and Malcolm X, who highlighted black self-respect, black self-defense, and black self-determination. He also knew that his Southern Christian style did not always resonate with Northern urban youth. Yet King always extended his radical love to them—in a sincere and authentic way. In his speech to high school students in Philadelphia, we see another side of King: a love warrior focused on fostering black self-love in youth. Based on my own teaching, including work in high schools and prisons, I decided to end part 1 with King's more personal and intimate directive to black youth and their future.

ONE

THE VIOLENCE OF DESPERATE MEN

The following is a chapter from Dr. King's memoir of the Montgomery bus boycott, *Stride Toward Freedom* (1958), which King described as "the chronicle of 50,000 Negroes who took to heart the principles of nonviolence, who learned to fight for their rights with the weapon of love, and who, in the process, acquired a new estimate of their own human worth."

After the "get-tough" policy failed to stop the movement the diehards became desperate, and we waited to see what their next move would be. Almost immediately after the protest started we had begun to receive threatening telephone calls and letters. Sporadic in the beginning, they increased as time went on. By the middle of January, they had risen to thirty and forty a day.

Postcards, often signed "KKK," said simply "get out of town or else." Many misspelled and crudely written letters presented religious half-truths to prove that "God do not intend the White People and the Negro to go to gather if he did we would be the same." Others enclosed mimeographed and printed materials combining anti-Semitic and anti-Negro sentiments. One of these contained a handwritten postscript: "You niggers are getting your self in a bad place. The Bible is strong for segregation as of the jews [*sic*] concerning other races. It is even for segregation between the 12 tribes of Israel. We need and will have a Hitler to get our country straightened out." Many of the letters were unprintable catalogues of blasphemy and obscenity.

Meanwhile the telephone rang all day and most of the night. Often Coretta was alone in the house when the calls came, but the insulting voices did not spare her. Many times the person on the other end simply waited until we answered and then hung up.

A large percentage of the calls had sexual themes. One woman, whose voice I soon came to recognize, telephoned day after day to hurl her sexual accusations at the Negro. Whenever I tried to answer, as I frequently did in an effort to explain our case calmly, the caller would cut me off. Occasionally, we would leave the telephone off the hook, but we could not do this for long because we never knew when an important call would come in.

When these incidents started, I took them in stride, feeling that they were the work of a few hotheads who would soon be discouraged when they discovered that we would not fight back. But as the weeks passed, I began to see that many of the threats were in earnest. Soon I felt myself faltering and growing in fear. One day, a white friend told me that he had heard from reliable sources that plans were being made to take my life. For the first time I realized that something could happen to me.

One night at a mass meeting, I found myself saying: "If one day you find me sprawled out dead, I do not want you to retaliate with a single act of violence. I urge you to continue protesting with the same dignity and discipline you have shown so far." A strange silence came over the audience.

Afterward, to the anxious group that gathered around, I tried to make light of the incident by saying that my words had not grown from any specific cause, but were just a general statement of principle that should guide our actions in the event of any fatality. But Ralph Abernathy was not satisfied. As he drove me home that night, he said:

"Something is wrong. You are disturbed about something."

I tried to evade the issue by repeating what I had just told the group at the church. But he persisted.

"Martin," he said, "you were not talking about some general principle. You had something specific in mind."

Unable to evade any longer, I admitted the truth. For the first time I told him about the threats that were harassing my family. I told him about the conversation with my white friend. I told him about the fears that were creeping up on my soul. Ralph tried to reassure me, but I was still afraid.

The threats continued. Almost every day someone warned me that he had overheard white men making plans to get rid of me. Almost every night I went to bed faced with the uncertainty of the next moment. In the morning I would look at Coretta and "Yoki" and say to myself: "They can be taken away from me at any moment; I can be taken away from them at any moment." For once I did not even share my thoughts with Coretta.

One night toward the end of January I settled into bed late, after a strenuous day. Coretta had already fallen asleep and just as I was about to doze off the telephone rang. An angry voice said, "Listen, nigger, we've taken all we want from you; before next week you'll be sorry you ever came to Montgomery." I hung up, but I couldn't sleep. It seemed that all of my fears had come down on me at once. I had reached the saturation point.

I got out of bed and began to walk the floor. Finally I went to the kitchen and heated a pot of coffee. I was ready to give up. With my cup of coffee sitting untouched before me I tried to think of a way to move out of the picture without appearing a coward. In this state of exhaustion, when my courage had all but gone, I decided to take my problem to God. With my head in my hands, I bowed over the kitchen table and prayed aloud. The words I spoke to God that midnight are still vivid in my memory. "I am here taking a stand for what I believe is right. But now I am afraid. The people are looking to me for leadership, and if I stand before them without strength and courage, they too will falter. I am at the end of my powers. I have nothing left. I've come to the point where I can't face it alone."

At that moment I experienced the presence of the Divine as I had never experienced Him before. It seemed as though I could hear the quiet assurance of an inner voice saying: "Stand up for righteousness, stand up for truth; and God will be at your side forever." Almost at once my fears began to go. My uncertainty disappeared. I was ready to face anything.

Three nights later, on January 30, I left home a little before seven to attend our Monday evening mass meeting at the First Baptist Church. A member of my congregation, Mrs. Mary Lucy Williams, had come to the parsonage to keep my wife company in my absence. After putting the baby to bed, Coretta and Mrs. Williams went to the living room to look at television. About nine-thirty they heard a noise in front that sounded as though someone had thrown a brick. In a matter of seconds an explosion rocked the house. A bomb had gone off on the porch.

The sound was heard many blocks away, and word of the bombing reached the mass meeting almost instantly. Toward the close of the meeting, as I stood on the platform helping to take the collection, I noticed an usher rushing to give Ralph Abernathy a message. Abernathy turned and ran downstairs, soon to reappear with a worried look on his face. Several others rushed in and out of the church. People looked at me and then away; one or two seemed about to approach me and then changed their minds. An usher called me to the side of the platform, presumably to give me a message, but before I could get there S. S. Seay had sent him away. By now I was convinced that whatever had happened affected me. I called Ralph Abernathy, S. S. Seay, and E. N. French and asked them to tell me what was wrong. Ralph looked at Seay and French and then turned to me and said hesitantly:

"Your house has been bombed."

I asked if my wife and baby were all right.

They said, "We are checking on that now."

Strangely enough, I accepted the word of the bombing calmly. My religious experience a few nights before had given me the strength to face it. I interrupted the collection and asked all present to give me their undivided attention. After telling them why I had to leave, I urged each person to go straight home after the meeting and adhere strictly to our philosophy of nonviolence. I admonished them not to become panicky and lose their heads. "Let us keep moving," I urged them, "with the faith that what we are doing is right, and with the even greater faith that God is with us in the struggle."

I was immediately driven home. As we neared the scene I noticed hundreds of people with angry faces in front of the house. The policemen were trying, in their usual rough manner, to clear the streets, but they were ignored by the crowd. One Negro was saying to a policeman, who was attempting to push him aside: "I ain't gonna move nowhere. That's the trouble now; you white folks is always pushin' us around. Now you got your .38 and I got mine; so let's battle it out." As I walked toward the front porch I realized that many people were armed. Nonviolent resistance was on the verge of being transformed into violence.

I rushed into the house to see if Coretta and "Yoki" were safe. When I walked into the bedroom and saw my wife and daughter uninjured, I drew my first full breath in many minutes. I learned that fortunately when Coretta and Mrs. Williams had heard the sound of something falling on the front porch, they had jumped up and run to the back of the house. If instead they had gone to the porch to investigate, the outcome might have been fatal. Coretta was neither bitter nor panicky. She had accepted the whole thing with unbelievable composure. As I noticed her calmness I became even more calm myself.

Mayor Gayle, Commissioner Sellers, and several white reporters had reached the house before I did and were standing in the dining room. After reassuring myself about my family's safety, I went to speak to them. Both Gayle and Sellers expressed their regret that "this unfortunate incident has taken place in our city." One of the trustees of my church, who is employed in the public school system of Montgomery, was standing beside me when the mayor and the commissioner spoke. Although in a vulnerable position, he turned to the mayor and said: "You may express your regrets, but you must face the fact that your public statements created the atmosphere for this bombing. This is the end result of your 'get-tough' policy." Neither Mayor Gayle nor Commissioner Sellers could reply.

By this time the crowd outside was getting out of hand. The policemen had failed to disperse them, and throngs of additional people were arriving every minute. The white reporters inside the house wanted to leave to get their stories on the wires, but they were afraid to face the angry crowd. The mayor and police commissioner, though they might not have admitted it, were very pale.

In this atmosphere I walked out to the porch and asked the crowd to come to order. In less than a moment there was complete silence. Quietly I told them that I was all right and that my wife and baby were all right. "Now let's not become panicky," I continued. "If you have weapons, take them home; if you do not have them, please do not seek to get them. We cannot solve this problem through retaliatory violence. We must meet violence with nonviolence. Remember the words of Jesus: 'He who lives by the sword will perish by the sword.'" I then urged them to leave peacefully. "We must love our white brothers," I said, "no matter what they do to us. We must make them know that we love them. Jesus still cries out in words that echo across the centuries: 'Love your enemies; bless them that curse you; pray for them that despitefully use you.' This is what we must live by. We must meet hate with love. Remember," I ended, "if I am stopped, this movement will not stop, because God is with the movement. Go home with this glowing faith and this radiant assurance."

As I finished speaking there were shouts of "Amen" and "God bless you." I could hear voices saying: "We are with you all the way, Reverend." I looked out over that vast throng of people and noticed tears on many faces.

After I finished, the police commissioner began to address the crowd. Immediately there were boos. Police officers tried to get the attention of the Negroes by saying, "Be quiet—the commissioner is speaking." To this the crowd responded with even louder boos. I came back to the edge of the porch and raised my hand for silence. "Remember what I just said. Let us hear the commissioner." In the ensuing lull, the commissioner spoke and offered a reward to the person or persons who could report the offenders. Then the crowd began to disperse.

Things remained tense the whole of that night. The Negroes had had enough. They were ready to meet violence with violence. One policeman later told me that if a Negro had fallen over a brick that night a race riot would probably have broken out because the Negro would have been convinced that a white person had pushed him. This could well have been the darkest night in Montgomery's history. But something happened to avert it: the spirit of God was in our hearts; and a night that seemed destined to end in unleashed chaos came to a close in a majestic group demonstration of nonviolence.

After our many friends left the house late that evening, Coretta, "Yoki," and I were driven to the home of one of our church members to spend the night. I could not get to sleep. While I lay in that quiet front bedroom, with a distant street lamp throwing a reassuring glow through the curtained window, I began to think of the viciousness of people who would bomb my home. I could feel the anger rising when I realized that my wife and baby could have been killed. I thought about the city commissioners and all the statements that they had made about me and the Negro generally. I was once more on the verge of corroding hatred. And once more I caught myself and said: "You must not allow yourself to become bitter."

I tried to put myself in the place of the three commissioners. I said to myself these men are not bad men. They are misguided. They have fine reputations in the community. In their dealings with white people they are respectable and gentlemanly. They probably think they are right in their methods of dealing with Negroes. They say the things they say about us and treat us as they do because they have been taught these things. From the cradle to the grave, it is instilled in them that the Negro is inferior. Their parents probably taught them that; the schools they attended taught them that; the books they read, even their churches and ministers, often taught them that; and above all the very concept of segregation teaches them that. The whole cultural tradition under which they have grown—a tradition blighted with more than 250 years of slavery and more than 90 years of segregation—teaches them that Negroes do not deserve certain things. So these men are merely the children of their culture. When they seek to preserve segregation they are seeking to preserve only what their local folkways have taught them was right.

Midnight had long since passed. Coretta and the baby were sound asleep. It was time for me too to get some rest. At about two-thirty I turned over in bed and fell into a dazed slumber. But the night was not yet over. Some time later Coretta and I were awakened by a slow, steady knocking at the front door. We looked at each other wordlessly in the dim light, and listened as the knocking began again. Through the window we could see the dark outline of a figure on the front porch. Our hosts were sound asleep in the back of the house, and we lay in the front, frozen into inaction. Eventually the sounds stopped and we saw a shadowy figure move across the porch and start down the steps to the street. I pulled myself out of bed, peered through the curtains, and recognized the stocky, reassuring back of Coretta's father.

Obie Scott had heard the news of the bombing over the radio in Marion, and had driven to Montgomery to take Coretta and "Yoki" home with him, "until this thing cools off." We talked together for some time, but although Coretta listened respectfully to her father's persuasions, she would not leave. "I'm sorry, Dad," she said, "but I belong here with Martin." And so Obie Scott drove back to Marion alone.

Just two nights later, a stick of dynamite was thrown on the lawn of E. D. Nixon. Fortunately, again no one was hurt. Once more a large crowd of Negroes assembled, but they did not lose control. And so nonviolence had won its first and its second tests.

After the bombings, many of the officers of my church and other trusted friends urged me to hire a bodyguard and armed watchmen for my house. I tried to tell them that I had no fears now, and consequently needed no protection. But they were insistent, so I agreed to consider the question. I also went down to the sheriff's office and applied for a license to carry a gun in the car; but this was refused.

Meanwhile I reconsidered. How could I serve as one of the leaders of a nonviolent movement and at the same time use weapons of violence for my personal protection? Coretta and I talked the matter over for several days and finally agreed that arms were no solution. We decided then to get rid of the one weapon we owned. We tried to satisfy our friends by having floodlights mounted around the house, and hiring unarmed watchmen around the clock. I also promised that I would not travel around the city alone.

This was a comparatively easy promise to keep, thanks to our friend, Bob Williams, professor of music at Alabama State College and a former collegemate of mine at Morehouse. When I came to Montgomery, I had found him here, and from the moment the protest started he was seldom far from my side or Coretta's. He did most of my driving around Montgomery and accompanied me on several out-of-town trips. Whenever Coretta and "Yoki" went to Atlanta or Marion, he was always there to drive them down and to bring them back. Almost imperceptibly he had become my voluntary "bodyguard," though he carried no arms and could never have been as fierce as the name implied.

In this crisis the officers and members of my church were always nearby to lend their encouragement and active support. As I gradually lost my role as husband and father, having to be away from home for hours and sometimes days at a time, the women of the church came into the house to keep Coretta company. Often they volunteered to cook the meals and clean, or help with the baby. Many of the men took turns as watchmen, or drove me around when Bob Williams was not available. Nor did my congregation ever complain when the multiplicity of my new responsibilities caused me to lag in my pastoral duties. For months my day-to-day contact with my parishioners had almost ceased. I had become no more than a Sunday preacher. But my church willingly shared me with the community, and threw their own considerable resources of time and money into the struggle.

Our local white friends, too, came forward with their support. Often they called Coretta to say an encouraging word, and when the house was bombed several of them, known and unknown to us, came by to express their regret. Occasionally the mail would bring a letter from a white Montgomerian saying, "Carry on, we are with you a hundred percent." Frequently these were simply signed "a white friend."

Interestingly enough, for some time after the bombings the threatening telephone calls slowed up. But this was only a lull; several months later they had begun again in full force. In order to sleep at night, it finally became necessary to apply for an unlisted number. This number was passed out to all the members of the church, the members of the MIA, and other friends across the country. And although it had sometimes been suggested that our own group was responsible for the threats, we never received another hostile call. Of course, the letters still came, but my secretaries were discreet enough to keep as many of them as possible from my attention.

When the opposition discovered that violence could not block the protest, they resorted to mass arrests. As early as January 9, a Montgomery attorney had called the attention of the press to an old state law against boycotts. He referred to Title 14, Section 54, which provides that when two or more persons enter into a conspiracy to prevent the operation of a lawful business, without just cause or legal excuse, they shall be guilty of a misdemeanor. On February 13 the Montgomery County grand jury was called to determine whether Negroes who were boycotting the buses were violating this law. After about a week of deliberations, the jury, composed of seventeen whites and one Negro, found the boycott illegal and indicted more than one hundred persons. My name, of course, was on the list.

At the time of the indictments I was at Fisk University in Nashville, giving a series of lectures. During this period I was talking to Montgomery on the phone at least three times a day in order to keep abreast of developments. Thus I heard of the indictments first in a telephone call from Ralph Abernathy, late Tuesday night, February 21. He said that the arrests were scheduled to begin the following morning. Knowing that he would be one of the first to be arrested, I assured him that I would be with him and the others in my prayers. As usual he was unperturbed. I told him that I would cut my trip short in Nashville and come to Montgomery the next day.

I booked an early morning flight. All night long I thought of the people in Montgomery. Would these mass arrests so frighten them that they would urge us to call off the protest? I knew how hard-pressed they had been. For more than thirteen weeks they had walked, and sacrificed, and worn down their cars. They had been harassed and intimidated on every hand. And now they faced arrest on top of all this. Would they become battle-weary, I wondered. Would they give up in despair? Would this be the end of our movement?

I arose early Wednesday morning and notified the officials of Fisk that I had to leave ahead of time because of the situation in Montgomery. I flew to Atlanta to pick up my wife and daughter, whom I had left at my parents' home while I was in Nashville. My wife, my mother, and father met me at the airport. I had told them about the indictments over the phone, and they had gotten additional information from a radio broadcast. Coretta showed her usual composure; but my parents' faces wore signs of deep perturbation.

My father, so unafraid for himself, had fallen into a constant state of terror for me and my family. Since the protest began he had beaten a path between Atlanta and Montgomery to be at our side. Many times he had sat in on our board meetings and never shown any doubt about the justice of our actions. Yet this stern and courageous man had reached the point where he could scarcely mention the protest without tears. My mother too had suffered. After the bombing she had had to take to bed under doctor's orders, and she was often ill later. Their expressions—even the way they walked, I realized as they came toward me at the airport—had begun to show the strain.

As we drove to their house, my father said that he thought it would be unwise for me to return to Montgomery now. "Although many others have been indicted," he said, "their main concern is to get you. They might even put you in jail without a bond." He went on to tell me that the law enforcement agencies in Montgomery had been trying to find something on my record in Atlanta which would make it possible to deport me from Alabama. They had gone to the Atlanta police department, and were disappointed when Chief Jenkins informed them that I did not have even a minor police record. "All of this shows," my father concluded, "that they are out to get you."

I listened to him attentively, and yet I knew that I could not follow his suggestion and stay in Atlanta. I was profoundly concerned about my parents. I was worried about their worry. I knew that if I continued the struggle I would be plagued by the pain that I was inflicting on them. But if I eased out now I would be plagued by my own conscience, reminding me that I lacked the moral courage to stand by a cause to the end. No one can understand my conflict who has not looked into the eyes of those he loves, knowing that he has no alternative but to take a dangerous stand that leaves them tormented.

My father told me that he had asked several trusted friends to come to the house in the early afternoon to discuss the whole issue. Feeling that this exchange of ideas might help to relieve his worries, I readily agreed to stay over and talk to them. Among those who came were A. T. Walden, a distinguished attorney; C. R. Yates and T. M. Alexander, both prominent businessmen; C. A. Scott, editor of the *Atlanta Daily World*; Bishop Sherman L. Green of A. M. E. Church; Benjamin E. Mays, president of Morehouse College; and Rufus E. Clement, president of Atlanta University. Coretta and my mother joined us.

My father explained to the group that because of his respect for their judgment he was calling on them for advice on whether I should return to Montgomery. He gave them a brief history of the attempts that had been made to get me out of Montgomery. He admitted that the fear of what might happen to me had caused him and my mother many restless nights. He concluded by saying that he had talked to a liberal white attorney a few hours earlier, who had confirmed his feeling that I should not go back at this time.

There were murmurs of agreement in the room, and I listened as sympathetically and objectively as I could while two of the men gave their reasons for concurring. These were my elders, leaders among my people. Their words commanded respect. But soon I could not restrain myself any longer. "I must go back to Montgomery," I protested. "My friends and associates are being arrested. It would be the height of cowardice for me to stay away. I would rather be in jail ten years than desert my people now. I have begun the struggle, and I can't turn back. I have reached the point of no return." In the moment of silence that followed I heard my father break into tears. I looked at Dr. Mays, one of the great influences in my life. Perhaps he heard my unspoken plea. At any rate, he was soon defending my position strongly. Then others joined him in supporting me. They assured my father that things were not so bad as they seemed. Mr. Walden put through two calls on the spot to Thurgood Marshall, general counsel of the NAACP, and Arthur Shores, NAACP counsel in Alabama, both of whom assured him that I would have the best legal protection. In the face of all of these persuasions, my father began to be reconciled to my return to Montgomery.

After everybody had gone, Coretta and I went upstairs to our room and had a long talk. She, too, I was glad to find, had no doubt that I must go back immediately. With my own feelings reinforced by the opinions of others I trusted, and with my father's misgivings at rest, I felt better and more prepared to face the experience ahead.

Characteristically, my father, having withdrawn his objections to our return to Montgomery, decided to go along with us, unconcerned with any possible danger or unpleasantness to himself. He secured a driver and at six o'clock Thursday morning we were on the highway headed for Montgomery, arriving about nine. Before we could get out of the car, several television cameras were trained on us. The reporters had somehow discovered the time of our arrival. A few minutes later Ralph Abernathy, released on bail after his arrest the previous day, came to the house. With Ralph and my father, I set out for the county jail, several of my church members following after.

At the jail, an almost holiday atmosphere prevailed. On the way Ralph Abernathy told me how people had rushed down to get arrested the day before. No one, it seems, had been frightened. No one had tried to evade arrest. Many Negroes had gone voluntarily to the sheriff's office to see if their names were on the list, and were even disappointed when they were not. A once fear-ridden people had been transformed. Those who had previously trembled before the law were now proud to be arrested for the cause of freedom. With this feeling of solidarity around me, I walked with firm steps toward the rear of the jail. After I had received a number and had been photographed and fingerprinted, one of my church members paid my bond and I left for home.

The trial was set for March 19. Friends from all over the country came to Montgomery to be with us during the proceedings. Ministers from as far north as New York were present. Negro congressman Charles C. Diggs (D-Mich.) was on hand. Scores of reporters representing publications in the United States, India, France, and England were there to cover the trial. More than five hundred Negroes stood in the halls and the streets surrounding the small courthouse. Several of them wore crosses on their lapels reading, "Father, forgive them."

Judge Eugene Carter brought the court to order, and after the necessary preliminaries the state called me up as the first defendant. For four days I sat in court listening to arguments and waiting for a verdict. William F. Thetford, solicitor for the state, was attempting to prove that I had disobeyed a law by organizing an illegal boycott. The defense attorneys—Arthur Shores, Peter Hall, Ozell Billingsley, Fred Gray, Charles Langford, and Robert Carter—presented arguments to show that the prosecution's evidence was insufficient to prove that I had violated Alabama's antiboycott law. Even if the state had proved such action, they asserted, no evidence was produced to show that the Negroes did not have just cause or legal excuse.

In all, twenty-eight witnesses were brought to the stand by the defense. I listened with a mixture of sadness and awe as these simple people—most of them unlettered—sat on the witness stand without fear and told their stories. They looked the solicitor and the judge in the eye with a courage and dignity to which there was no answer.

Perhaps the most touching testimony was that of Mrs. Stella Brooks. Her husband had climbed on a bus. After paying his fare he was ordered by the driver to get off and reboard by the back door. He looked through the crowded bus and seeing that there was no room in back he said that he would get off and walk if the driver would return his dime. The driver refused; an argument ensued; and the driver called the police. The policeman arrived, abusing Brooks, who still refused to leave the bus unless his dime was returned. The policeman shot him. It happened so suddenly that everybody was dazed. Brooks died of his wounds.

Mrs. Martha Walker testified about the day when she was leading her blind husband from the bus. She had stepped down and as her husband was following the driver slammed the door and began to drive off. Walker's leg was caught. Although Mrs. Walker called out, the driver failed to stop, and her husband was dragged some distance before he could free himself. She reported the incident, but the bus company did nothing about it.

The stories continued. Mrs. Sadie Brooks testified that she heard a Negro passenger threatened because he did not have the correct change. "The driver whipped out a pistol and drove the man off the bus." Mrs. Della Perkins described being called an "ugly black ape" by a driver.

I will always remember my delight when Mrs. Georgia Gilmore—an unlettered woman of unusual intelligence—told how an operator demanded that she get off the bus after paying her fare and board it again by the back door, and then drove away before she could get there. She turned to Judge Carter and said: "When they count the money, they do not know Negro money from white money."

On Thursday afternoon, March 22, both sides rested. All eyes were turned toward Judge Carter, as with barely a pause he rendered his verdict: "I declare the defendant guilty of violating the state's anti-boycott law." The penalty was a fine of $500 and court costs, or 386 days at hard labor in the County of Montgomery. Then Judge Carter announced that he was giving a minimum penalty because of what I had done to prevent violence. In the cases of the other Negroes charged with the same violation—the number had now boiled down to 89—Judge Carter entered a continuance until a final appeal was complete in my case.

In a few minutes several friends had come up to sign my bond, and the lawyers had notified the judge that the case would be appealed. Many people stood around the courtroom in tears. Others walked out with their heads bowed. I came to the end of my trial with a feeling of sympathy for Judge Carter in his dilemma. To convict me he had to face the condemnation of the nation and world opinion; to acquit me he had to face the condemnation of the local community and those voters who kept him in office. Throughout the proceedings he had treated me with great courtesy, and he had rendered a verdict which he probably thought was the best way out. After the trial he left town for a "welcomed rest."

I left the courtroom with my wife at my side and a host of friends following. In front of the courthouse hundreds of Negroes and whites, including television cameramen and photographers, were waiting. As I waved my hand, they shouted: "God bless you," and began to sing, "We ain't gonna ride the buses no more."

Ordinarily, a person leaving a courtroom with a conviction behind him would wear a somber face. But I left with a smile. I knew that I was a convicted criminal, but I was proud of my crime. It was the crime of joining my people in a nonviolent protest against injustice. It was the crime of seeking to instill within my people a sense of dignity and self-respect. It was the crime of desiring for my people the unalienable rights of life, liberty, and the pursuit of happiness. It was above all the crime of seeking to convince my people that noncooperation with evil is just as much a moral duty as is cooperation with good.

So ended another effort to halt the protest. Instead of stopping the movement, the opposition's tactics had only served to give it greater momentum, and to draw us closer together. What the opposition failed to see was that our mutual sufferings had wrapped us all in a single garment of destiny. What happened to one happened to all.

On that cloudy afternoon in March, Judge Carter had convicted more than Martin Luther King, Jr., Case No. 7399; he had convicted every Negro in Montgomery. It is no wonder that the movement couldn't be stopped. It was too large to be stopped. Its links were too well bound together in a powerfully effective chain. There is amazing power in unity. Where there is true unity, every effort to disunite only serves to strengthen the unity. This is what the opposition failed to see.

The members of the opposition had also revealed that they did not know the Negroes with whom they were dealing. They thought they were dealing with a group who could be cajoled or forced to do whatever the white man wanted them to do. They were not aware that they were dealing with Negroes who had been freed from fear. And so every move they made proved to be a mistake. It could not be otherwise, because their methods were geared to the "old Negro," and they were dealing with a "new Negro."

From *Stride Toward Freedom: The Montgomery Story*
(Harper & Row, 1958, reprinted by Beacon Press, 2010).

TWO

PALM SUNDAY SERMON ON MOHANDAS K. GANDHI

On March 22, 1959, Dr. King returned to his pulpit after an absence of nearly two months and discussed the life of Gandhi, suggesting that "more than anybody else in the modern world" he had "caught the spirit of Jesus Christ, and lived it more completely in his life."

To the cross and its significance in human experience. This is the time in the year when we think of the love of God breaking forth into time out of eternity. This is the time of the year when we come to see that the most powerful forces in the universe are not those forces of military might but those forces of spiritual might. And as we sing together this great hymn of our church, the Christian church, hymn number 191, let us think about it again:

When I survey the wondrous cross,
On which the prince of glory died,
I count my richest gains but loss
And pour contempt on all my pride.

A beautiful hymn. I think if there is any hymn of the Christian church that I would call a favorite hymn, it is this one. And then it goes on to say, in that last stanza:

Were the whole realm of nature mine,
That was a present far too small.
Love so amazing, so divine,
Demands my life, my all and my all.

We think about Christ and the cross in the days ahead as he walks through Jerusalem and he's carried from Jerusalem to Calvary Hill, where he is crucified. Let us think of this wondrous cross.

This, as you know, is what has traditionally been known in the Christian church as Palm Sunday. And ordinarily the preacher is expected to preach a sermon on the Lordship or the Kingship of Christ—the triumphal entry, or something that relates to this great event as Jesus entered Jerusalem, for it was after this that Jesus was crucified. And I remember, the other day, about seven or eight days ago, standing on the Mount of Olives and looking across just a few feet and noticing that gate that still stands there in Jerusalem, and through which Christ passed into Jerusalem, into the old city. The ruins of that gate stand there, and one feels the sense of Christ's mission as he looks at the gate. And he looks at Jerusalem, and he sees what could take place in such a setting. And you notice there also the spot where the temple stood, and it was here that Jesus passed and he went into the temple and ran the money-changers out.

And so that, if I talked about that this morning, I could talk about it not only from what the Bible says but from personal experience, first-hand experience. But I beg of you to indulge me this morning to talk about the life of a man who lived in India. And I think I'm justified in doing this because I believe this man, more than anybody else in the modern world, caught the spirit of Jesus Christ and lived it more completely in his life. His name was Gandhi, Mohandas K. Gandhi. And after he lived a few years, the poet Tagore, who lived in India, gave him another name: "Mahatma," the great soul. And we know him as Mahatma Gandhi.

I would like to use a double text for what I have to say this morning, both of them are found in the gospel as recorded by Saint John. One found in the tenth chapter, and the sixteenth verse, and it reads, "I have other sheep, which are not of this fold." "I have other sheep, which are not of this fold." And then the other one is found in the fourteenth chapter of John, in the twelfth verse. It reads, "Verily, verily, I say unto you, he that believeth on me, the works that I do, shall he do also. And greater works than these shall he do because I go unto my Father."

I want you to notice these two passages of scripture. On the one hand, "I have other sheep that are not of this fold." I think Jesus is saying here in substance that "I have followers who are not in this inner circle." He's saying in substance that "I have people dedicated and following my ways who have not become attached to the institution surrounding my name. I have other sheep that are not of this fold. And my influence is not limited to the institutional Christian church." I think this is what Jesus would say if he were living today concerning this passage, that "I have people who are following me who've never joined the Christian church as an institution."

And then that other passage, I think Jesus was saying this—it's a strange thing, and I used to wonder what Jesus meant when he said, "There will be people who will do greater things than I did." And I have thought about the glory and honor surrounding the life of Christ, and I thought about the fact that he represented the absolute revelation of God. And I've thought about the fact that in his life, he represented all of the glory of eternity coming into time. And how would it be possible for anybody to do greater works than Christ? How would it be possible for anybody even to match him, or even to approximate his work?

But I've come to see what Christ meant. Christ meant that in his life he would only touch a few people. And in his lifetime—and if you study the life of Christ, and if you know your Bible you realize that Christ never traveled outside of Palestine, and his influence in his own lifetime was limited to a small group of people. He never had more than twelve followers in his lifetime; others heard about him and others came to see him, but he never had but twelve real followers, and three of them turned out to be not too good. But he pictured the day that his spirit and his influence would go beyond the borders of Palestine, and that men would catch his message and carry it over the world, and that men all over the world would grasp the truth of his gospel. And they would be able to do things that he couldn't do. They were able, be able to travel places that he couldn't travel. And they would be able to convert people that he couldn't convert in his lifetime. And this is what he meant when he said, "Greater works shall ye do, for an Apostle Paul will catch my work."

And I remember just last Tuesday morning standing on that beautiful hill called the Acropolis in Athens. And there, standing around the Parthenon, as it stands still in all of its beautiful and impressive proportions, although it has been torn somewhat through wars, but it still stands there. And right across from the Acropolis you see Mars Hill. And I remember when our guide said, "That's the hill where the Apostle Paul preached."

Now when you think of the fact that Athens is a long ways from Jerusalem, for we traveled right over Damascus where Paul was converted, and Damascus is at least five hours by flight from Athens. And you think about the fact that Paul had caught this message and carried it beyond the Damascus Road all over the world, and he had gone as far as Greece, as far as Athens, to preach the gospel of Jesus Christ. This is what Jesus meant, that "somebody will catch my message, and they would be able to carry it in places that I couldn't carry it, and they would be able to do things in their lives that I couldn't do."

And I believe these two passages of scripture apply more uniquely to the life and work of Mahatma Gandhi than to any other individual in the history of the world. For here was a man who was not a Christian in terms of being a member of the Christian church but who was a Christian. And it is one of the strange ironies of the modern world that the greatest Christian of the twentieth century was not a member of the Christian church. And the second thing is, that this man took the message of Jesus Christ and was able to do even greater works than Jesus did in his lifetime. Jesus himself predicted this: "Ye shall do even greater works."

Now let us look at the life, as briefly as possible, the life of this man and his work, and see just what it gives us, and what this life reveals to us in terms of the struggles ahead. I would say the first thing that we must see about this life is that Mahatma Gandhi was able to achieve for his people independence through nonviolent means. I think you should underscore this. He was able to achieve for his people independence from the domination of the British Empire without lifting one gun or without uttering one curse word. He did it with the spirit of Jesus Christ in his heart and the love of God, and this was all he had. He had no weapons. He had no army, in terms of military might. And yet he was able to achieve independence from the largest empire in the history of this world without picking up a gun or without any ammunition.

Gandhi was born in India in a little place called Porbandar, down almost in central India. And he had seen the conditions of this country. India had been under the domination of the British Empire for many years. And under the domination of the British Empire, the people of India suffered all types of exploitation. And you think about the fact that while Britain was in India, that out of a population of four hundred million people, more than three hundred and sixty-five million of these people made less than fifty dollars a year. And more than half of this had to be spent for taxes.

Gandhi looked at all of this. He looked at his people as they lived in ghettos and hovels and as they lived out on the streets, many of them. And even today, after being exploited so many years, they haven't been able to solve those problems. For we landed in Bombay, India, and I never will forget it, that night. We got up early in the morning to take a plane for Delhi. And as we rode out to the airport we looked out on the street and saw people sleeping out on the sidewalks and out in the streets, and everywhere we went to. Walk through the train station, and you can't hardly get to the train, because people are sleeping on the platforms of the train station. No homes to live in. In Bombay, India, where they have a population of three million people, five hundred thousand of these people sleep on the streets at night. Nowhere to sleep, no homes to live in, making no more than fifteen or twenty dollars a year or even less than that.

And this was the exploitation that Mahatma Gandhi noticed years ago. And even more than that, these people were humiliated and embarrassed and segregated in their own land. There were places that the Indian people could not even go in their own land. The British had come in there and set up clubs and other places and even hotels where Indians couldn't even enter in their own land. Gandhi looked at all of this, and as a young lawyer, after he had just left England and gotten his law—received his law training, he went over to South Africa. And there he saw in South Africa, and Indians were even exploited there.

And one day he was taking a train to Pretoria, and he had first-class accommodations on that train. And when they came to pick up the tickets they noticed that he was an Indian, that he had a brown face, and they told him to get out and move on to the third-class accommodation, that he wasn't supposed to be there with any first-class accommodation. And Gandhi that day refused to move, and they threw him off the train. And there, in that cold station that night, he stayed all night, and he started meditating on his plight and the plight of his people. And he decided from that point on that he would never submit himself to injustice, or to exploitation.

It was there on the next day that he called a meeting of all of the Indians in South Africa, in that particular region of South Africa, and told them what had happened, and told them what was happening to them every day, and said that, "We must do something about it. We must organize ourselves to rid our community, the South African community, and also the Indian community back home, of the domination and the exploitation of foreign powers."

But Mahatma Gandhi came to something else in that moment. As he started organizing his forces in South Africa, he read the Sermon on the Mount. He later read the works of the American poet Thoreau. And he later read the Russian author Tolstoy. And he found something in all of this that gave him insights. Started reading in the Bible, "turn the other cheek," "resist evil with good," "blessed are the meek, for they shall inherit the earth." And all of these things inspired him to no end. He read Thoreau as he said that no just man can submit to anything evil, even if it means standing up and being disobedient to the laws of the state. And so this he combined into a new method, and he said to his people, "Now, it's possible to resist evil; this is your first responsibility; never adjust to evil, resist it. But if you can resist it without resorting to violence or to hate, you can stand up against it and still love the individuals that carry on the evil system that you are resisting."

And a few years later, after he won a victory in South Africa, he went back to India. And there his people called on him, called on his leadership, to organize them and get ready for the trials ahead, and he did just that. He went back, and in 1917 he started his first campaign in India. And throughout his long struggle there, he followed the way of nonviolent resistance. Never uttered a curse word, mark you. He never owned an instrument of violence. And he had nothing but love and understanding goodwill in his heart for the people who were seeking to defeat him and who were exploiting and humiliating his people.

And then came that day when he said to the people of India, "I'm going to leave this community." He had set up in a place called Ahmadabad, and there was the Sabarmati ashram. He lived there with a group of people; his ashram was a place of quiet and meditation where the people lived together. And one day he said to those people, "I'm going to leave this place, and I will not return until India has received her independence." And this was in 1930. And he had so organized the whole of India then; people had left their jobs. People with tremendous and powerful law practices had left their jobs. The president of India was a lawyer who had made almost a million rupees—a million dollars—and he left it, turned it all over to the movement. The father, the president of—the prime minister of India, Mr. Nehru, left his law practice to get in the freedom movement with Gandhi, and he had organized the whole of India.

And you have read of the Salt March, which was a very significant thing in the Indian struggle. And this demonstrates how Gandhi used this method of nonviolence and how he would mobilize his people and galvanize the whole of the nation to bring about victory. In India, the British people had come to the point where they were charging the Indian people a tax on all of the salt, and they would not allow them even to make their own salt from all of the salt seas around the country. They couldn't touch it; it was against the law. And Gandhi got all of the people of India to see the injustice of this. And he decided one day that they would march from Ahmadabad down to a place called Dandi.

We had the privilege of spending a day or so at Ahmadabad at that Sabarmati ashram, and we stood there at the point where Gandhi started his long walk of two hundred and eighteen miles. And he started there walking with eighty people. And gradually the number grew to a million, and it grew to millions and millions. And finally, they kept walking and walking until they reached the little village of Dandi. And there, Gandhi went on and reached down in the river, or in the sea rather, and brought up a little salt in his hand to demonstrate and dramatize the fact that they were breaking this law in protest against the injustices they had faced all over the years with these salt laws.

And Gandhi said to his people, "If you are hit, don't hit back; even if they shoot at you, don't shoot back; if they curse you, don't curse back, but just keep moving. Some of us might have to die before we get there; some of us might be thrown in jail before we get there, but let us just keep moving." And they kept moving, and they walked and walked, and millions of them had gotten together when they finally reached that point. And the British Empire knew, then, that this little man had mobilized the people of India to the point that they could never defeat them. And they realized, at that very point, that this was the beginning of the end of the British Empire as far as India was concerned.

He was able to mobilize and galvanize more people than, in his lifetime, than any other person in the history of this world. And just with a little love in his heart and understanding goodwill and a refusal to cooperate with an evil law, he was able to break the backbone of the British Empire. And this, I think, is one of the most significant things that has ever happened in the history of the world, and more than three hundred and ninety million people achieved their freedom. And they achieved it nonviolently when a man refused to follow the way of hate, and he refused to follow the way of violence, and only decided to follow the way of love and understanding goodwill and refused to cooperate with any system of evil.

And the significant thing is that when you follow this way, when the battle is almost over, and a new friendship and reconciliation exists between the people who have been the oppressors and the oppressed. There is no greater friendship anywhere in the world today than between the Indian people and the British people. If you ask the Indian people today who they love more, what people, whether they love Americans more, British more, they will say to you immediately that they love the British people more.

The night we had dinner with Prime Minister Nehru the person who sat at that dinner table with us, as a guest of the prime minister at that time, was Lady Mountbatten with her daughter, the wife of Lord Mountbatten, who was the viceroy of India when it received its independence. And they're marvelous and great and lasting friends. There is a lasting friendship there. And this is only because Gandhi followed the way of love and nonviolence, refusing to hate and refusing to follow the way of violence. And a new friendship exists. The aftermath of violence is always bitterness; the aftermath of nonviolence is the creation of the beloved community so that when the battle is over, it's over, and a new love and a new understanding and a new relationship comes into being between the oppressed and the oppressor.

This little man, one of the greatest conquerors that the world has ever known. Somebody said that when Mahatma Gandhi was coming over to England for the roundtable conference in 1932, a group of people stood there waiting. And somebody pointed out—And while they were waiting somebody said, "You see around that cliff? That was where Julius Caesar came, the way he came in when he invaded Britain years ago." And then somebody pointed over to another place and said, "That was the way William the Conqueror came in. They invaded years ago in the Battle of Hastings." Then somebody else looked over and said, "There is another conqueror coming in. In just a few minutes the third and greatest conqueror that has ever come into Great Britain." And strangely enough, this little man came in with no armies, no guards around him, no military might, no beautiful clothes, just loin cloth, but this man proved to be the greatest conqueror that the British Empire ever faced. He was able to achieve, through love and nonviolence, the independence of his people and break the backbone of the British Empire. "Ye shall do greater works than I have done." And this is exemplified in the life of Mahatma Gandhi.

Let me rush on to say a second thing: here is a man who achieved in his life absolute self-discipline. Absolute self-discipline. So that in his life there was no gulf between the private and the public; there was no gulf in his life between the "is" and the "oughts." Here was a man who had absolved the "isness" of his being and the "oughtness" of his being. And this was one of the greatest accomplishments in his life. Gandhi used to say to his people, "I have no secrets. My life is an open book." And he lived that every day. He achieved in his life absolute self-discipline.

He started out as a young lawyer. He went to South Africa, and he became a thriving, promising lawyer making more than thirty thousand dollars a year. And then he came to see that he had a task ahead to free his people. And he vowed poverty, decided to do away with all of the money that he had made, and he went back to India and started wearing the very clothes that all of these disinherited masses of people of India had been wearing. He had been a popular young man in England, worn all of the beautiful clothes and his wife the beautiful saris of India with all of its silk beauty, but then he came to that point of saying to his wife, "You've got to drop this." And he started wearing what was called the dhoti, loin cloth, the same thing that these masses of people wore. He did it, identified himself with them absolutely.

And he had no income; he had nothing in this world, not even a piece of property. This man achieved in his life absolute self-discipline to the point of renouncing the world. And when he died, the only thing that he owned was a pair of glasses, a pair of sandals, a loin cloth, some false teeth, and some little monkeys who saw no evil, who said no evil, and who somehow didn't see any evil. This is all he had. And if you ask people in India today why was it that Mahatma Gandhi was able to do what he did in India, they would say they followed him because of his absolute sincerity and his absolute dedication. Here was a man who achieved in his life this bridging of the gulf between the "ought" and the "is." He achieved in his life absolute self-discipline.

And there is a final thing Mahatma Gandhi was able to do. He had the amazing capacity, the amazing capacity for internal criticism. Most others have the amazing capacity for external criticism. We can always see the evil in others; we can always see the evil in our oppressors. But Gandhi had the amazing capacity to see not only the splinter in his opponent's eye but also the planks in his own eye and the eye of his people. He had the amazing capacity for self-criticism. And this was true in his individual life; it was true in his family life; and it was true in his people's life. He not only criticized the British Empire, but he criticized his own people when they needed it, and he criticized himself when he needed it.

And whenever he made a mistake, he confessed it publicly. Here was a man who would say to his people, "I'm not perfect. I'm not infallible. I don't want you to start a religion around me. I'm not a god." And I'm convinced that today there would be a religion around Gandhi if Gandhi had not insisted all through his life that "I don't want a religion around me because I'm too human. I'm too fallible. Never think that I'm infallible."

And any time he made a mistake, even in his personal life or even in decisions that he made in the independence struggle, he came out in the public and said, "I made a mistake." In 1922, when he had started one of his first campaigns of nonviolence and some of the people started getting violent, some of the Indian people started getting violent, and they killed twenty some, twenty-eight of the British people in this struggle. And in the midst of this struggle, Gandhi came to the forefront of the scene and called the campaign off. And he stood up before the Indian people and before the British people and said, "I made a Himalayan blunder. I thought my people were ready; I thought they were disciplined for this task." And people around Gandhi were angry with him. Even Prime Minister Nehru says in *Toward Freedom* that he was angry. His father was angry. All of these people who had left their hundreds and thousands of dollars to follow Gandhi and his movement were angry when he called this movement off. But he called it off because, as he said, "I've made a blunder." And he never hesitated to acknowledge before the public when he made a mistake. And he always went back and said, "I made a mistake. I'm going back to rethink it, I'm going back to meditate over it. And I'll be coming back. Don't think the struggle is over, don't think I'm retreating from this thing permanently and ultimately. I'm just taking a temporary retreat, because I made a mistake."

But not only that, he confessed the errors and the mistakes of his family. Even when his son, one of his sons, went wrong he wrote in his paper about it. And his wife committed an act once that was sinful to him. He had pledged himself to poverty, and he would never use any of the money that came in for his personal benefit. And one day his wife, feeling the need for some of that money that had come in, decided to use it. And Gandhi discovered it, and he wrote in his paper that his wife had committed a grave sin. He didn't mind letting the world know it. Here was a man who confessed his errors publicly and didn't mind if you saw him fail. He saw his own shortcomings, the shortcomings of his family, and then he saw the shortcomings of his own people.

We went in some little villages, and in these villages we saw hundreds of people sleeping on the ground. They didn't have any beds to sleep in. We looked in these same villages; there was no running water there, nothing to wash with. We looked in these villages, and we saw people there in their little huts and in their little rooms, and the cow, their little cow, or their calves slept in the same room with them. If they had a few chickens, the chickens slept in the same room with them. We looked at these people, and they had nothing that we would consider convenient, none of the comforts of life. Here they are, sleeping in the same room with the beast of the field. This is all they had. Pretty soon we discovered that these people were the untouchables.

Now you know in India you have what is known as the caste system, and that existed for years. And there were those people who were the outcasts, some seventy million of them. They were called untouchables. And these were the people who were exploited, and they were trampled over even by the Indian people themselves. And Gandhi looked at this system. Gandhi couldn't stand this system, and he looked at his people, and he said, "Now, you have selected me and you've asked me to free you from the political domination and the economic exploitation inflicted upon you by Britain. And here you are trampling over and exploiting seventy million of your brothers." And he decided that he would not ever adjust to that system and that he would speak against it and stand up against it the rest of his life.

And you read, back in his early life, the first thing he did when he went to India was to adopt an untouchable girl as his daughter. And his wife thought he was going crazy because she was a member of one of the high castes. And she said, "What in the world are you doing adopting an untouchable? We are not supposed to touch these people." And he said, "I am going to have this young lady as my daughter." And he brought her into his ashram, and she lived there, and she lives in India today. And he demonstrated in his own life that untouchability had to go. And one of the greatest tasks ever performed by Mahatma Gandhi was against untouchability.

One day he stood before his people and said, "You are exploiting these untouchables. Even though we are fighting with all that we have in our bodies and our souls to break loose from the bondage of the British Empire, we are exploiting these people, and we're taking from them their selfhood and their self-respect." And he said, "We will not even allow these people to go into temple." They couldn't go in the temple and worship God like other people. They could not draw water like other people, and there were certain streets they couldn't even walk on.

And he looked at all of this. One day he said, "Beginning on the twenty-first of September at twelve o'clock, I will refuse to eat. And I will not eat any more until the leaders of the caste system will come to me with the leaders of the untouchables and say that there will be an end to untouchability. And I will not eat any more until the Hindu temples of India will open their doors to the untouchables." And he refused to eat. And days passed. Nothing happened. Finally, when Gandhi was about to breathe his last, breathe his last breath and his body—it was all but gone and he had lost many pounds—a group came to him. A group from the untouchables and a group from the Brahmin caste came to him and signed a statement saying that we will no longer adhere to the caste system and to untouchability. And the priests of the temple came to him and said now the temple will be open unto the untouchables. And that afternoon, untouchables from all over India went into the temples, and all of these thousands and millions of people put their arms around the Brahmins and peoples of other castes. Hundreds and millions of people who had never touched each other for two thousand years were now singing and praising God together. And this was the great contribution that Mahatma Gandhi brought about.

And today in India, untouchability is a crime punishable by the law. And if anybody practices untouchability, he can be put in prison for as long as three years. And as one political leader said to me, "You cannot find in India one hundred people today who would sign the public statement endorsing untouchability." Here was a man who had the amazing capacity for internal criticism to the point that he saw the shortcomings of his own people. And he was just as firm against doing something about that as he was about doing away with the exploitation of the British Empire. And this is what makes him one of the great men of history.

And the final thing that I would like to say to you this morning is that the world doesn't like people like Gandhi. That's strange, isn't it? They don't like people like Christ. They don't like people like Abraham Lincoln. They kill them. And this man, who had done all of that for India, this man who had given his life and who had mobilized and galvanized four hundred million people for independence so that in 1947 India received its independence, and he became the father of that nation. This same man because he decided that he would not rest until he saw the Muslims and the Hindus together; they had been fighting among themselves, they had been in riots among themselves, and he wanted to see this straight. And one of his own fellow Hindus felt that he was a little too favorable toward the Muslims, felt that he was giving in a little too much toward the Muslims.

And one afternoon, when he was at Birla House, living there with one of the big industrialists for a few days in Delhi, he walked out to his evening prayer meeting. Every evening he had a prayer meeting where hundreds of people came, and he prayed with them. And on his way out there that afternoon, one of his fellow Hindus shot him. And here was a man of nonviolence, falling at the hand of a man of violence. Here was a man of love falling at the hands of a man of hate. This seems the way of history.

And isn't it significant that he died on the same day that Christ died; it was on a Friday. This is the story of history. But thank God it never stops here. Thank God Good Friday is never the end. And the man who shot Gandhi only shot him into the hearts of humanity. And just as when Abraham Lincoln was shot—mark you, for the same reason that Mahatma Gandhi was shot, that is, the attempt to heal the wounds of a divided nation—when the great leader Abraham Lincoln was shot, Secretary Stanton stood by the body of this leader and said, "Now he belongs to the ages." And that same thing can be said about Mahatma Gandhi now. He belongs to the ages, and he belongs especially to this age, an age drifting once more to its doom. And he has revealed to us that we must learn to go another way.

For in a day when Sputniks and Explorers are dashing through outer space and guided ballistic missiles are carving highways of death through the stratosphere, no nation can win a war. Today it is no longer a choice between violence and nonviolence; it is either nonviolence or nonexistence. It may not be that Mahatma Gandhi is God's appeal to this age, an age drifting to its doom. And that warning—And that appeal is always in the form of a warning: "He who lives by the sword will perish by the sword." Jesus said it years ago. Whenever men follow that and see that way, new horizons begin to emerge and a new world unfolds. Who today will follow Christ in his way and follow it so much that we'll be able to do greater things even than he did because we will be able to bring about the peace of the world and mobilize hundreds and thousands of men to follow the way of Christ?

I close by quoting the words of John Oxenham:

To every man there openeth a way, and ways, and a way
The high soul climbs the high way, and the low soul gropes the low,
And in between on the misty flats, the rest drift to and fro.

*But to every man — to every nation, to every civilization —
there openeth a high and a low way.
Every soul decideth which way it shall go.*

And God grant that we shall choose the high way, even if it will mean assassination, even if it will mean crucifixion, for by going this way we will discover that death would be only the beginning of our influence.

"I have other sheep," says Jesus, "which are not of this fold. And if you will believe in me and follow my way, you will be even, you will be able to do even greater works than I did in my lifetime."

O God, our gracious Heavenly Father, we thank Thee for the fact that you have inspired men and women in all nations and in all cultures. We call you different names: some call Thee Allah; some call you Elohim; some call you Jehovah; some call you Brahma; and some call you the Unmoved Mover; some call you the Architectonic Good. But we know that these are all names for one and the same God, and we know you are one.

And grant, O God, that we will follow Thee and become so committed to Thy way and Thy kingdom that we will be able to establish in our lives and in this world a brotherhood. We will be able to establish here a kingdom of understanding, where men will live together as brothers and respect the dignity and worth of all human personality.

In the name and spirit of Jesus we pray. Amen.

We open the doors of the church now. Is there one who will accept the Christ this morning just as you are? Who will make that decision as we stand and sing together? One hundred and sixty-two.

Let us remain standing now for the recessional hymn. We are grateful to God for these persons who have come to unite with the church.

> Delivered at Dexter Avenue Baptist Church,
> Montgomery, Alabama, March 22, 1959.

THREE

PILGRIMAGE TO NONVIOLENCE

This piece, published in 1958 as a chapter in *Stride Toward Freedom*, traces the philosophical and theoretical evolution of Dr. King's personal commitment to nonviolence. It was later published, in 1960, in *Christian Century* magazine as part of its famous series, "How My Mind Has Changed."

Often the question has arisen concerning my own intellectual pilgrimage to nonviolence. In order to get at this question it is necessary to go back to my early teens in Atlanta. I had grown up abhorring not only segregation but also the oppressive and barbarous acts that grew out of it. I had passed spots where Negroes had been savagely lynched, and had watched the Ku Klux Klan on its rides at night. I had seen police brutality with my own eyes, and watched Negroes receive the most tragic injustice in the courts. All of these things had done something to my growing personality. I had come perilously close to resenting all white people.

I had also learned that the inseparable twin of racial injustice was economic injustice. Although I came from a home of economic security and relative comfort, I could never get out of my mind the economic insecurity of many of my playmates and the tragic poverty of those living around me. During my late teens I worked two summers, against my father's wishes—he never wanted my brother and me to work around white people because of the oppressive conditions—in a plant that hired both Negroes and whites. Here I saw economic injustice firsthand, and realized that the poor white was exploited just as much as the Negro. Through these early experiences I grew up deeply conscious of the varieties of injustice in our society.

So when I went to Atlanta's Morehouse College as a freshman in 1944 my concern for racial and economic justice was already substantial. During my student days at Morehouse I read Thoreau's essay "Civil Disobedience" for the first time. Fascinated by the idea of refusing to cooperate with an evil system, I was so deeply moved that I reread the work several times. This was my first intellectual contact with the theory of nonviolent resistance.

Not until I entered Crozer Theological Seminary in 1948, however, did I begin a serious intellectual quest for a method to eliminate social evil. Although my major interest was in the fields of theology and philosophy, I spent a great deal of time reading the works of the great social philosophers. I came early to Walter Rauschenbusch's *Christianity and the Social Crisis*, which left an indelible imprint on my thinking by giving me a theological basis for the social concern which had already grown up in me as a result of my early experiences. Of course there were points at which I differed with Rauschenbusch. I felt that he had fallen victim to the nineteenth-century "cult of inevitable progress" which led him to a superficial optimism concerning man's nature. Moreover, he came perilously close to identifying the Kingdom of God with a particular social and economic system—a tendency which should never befall the Church. But in spite of these shortcomings Rauschenbusch had done a great service for the Christian Church by insisting that the gospel deals with the whole man, not only his soul but his body; not only his spiritual well-being but his material well-being. It has been my conviction ever since reading Rauschenbusch that any religion which professes to be concerned about the souls of men and is not concerned about the social and economic conditions that scar the soul is a spiritually moribund religion only waiting for the day to be buried. It well has been said: "A religion that ends with the individual, ends."

After reading Rauschenbusch, I turned to a serious study of the social and ethical theories of the great philosophers, from Plato and Aristotle down to Rousseau, Hobbes, Bentham, Mill, and Locke. All of these masters stimulated my thinking—such as it was—and, while finding things to question in each of them, I nevertheless learned a great deal from their study.

During the Christmas holidays of 1949 I decided to spend my spare time reading Karl Marx to try to understand the appeal of communism for many people. For the first time I carefully scrutinized *Das Kapital* and *The Communist Manifesto.* I also read some interpretive works on the thinking of Marx and Lenin. In reading such Communist writings I drew certain conclusions that have remained with me as convictions to this day. First I rejected their materialistic interpretation of history. Communism, avowedly secularistic and materialistic, has no place for God. This I could never accept, for as a Christian I believe that there is a creative personal power in this universe who is the ground and essence of all reality—a power that cannot be explained in materialistic terms. History is ultimately guided by spirit, not matter. Second, I strongly disagreed with communism's ethical relativism. Since for the Communist there is no divine government, no absolute moral order, there are no fixed, immutable principles; consequently almost anything—force, violence, murder, lying—is a justifiable means to the "millennial" end. This type of relativism was abhorrent to me. Constructive ends can never give absolute moral justification to destructive means, because in the final analysis the end is preexistent in the mean. Third, I opposed communism's political totalitarianism. In communism the individual ends up in subjection to the state. True, the Marxist would argue that the state is an "interim" reality which is to be eliminated when the classless society emerges; but the state is the end while it lasts, and man only a means to that end. And if any man's so-called rights or liberties stand in the way of that end, they are simply swept aside. His liberties of expression, his freedom to vote, his freedom to listen to what news he likes or to choose his books are all restricted. Man becomes hardly more, in communism, than a depersonalized cog in the turning wheel of the state.

This deprecation of individual freedom was objectionable to me.

I am convinced now, as I was then, that man is an end because he is a child of God. Man is not made for the state; the state is made for man. To deprive man of freedom is to relegate him to the status of a thing, rather than elevate him to the status of a person. Man must never be treated as a means to the end of the state, but always as an end within himself.

Yet, in spite of the fact that my response to communism was and is negative, and I considered it basically evil, there were points at which I found it challenging. The late Archbishop of Canterbury, William Temple, referred to communism as a Christian heresy. By this he meant that communism had laid hold of certain truths which are essential parts of the Christian view of things, but that it had bound up with them concepts and practices which no Christian could ever accept or profess. Communism challenged the late archbishop and it should challenge every Christian—as it challenged me—to a growing concern about social justice. With all of its false assumptions and evil methods, communism grew as a protest against the hardships of the underprivileged. Communism in theory emphasized a classless society, and a concern for social justice, though the world knows from sad experience that in practice it created new classes and a new lexicon of injustice. The Christian ought always to be challenged by any protest against unfair treatment of the poor, for Christianity is itself such a protest, nowhere expressed more eloquently than in Jesus's words: "The Spirit of the Lord is upon me, because he hath anointed me to preach the gospel to the poor; he hath sent me to heal the brokenhearted, to preach deliverance to the captives, and recovering of sight to the blind, to set at liberty them that are bruised, to preach the acceptable year of the Lord."

I also sought systematic answers to Marx's critique of modern bourgeois culture. He presented capitalism as essentially a struggle between the owners of the productive resources and the workers, whom Marx regarded as the real producers. Marx interpreted economic forces as the dialectical process by which society moved from feudalism through capitalism to socialism, with the primary mechanism of this historical movement being the struggle between economic classes whose interests were irreconcilable. Obviously this theory left out of account the numerous and significant complexities—political, economic, moral, religious, and psychological—which played a vital role in shaping the constellation of institutions and ideas known today as Western civilization. Moreover, it was dated in the sense that the capitalism Marx wrote about bore only a partial resemblance to the capitalism we know in this country today.

But in spite of the shortcomings of his analysis, Marx had raised some basic questions. I was deeply concerned from my early teen days about the gulf between superfluous wealth and abject poverty, and my reading of Marx made me ever more conscious of this gulf. Although modern American capitalism had greatly reduced the gap through social reforms, there was still need for a better distribution of wealth. Moreover, Marx had revealed the danger of the profit motive as the sole basis of an economic system: capitalism is always in danger of inspiring men to be more concerned about making a living than making a life. We are prone to judge success by the index of our salaries or the size of our automobiles, rather than by the quality of our service and relationship to humanity—thus capitalism can lead to a practical materialism that is as pernicious as the materialism taught by communism.

In short, I read Marx as I read all of the influential historical thinkers—from a dialectical point of view, combining a partial yes and a partial no. Insofar as Marx posited a metaphysical materialism, an ethical relativism, and a strangulating totalitarianism, I responded with an unambiguous "no"; but insofar as he pointed to weaknesses of traditional capitalism, contributed to the growth of a definite self-consciousness in the masses, and challenged the social conscience of the Christian churches, I responded with a definite "yes."

My reading of Marx also convinced me that truth is found neither in Marxism nor in traditional capitalism. Each represents a partial truth. Historically capitalism failed to see the truth in collective enterprise and Marxism failed to see the truth in individual enterprise. Nineteenth-century capitalism failed to see that life is social and Marxism failed and still fails to see that life is individual and personal.

The Kingdom of God is neither the thesis of individual enterprise nor the antithesis of collective enterprise, but a synthesis which reconciles the truths of both.

During my stay at Crozer, I was also exposed for the first time to the pacifist position in a lecture by Dr. A. J. Muste. I was deeply moved by Dr. Muste's talk, but far from convinced of the practicability of his position. Like most of the students of Crozer, I felt that while war could never be a positive or absolute good, it could serve as a negative good in the sense of preventing the spread and growth of an evil force. War, horrible as it is, might be preferable to surrender to a totalitarian system—Nazi, Fascist, or Communist.

During this period I had about despaired of the power of love in solving social problems. Perhaps my faith in love was temporarily shaken by the philosophy of Nietzsche. I had been reading parts of *The Genealogy of Morals* and the whole of *The Will to Power*. Nietzsche's glorification of power—in his theory all life expressed the will to power—was an outgrowth of his contempt for ordinary morals. He attacked the whole of the Hebraic-Christian morality—with its virtues of piety and humility, its otherworldliness, and its attitude toward suffering—as the glorification of weakness, as making virtues out of necessity and impotence. He looked to the development of a superman who would surpass man as man surpassed the ape.

Then one Sunday afternoon I traveled to Philadelphia to hear a sermon by Dr. Mordecai Johnson, president of Howard University. He was there to preach for the Fellowship House of Philadelphia. Dr. Johnson had just returned from a trip to India, and, to my great interest, he spoke of the life and teachings of Mahatma Gandhi. His message was so profound and electrifying that I left the meeting and bought a half dozen books on Gandhi's life and works.

Like most people, I had heard of Gandhi, but I had never studied him seriously. As I read I became deeply fascinated by his campaigns of nonviolent resistance. I was particularly moved by the Salt March to the Sea and his numerous fasts. The whole concept of "Satyagraha" (*Satya* is truth which equals love, and *agraha* is force; "Satyagraha," therefore, means truth-force or love-force) was profoundly significant to me. As I delved deeper into the philosophy of Gandhi my skepticism concerning the power of love gradually diminished, and I came to see for the first time its potency in the area of social reform. Prior to reading Gandhi, I had about concluded that the ethics of Jesus were only effective in individual relationships. The "turn the other cheek" philosophy and the "love your enemies" philosophy were only valid, I felt, when individuals were in conflict with other individuals; when racial groups and nations were in conflict a more realistic approach seemed necessary. But after reading Gandhi, I saw how utterly mistaken I was.

Gandhi was probably the first person in history to lift the love ethic of Jesus above mere interaction between individuals to a powerful and effective social force on a large scale. Love for Gandhi was a potent instrument for social and collective transformation. It was in this Gandhian emphasis on love and nonviolence that I discovered the method for social reform that I had been seeking for so many months. The intellectual and moral satisfaction that I failed to gain from the utilitarianism of Bentham and Mill, the revolutionary methods of Marx and Lenin, the social-contracts theory of Hobbes, the "back to nature" optimism of Rousseau, and the superman philosophy of Nietzsche, I found in the nonviolent resistance philosophy of Gandhi. I came to feel that this was the only morally and practically sound method open to oppressed people in their struggle for freedom.

But my intellectual odyssey to nonviolence did not end here. During my last year in theological school, I began to read the works of Reinhold Niebuhr. The prophetic and realistic elements in Niebuhr's passionate style and profound thought were appealing to me, and I became so enamored of his social ethics that I almost fell into the trap of accepting uncritically everything he wrote.

About this time I read Niebuhr's critique of the pacifist position. Niebuhr had himself once been a member of the pacifist ranks. For several years, he had been national chairman of the Fellowship of Reconciliation. His break with pacifism came in the early thirties, and the first full statement of his criticism of pacifism was in *Moral Man and Immoral Society*. Here he argued that there was no intrinsic moral difference between violent and nonviolent resistance. The social consequences of the two methods were different, he contended, but the differences were in degree rather than kind. Later Niebuhr began emphasizing the irresponsibility of relying on nonviolent resistance when there was no ground for believing that it would be successful in preventing the spread of totalitarian tyranny. It could only be successful, he argued, if the groups against whom the resistance was taking place had some degree of moral conscience, as was the case in Gandhi's struggle against the British. Niebuhr's ultimate rejection of pacifism was based primarily on the doctrine of man. He argued that pacifism failed to do justice to the reformation doctrine of justification by faith, substituting for it a sectarian perfectionism which believes "that divine grace actually lifts men out of the sinful contradictions of history and establishes him above the sins of the world."

At first, Niebuhr's critique of pacifism left me in a state of confusion. As I continued to read, however, I came to see more and more the shortcomings of his position. For instance, many of his statements revealed that he interpreted pacifism as a sort of passive nonresistance to evil expressing naive trust in the power of love. But this was a serious distortion. My study of Gandhi convinced me that true pacifism is not nonresistance to evil, but nonviolent resistance to evil. Between the two positions, there is a world of difference. Gandhi resisted evil with as much vigor and power as the violent resister, but he resisted with love instead of hate. True pacifism is not unrealistic submission to evil power, as Niebuhr contends. It is rather a courageous confrontation of evil by the power of love, in the faith that it is better to be the recipient of violence than the inflicter of it, since the latter only multiplies the existence of violence and bitterness in the universe, while the former may develop a sense of shame in the opponent, and thereby bring about a transformation and change of heart.

In spite of the fact that I found many things to be desired in Niebuhr's philosophy, there were several points at which he constructively influenced my thinking. Niebuhr's great contribution to contemporary theology is that he has refuted the false optimism characteristic of a great segment of Protestant liberalism, without falling into the anti-rationalism of the continental theologian Karl Barth, or the semi-fundamentalism of other dialectical theologians. Moreover, Niebuhr has extraordinary insight into human nature, especially the behavior of nations and social groups. He is keenly aware of the complexity of human motives and of the relation between morality and power. His theology is a persistent reminder of the reality of sin on every level of man's existence. These elements in Niebuhr's thinking helped me to recognize the illusions of a superficial optimism concerning human nature and the dangers of a false idealism. While I still believed in man's potential for good, Niebuhr made me realize his potential for evil as well. Moreover, Niebuhr helped me to recognize the complexity of man's social involvement and the glaring reality of collective evil.

Many pacifists, I felt, failed to see this. All too many had an unwarranted optimism concerning man and leaned unconsciously toward self-righteousness. It was my revolt against these attitudes under the influence of Niebuhr that accounts for the fact that in spite of my strong leaning toward pacifism, I never joined a pacifist organization. After reading Niebuhr, I tried to arrive at a realistic pacifism. In other words, I came to see the pacifist position not as sinless but as the lesser evil in the circumstances. I felt then, and I feel now, that the pacifist would have a greater appeal if he did not claim to be free from the moral dilemmas that the Christian nonpacifist confronts.

The next stage of my intellectual pilgrimage to nonviolence came during my doctoral studies at Boston University. Here I had the opportunity to talk to many exponents of nonviolence, both students and visitors to the campus. Boston University School of Theology, under the influence of Dean Walter Muelder and Professor Allen Knight Chalmers, had a deep sympathy for pacifism. Both Dean Muelder and Dr. Chalmers had a passion for social justice that stemmed, not from a superficial optimism, but from a deep faith in the possibilities of human beings when they allowed themselves to become co-workers with God. It was at Boston University that I came to see that Niebuhr had overemphasized the corruption of human nature. His pessimism concerning human nature was not balanced by an optimism concerning divine nature. He was so involved in diagnosing man's sickness of sin that he overlooked the cure of grace.

I studied philosophy and theology at Boston University under Edgar S. Brightman and L. Harold DeWolf. Both men greatly stimulated my thinking. It was mainly under these teachers that I studied personalistic philosophy—the theory that the clue to the meaning of ultimate reality is found in personality. This personal idealism remains today my basic philosophical position. Personalism's insistence that only personality—finite and infinite—is ultimately real strengthened me in two convictions: it gave me metaphysical and philosophical grounding for the idea of a personal God, and it gave me a metaphysical basis for the dignity and worth of all human personality.

Just before Dr. Brightman's death, I began studying the philosophy of Hegel with him. Although the course was mainly a study of Hegel's monumental work, *Phenomenology of Mind*, I spent my spare time reading his *Philosophy of History* and *Philosophy of Right*. There were points in Hegel's philosophy that I strongly disagreed with. For instance, his absolute idealism was rationally unsound to me because it tended to swallow up the many in the one. But there were other aspects of his thinking that I found stimulating. His contention that "truth is the whole" led me to a philosophical method of rational coherence. His analysis of the dialectical process, in spite of its shortcomings, helped me to see that growth comes through struggle.

In 1954 I ended my formal training with all of these relatively divergent intellectual forces converging into a positive social philosophy. One of the main tenets of this philosophy was the conviction that nonviolent resistance was one of the most potent weapons available to oppressed people in their quest for social justice. At this time, however, I had merely an intellectual understanding and appreciation of the position, with no firm determination to organize it in a socially effective situation.

When I went to Montgomery as a pastor, I had not the slightest idea that I would later become involved in a crisis in which nonviolent resistance would be applicable. I neither started the protest nor suggested it. I simply responded to the call of the people for a spokesman. When the protest began, my mind, consciously or unconsciously, was driven back to the Sermon on the Mount, with its sublime teachings on love, and the Gandhian method of nonviolent resistance. As the days unfolded, I came to see the power of nonviolence more and more. Living through the actual experience of the protest, nonviolence became more than a method to which I gave intellectual assent; it became a commitment to a way of life. Many of the things that I had not cleared up intellectually concerning nonviolence were now solved in the sphere of practical action.

Since the philosophy of nonviolence played such a positive role in the Montgomery movement, it may be wise to turn to a brief discussion of some basic aspects of this philosophy.

First, it must be emphasized that nonviolent resistance is not a method for cowards; it does resist. If one uses this method because he is afraid or merely because he lacks the instruments of violence, he is not truly nonviolent. This is why Gandhi often said that if cowardice is the only alternative to violence, it is better to fight. He made this statement conscious of the fact that there is always another alternative: no individual or group need submit to any wrong, nor need they use violence to right the wrong; there is the way of nonviolence resistance. This is ultimately the way of the strong man. It is not a method of stagnant passivity. The phrase "passive resistance" often gives the false impression that this is a sort of "do-nothing method" in which the resister quietly and passively accepts evil. But nothing is further from the truth. For while the nonviolent resister is passive in the sense that he is not physically aggressive toward his opponent, his mind and emotions are always active, constantly seeking to persuade his opponent that he is wrong. The method is passive physically, but strongly active spiritually. It is not passive nonresistance to evil, it is active nonviolent resistance to evil.

A second basic fact that characterizes nonviolence is that it does not seek to defeat or humiliate the opponent, but to win his friendship and understanding. The nonviolent resister must often express his protest through noncooperation or boycotts, but he realizes that these are not ends themselves; they are merely means to awaken a sense of moral shame in the opponent. The end is redemption and reconciliation. The aftermath of nonviolence is the creation of the beloved community, while the aftermath of violence is tragic bitterness.

A third characteristic of this method is that the attack is directed against forces of evil rather than against persons who happen to be doing the evil. It is evil that the nonviolent resister seeks to defeat, not the persons victimized by evil. If he is opposing racial injustice, the nonviolent resister has the vision to see that the basic tension is not between races. As I like to say to the people in Montgomery: "The tension in this city is not between white people and Negro people. The tension is, at bottom, between justice and injustice, between the forces of light and the forces of darkness. And if there is a victory, it will be a victory not merely for fifty thousand Negroes, but a victory for justice and the forces of light. We are out to defeat injustice and not white persons who may be unjust."

A fourth point that characterizes nonviolent resistance is a willingness to accept suffering without retaliation, to accept blows from the opponent without striking back. "Rivers of blood may have to flow before we gain our freedom, but it must be our blood," Gandhi said to his countrymen. The nonviolent resister is willing to accept violence if necessary, but never to inflict it. He does not seek to dodge jail. If going to jail is necessary, he enters it "as a bridegroom enters the bride's chamber."

One may well ask: "What is the nonviolent resister's justification for this ordeal to which he invites men, for this mass political application of the ancient doctrine of turning the other cheek?" The answer is found in the realization that unearned suffering is redemptive. Suffering, the nonviolent resister realizes, has tremendous educational and transforming possibilities. "Things of fundamental importance to people are not secured by reason alone, but have to be purchased with their suffering," said Gandhi. He continues: "Suffering is infinitely more powerful than the law of the jungle for converting the opponent and opening his ears which are otherwise shut to the voice of reason."

A fifth point concerning nonviolent resistance is that it avoids not only external physical violence but also internal violence of spirit. The nonviolent resister not only refuses to shoot his opponent but he also refuses to hate him. At the center of nonviolence stands the principle of love. The nonviolent resister would contend that in the struggle for human dignity, the oppressed people of the world must not succumb to the temptation of becoming bitter or indulging in hate campaigns. To retaliate in kind would do nothing but intensify the existence of hate in the universe. Along the way of life, someone must have sense enough and morality enough to cut off the chain of hate. This can only be done by projecting the ethic of love to the center of our lives.

In speaking of love at this point, we are not referring to some sentimental or affectionate emotion. It would be nonsense to urge men to love their oppressors in an affectionate sense. Love in this connection means understanding, redemptive goodwill. Here the Greek language comes to our aid. There are three words for love in the Greek New Testament. First, there is *eros*. In Platonic philosophy *eros* meant the yearning of the soul for the realm of the divine. It has come now to mean a sort of aesthetic or romantic love. Second, there is *philia*, which means intimate affection between personal friends. *Philia* denotes a sort of reciprocal love; the person loves because he is loved. When we speak of loving those who oppose us, we refer to neither *eros* nor *philia*; we speak of a love which is expressed in the Greek word *agape*. *Agape* means understanding, redeeming goodwill for all men. It is an overflowing love which is purely spontaneous, unmotivated, groundless, and creative. It is not set in motion by any quality or function of its object. It is the love of God operating in the human heart.

Agape is disinterested love. It is a love in which the individual seeks not his own good, but the good of his neighbor (I Cor. 10:24). *Agape* does not begin by discriminating between worthy and unworthy people, or any qualities people possess. It begins by loving others *for their sakes*. It is an entirely "neighbor-regarding concern for others," which discovers the neighbor in every man it meets. Therefore, *agape* makes no distinction between friend and enemy; it is directed toward both.

If one loves an individual merely on account of his friendliness, he loves him for the sake of the benefits to be gained from the friendship, rather than for the friend's own sake. Consequently, the best way to assure oneself that love is disinterested is to have love for the enemy-neighbor from whom you can expect no good in return, but only hostility and persecution.

Another basic point about *agape* is that it springs from the *need* of the other person—his need for belonging to the best in the human family. The Samaritan who helped the Jew on the Jericho Road was "good" because he responded to the human need that he was presented with. God's love is eternal and fails not because man needs his love. St. Paul assures us that the loving act of redemption was done "while we were yet sinners"—that is, at the point of our greatest need for love. Since the white man's personality is greatly distorted by segregation, and his soul is greatly scarred, he needs the love of the Negro. The Negro must love the white man, because the white man needs his love to remove his tensions, insecurities, and fears.

Agape is not a weak, passive love. It is love in action. *Agape* is love seeking to preserve and create community. It is insistence on community even when one seeks to break it. *Agape* is a willingness to sacrifice in the interest of mutuality. *Agape* is a willingness to go to any length to restore community. It doesn't stop at the first mile, but it goes the second mile to restore community. It is a willingness to forgive, not seven times, but seventy times seven to restore community. The cross is the eternal expression of the length to which God will go in order to restore broken community. The resurrection is a symbol of God's triumph over all the forces that seek to block community. The Holy Spirit is the continuing community creating reality that moves through history. He who works against community is working against the whole of creation. Therefore, if I respond to hate with a reciprocal hate I do nothing but intensify the cleavage in broken community. I can only close the gap in broken community by meeting hate with love. If I meet hate with hate, I become depersonalized, because creation is so designed that my personality can only be fulfilled in the context of community. Booker T. Washington was right: "Let no man pull you so low as to make you hate him." When he pulls you that low he brings you to the point of working against community; he drags you to the point of defying creation, and thereby becoming depersonalized.

In the final analysis, *agape* means a recognition of the fact that all life is interrelated. All humanity is involved in a single process, and all men are brothers. To the degree that I harm my brother, no matter what he is doing to me, to that extent I am harming myself. For example, white men often refuse federal aid to education in order to avoid giving the Negro his rights; but because all men are brothers they cannot deny Negro children without harming their own. They end, all efforts to the contrary, by hurting themselves. Why is this? Because men are brothers. If you harm me, you harm yourself.

Love, *agape*, is the only cement that can hold this broken community together. When I am commanded to love, I am commanded to restore community, to resist injustice, and to meet the needs of my brothers.

A sixth basic fact about nonviolent resistance is that it is based on the conviction that the universe is on the side of justice. Consequently, the believer in nonviolence has deep faith in the future. This faith is another reason why the nonviolent resister can accept suffering without retaliation. For he knows that in his struggle for justice he has cosmic companionship. It is true that there are devout believers in nonviolence who find it difficult to believe in a personal God. But even these persons believe in the existence of some creative force that works for universal wholeness. Whether we call it an unconscious process, an impersonal Brahman, or a Personal Being of matchless power and infinite love, there is a creative force in this universe that works to bring the disconnected aspects of reality into a harmonious whole.

From *Stride Toward Freedom: The Montgomery Story*
(Harper & Row, 1958, reprinted by Beacon Press, 2010).

FOUR

LOVING
YOUR ENEMIES

Convicted in July 1962 for participating in Albany movement demonstrations the previous December, Dr. King and his close friend and movement colleague Ralph Abernathy refused to pay their fines and announced instead that they would serve five-day jail terms. After spending two nights in a jail that King described as "dirty, filthy, and ill-equipped . . . [the] worst I have ever seen," the two men were unexpectedly bailed out by an unidentified black man. When he was again jailed, later in July of that year, King used his two weeks of imprisonment to revise one of his favorite sermons, "Loving Your Enemies," for inclusion in the sermon book *Strength to Love,* published in 1963.

Ye have heard that it hath been said,
Thou shalt love thy neighbor, and hate
thine enemy. But I say unto you, Love
your enemies, bless them that curse you,
do good to them that hate you, and pray
for them which despitefully use you, and
persecute you; that ye may be children
of your Father which is in heaven.
　　　　　—MATTHEW 5:43–45

Probably no admonition of Jesus has been more difficult to follow than the command to "love your enemies." Some men have sincerely felt that its actual practice is not possible. It is easy, they say, to love those who love you, but how can one love those who openly and insidiously seek to defeat you? Others, like the philosopher Nietzsche, contend that Jesus' exhortation to love one's enemies is testimony to the fact that the Christian ethic is designed for the weak and cowardly, and not for the strong and courageous. Jesus, they say, was an impractical idealist.

In spite of these insistent questions and persistent objections, this command of Jesus challenges us with new urgency. Upheaval after upheaval has reminded us that modern man is traveling along a road called hate, in a journey that will bring us to destruction and damnation. Far from being the pious injunction of a Utopian dreamer, the command to love one's enemy is an absolute necessity for our survival. Love even for enemies is the key to the solution of the problems of our world. Jesus is not an impractical idealist: he is the practical realist.

I am certain that Jesus understood the difficulty inherent in the act of loving one's enemy. He never joined the ranks of those who talk glibly about the easiness of the moral life. He realized that every genuine expression of love grows out of a consistent and total surrender to God. So when Jesus said "Love your enemy," he was not unmindful of its stringent qualities. Yet he meant every word of it. Our responsibility as Christians is to discover the meaning of this command and seek passionately to live it out in our daily lives.

I

Let us be practical and ask the question, *How do we love our enemies?*

First, we must develop and maintain the capacity to forgive. He who is devoid of the power to forgive is devoid of the power to love. It is impossible even to begin the act of loving one's enemies without the prior acceptance of the necessity, over and over again, of forgiving those who inflict evil and injury upon us. It is also necessary to realize that the forgiving act must always be initiated by the person who has been wronged, the victim of some great hurt, the recipient of some tortuous injustice, the absorber of some terrible act of oppression. The wrongdoer may request forgiveness. He may come to himself, and, like the prodigal son, move up some dusty road, his heart palpitating with the desire for forgiveness. But only the injured neighbor, the loving father back home, can really pour out the warm waters of forgiveness.

Forgiveness does not mean ignoring what has been done or putting a false label on an evil act. It means, rather, that the evil act no longer remains as a barrier to the relationship. Forgiveness is a catalyst creating the atmosphere necessary for a fresh start and a new beginning. It is the lifting of a burden or the cancelling of a debt. The words "I will forgive you, but I'll never forget what you've done" never explain the real nature of forgiveness. Certainly one can never forget, if that means erasing it totally from his mind. But when we forgive, we forget in the sense that the evil deed is no longer a mental block impeding a new relationship. Likewise, we can never say, "I will forgive you, but I won't have anything further to do with you." Forgiveness means reconciliation, a coming together again. Without this, no man can love his enemies. The degree to which we are able to forgive determines the degree to which we are able to love our enemies.

Second, we must recognize that the evil deed of the enemy-neighbor, the thing that hurts, never quite expresses all that he is. An element of goodness may be found even in our worst enemy. Each of us is something of a schizophrenic personality, tragically divided against ourselves. A persistent civil war rages within all of our lives. Something within us causes us to lament with Ovid, the Latin poet, "I see and approve the better things, but follow worse," or to agree with Plato that human personality is like a charioteer having two headstrong horses, each wanting to go in a different direction, or to repeat with the Apostle Paul, "The good that I would I do not: but the evil which I would not, that I do."

This simply means that there is some good in the worst of us and some evil in the best of us. When we discover this, we are less prone to hate our enemies. When we look beneath the surface, beneath the impulsive evil deed, we see within our enemy-neighbor a measure of goodness and know that the viciousness and evilness of his acts are not quite representative of all that he is. We see him in a new light. We recognize that his hate grows out of fear, pride, ignorance, prejudice, and misunderstanding, but in spite of this, we know God's image is ineffably etched in his being. Then we love our enemies by realizing that they are not totally bad and that they are not beyond the reach of God's redemptive love.

Third, we must not seek to defeat or humiliate the enemy but to win his friendship and understanding. At times we are able to humiliate our worst enemy. Inevitably, his weak moments come and we are able to thrust in his side the spear of defeat. But this we must not do. Every word and deed must contribute to an understanding with the enemy and release those vast reservoirs of goodwill which have been blocked by impenetrable walls of hate.

The meaning of love is not to be confused with some sentimental outpouring. Love is something much deeper than emotional bosh. Perhaps the Greek language can clear our confusion at this point. In the Greek New Testament are three words for love. The word *eros* is a sort of aesthetic or romantic love. In the Platonic dialogues *eros* is a yearning of the soul for the realm of the divine. The second word is *philia*, a reciprocal love and the intimate affection and friendship between friends. We love those whom we like, and we love because we are loved. The third word is *agape* understanding and creative, redemptive goodwill for all men. An overflowing love which seeks nothing in return, *agape* is the love of God operating in the human heart. At this level, we love men not because we like them, nor because their ways appeal to us, nor even because they possess some type of divine spark; we love every man because God loves him. At this level, we love the person who does an evil deed, although we hate the deed that he does.

Now we can see what Jesus meant when he said, "Love your enemies." We should be happy that he did not say, "Like your enemies." It is almost impossible to like some people. "Like" is a sentimental and affectionate word. How can we be affectionate toward a person whose avowed aim is to crush our very being and place innumerable stumbling blocks in our path? How can we like a person who is threatening our children and bombing our homes? That is impossible. But Jesus recognized that *love* is greater than *like*. When Jesus bids us to love our enemies, he is speaking neither of *eros* nor *philia*; he is speaking of *agape* understanding and creative, redemptive goodwill for all men. Only by following this way and responding with this type of love are we able to be children of our Father who is in heaven.

II

Let us move now from the practical *how* to the theoretical *why: Why should we love our enemies?* The first reason is fairly obvious. Returning hate for hate multiplies hate, adding deeper darkness to a night already devoid of stars. Darkness cannot drive out darkness; only light can do that. Hate cannot drive out hate; only love can do that. Hate multiplies hate, violence multiplies violence, and toughness multiplies toughness in a descending spiral of destruction. So when Jesus says "Love your enemies," he is setting forth a profound and ultimately inescapable admonition. Have we not come to such an impasse in the modern world that we must love our enemies—or else? The chain reaction of evil—hate begetting hate, wars producing more wars—must be broken, or we shall be plunged into the dark abyss of annihilation.

Another reason why we must love our enemies is that hate scars the soul and distorts the personality. Mindful that hate is an evil and dangerous force, we too often think of what it does to the person hated. This is understandable, for hate brings irreparable damage to its victims. We have seen its ugly consequences in the ignominious deaths brought to six million Jews by a hate-obsessed madman named Hitler, in the unspeakable violence inflicted upon Negroes by bloodthirsty mobs, in the dark horrors of war, and in the terrible indignities and injustices perpetrated against millions of God's children by unconscionable oppressors.

But there is another side which we must never overlook. Hate is just as injurious to the person who hates. Like an unchecked cancer, hate corrodes the personality and eats away its vital unity. Hate destroys a man's sense of values and his objectivity. It causes him to describe the beautiful as ugly and the ugly as beautiful, and to confuse the true with the false and the false with the true.

Dr. E. Franklin Frazier, in an interesting essay entitled "The Pathology of Race Prejudice," included several examples of white persons who were normal, amiable, and congenial in their day-to-day relationships with other white persons but when they were challenged to think of Negroes as equals or even to discuss the question of racial injustice, they reacted with unbelievable irrationality and an abnormal unbalance. This happens when hate lingers in our minds. Psychiatrists report that many of the strange things that happen in the subconscious, many of our inner conflicts, are rooted in hate. They say, "Love or perish." Modern psychology recognizes what Jesus taught centuries ago: hate divides the personality and love in an amazing and inexorable way unites it.

A third reason why we should love our enemies is that love is the only force capable of transforming an enemy into a friend. We never get rid of an enemy by meeting hate with hate; we get rid of an enemy by getting rid of enmity. By its very nature, hate destroys and tears down; by its very nature, love creates and builds up. Love transforms with redemptive power.

Lincoln tried love and left for all history a magnificent drama of reconciliation. When he was campaigning for the presidency one of his arch-enemies was a man named Stanton. For some reason Stanton hated Lincoln. He used every ounce of his energy to degrade him in the eyes of the public. So deep rooted was Stanton's hate for Lincoln that he uttered unkind words about his physical appearance, and sought to embarrass him at every point with the bitterest diatribes. But in spite of this Lincoln was elected President of the United States. Then came the period when he had to select his cabinet, which would consist of the persons who would be his most intimate associates in implementing his program. He started choosing men here and there for the various secretaryships. The day finally came for Lincoln to select a man to fill the all-important post of Secretary of War. Can you imagine whom Lincoln chose to fill this post? None other than the man named Stanton. There was an immediate uproar in the inner circle when the news began to spread. Adviser after adviser was heard saying, "Mr. President, you are making a mistake. Do you know this man Stanton? Are you familiar with all of the ugly things he said about you? He is your enemy. He will seek to sabotage your program. Have you thought this through, Mr. President?" Mr. Lincoln's answer was terse and to the point: "Yes, I know Mr. Stanton. I am aware of all the terrible things he has said about me. But after looking over the nation, I find he is the best man for the job." So Stanton became Abraham Lincoln's Secretary of War and rendered an invaluable service to his nation and his President. Not many years later Lincoln was assassinated. Many laudable things were said about him. Even today millions of people still adore him as the greatest of all Americans. H. G. Wells selected him as one of the six great men of history. But of all the great statements made about Abraham Lincoln, the words of Stanton remain among the greatest. Standing near the dead body of the man he once hated, Stanton referred to him as one of the greatest men that ever lived and said "he now belongs to the ages." If Lincoln had hated Stanton both men would have gone to their graves as bitter enemies. But through the power of love Lincoln transformed an enemy into a friend. It was this same attitude that made it possible for Lincoln to speak a kind word about the South during the Civil War when feeling was most bitter. Asked by a shocked bystander how he could do this, Lincoln said, "Madam, do I not destroy my enemies when I make them my friends?" This is the power of redemptive love.

We must hasten to say that these are not the ultimate reasons why we should love our enemies. An even more basic reason why we are commanded to love is expressed explicitly in Jesus' words, "Love your enemies . . . *that ye may be children of your Father which is in heaven.*" We are called to this difficult task in order to realize a unique relationship with God. We are potential sons of God. Through love that potentiality becomes actuality. We must love our enemies, because only by loving them can we know God and experience the beauty of his holiness.

The relevance of what I have said to the crisis in race relations should be readily apparent. There will be no permanent solution to the race problem until oppressed men develop the capacity to love their enemies. The darkness of racial injustice will be dispelled only by the light of forgiving love. For more than three centuries American Negroes have been battered by the iron rod of oppression, frustrated by day and bewildered by night by unbearable injustice, and burdened with the ugly weight of discrimination. Forced to live with these shameful conditions, we are tempted to become bitter and to retaliate with a corresponding hate. But if this happens, the new order we seek will be little more than a duplicate of the old order. We must in strength and humility meet hate with love.

Of course, this is not *practical*. Life is a matter of getting even, of hitting back, of dog eat dog. Am I saying that Jesus commands us to love those who hurt and oppress us? Do I sound like most preachers—idealistic and impractical? Maybe in some distant Utopia, you say, that idea will work, but not in the hard, cold world in which we live.

My friends, we have followed the so-called practical way for too long a time now, and it has led inexorably to deeper confusion and chaos. Time is cluttered with the wreckage of communities which surrendered to hatred and violence. For the salvation of our nation and the salvation of mankind, we must follow another way. This does not mean that we abandon our righteous efforts. With every ounce of our energy we must continue to rid this nation of the incubus of segregation. But we shall not in the process relinquish our privilege and our obligation to love. While abhorring segregation, we shall love the segregationist. This is the only way to create the beloved community.

To our most bitter opponents we say: "We shall match your capacity to inflict suffering by our capacity to endure suffering. We shall meet your physical force with soul force. Do to us what you will, and we shall continue to love you. We cannot in all good conscience obey your unjust laws, because noncooperation with evil is as much a moral obligation as is cooperation with good. Throw us in jail, and we shall still love you. Send your hooded perpetrators of violence into our community at the midnight hour and beat us and leave us half dead, and we shall still love you. But be ye assured that we will wear you down by our capacity to suffer. One day we shall win freedom, but not only for ourselves. We shall so appeal to your heart and conscience that we shall win *you* in the process, and our victory will be a double victory."

Love is the most durable power in the world. This creative force, so beautifully exemplified in the life of our Christ, is the most potent instrument available in mankind's quest for peace and security. Napoleon Bonaparte, the great military genius, looking back over his years of conquest, is reported to have said: "Alexander, Caesar, Charlemagne and I have built great empires. But upon what did they depend? They depended on force. But centuries ago Jesus started an empire that was built on love, and even to this day millions will die for him." Who can doubt the veracity of these words? The great military leaders of the past have gone, and their empires have crumbled and burned to ashes. But the empire of Jesus, built solidly and majestically on the foundation of love, is still growing. It started with a small group of dedicated men, who, through the inspiration of their Lord, were able to shake the hinges from the gates of the Roman Empire, and carry the gospel into all the world. Today the vast earthly kingdom of Christ numbers more than 900,000,000 and covers every land and tribe. Today we hear again the promise of victory:

> *Jesus shall reign where'er the sun*
> *Does his successive journeys run;*
> *His kingdom stretch from shore to shore,*
> *Till moon shall wax and wane no more.*

Another choir joyously responds:

> *In Christ there is no East or West,*
> *In Him no South or North,*

But one great Fellowship of Love
Throughout the whole wide earth.

Jesus is eternally right. History is replete with the bleached bones of nations that refused to listen to him. May we in the twentieth century hear and follow his words—before it is too late. May we solemnly realize that we shall never be true sons of our heavenly Father until we love our enemies and pray for those who persecute us.

From *Strength to Love* (Harper & Row, 1963,
reprinted by Beacon Press in *A Gift of Love: Sermons
from Strength to Love and Other Preachings*, 2012).

FIVE

WHAT IS YOUR LIFE'S BLUEPRINT?

On October 26, 1967, six months before he was assassinated, Dr. King spoke to a group of students at Barratt Junior High School in Philadelphia.

I want to ask you a question, and that is, What is in your life's blueprint? This is a most important and crucial period of your lives, for what you do now and what you decide now at this age may well determine which way your life shall go. And whenever a building is constructed, you usually have an architect who draws a blueprint. And that blueprint serves as the pattern, as the guide, as the model for those who are to build the building. And a building is not well erected without a good, sound, and solid blueprint.

Now, each of you is in the process of building the structure of your lives. And the question is whether you have a proper, a solid, and a sound blueprint. And I want to suggest some of the things that should be in your life's blueprint.

Number one in your life's blueprint should be a deep belief in your own dignity, your own worth, and your own somebodiness. Don't allow anybody to make you feel that you are nobody. Always feel that you count. Always feel that you have worth. And always feel that your life has ultimate significance. Now, that means that you should not be ashamed of your color. You know, it's very unfortunate that in so many instances, our society has placed a stigma on the Negroes' color. And you know there are some Negroes who are ashamed of themselves. But don't be ashamed of your color. Don't be ashamed of your biological features. Somehow you must be able to say in your own lives—and really believe it—"I am black but beautiful," and believe it in your heart. And therefore you need not be lured into purchasing cosmetics advertised to make you lighter. Neither do you need to process your hair to make it appear straight. I have good hair, and it is good as anybody else's hair in the world, and we've got to believe that.

Now, in your life's blueprint, be sure that you have that principle of somebodiness. Secondly, in your life's blueprint, you must have as a basic principle the determination to achieve excellence in your various fields of endeavor. You're going to be deciding, as the days and the years unfold, what you will do in life, what your life's work will be. And once you discover what it will be, set out to do it, and to do it well. And I say to you, my young friends, that doors are opening to each of you, doors of opportunity are opening to each of you that were not open to your mothers and to your fathers. And the great challenge facing you is to be ready to enter these doors as they open.

Ralph Waldo Emerson, the great essayist, said in a lecture back in 1871 that if a man can write a better book or preach a better sermon or make a better mousetrap than his neighbor, even if he builds his house in the woods, the world will make a beaten path to his door. That hadn't always been true, but it will become increasingly true. And so I would urge you to study hard, to burn the midnight oil. I would say to you, "Don't drop out of school." And I understand all of the sociological reasons why we often drop out of school. But I urge you, in spite of your economic plight, in spite of the situation that you are forced to live so often with intolerable conditions, stay in school.

And when you discover what you're going to be in life, set out to do it as if God Almighty called you at this particular moment in history to do it. And just don't set out to do a good Negro job, but do a good job that anybody could do. Don't set out to be just a good Negro doctor, a good Negro lawyer, a good Negro schoolteacher, a good Negro preacher, a good Negro barber or beautician, a good Negro skilled laborer. For if you set out to do that, you have already flunked your matriculation exam for entrance into the University of Integration. Set out to do a good job, and do that job so well that the living, the dead, or the unborn couldn't do it any better.

If it falls to your lot to be a street sweeper, sweep streets like Michelangelo painted pictures. Sweep streets like Beethoven composed music. Sweep streets like Leontyne Price sings before the Metropolitan Opera. And sweep streets like Shakespeare wrote poetry. Sweep streets so well that all the hosts of Heaven and Earth will have to pause and say, "Here lived a great street sweeper who swept his job well."

If you can't be a pine on the top of the hill, be a scrub in the valley. But be the best little scrub on the side of the hill. Be a bush if you can't be a tree. If you can't be a highway, just be a trail. If you can't be the sun, be a star. For it isn't by size that you win or you fail. Be the best of whatever you are.

We already have some noble examples of black men and black women who demonstrated to us that human nature cannot be catalogued. They and their own lives have walked through long and desolate nights of oppression, and yet they've risen up and plunged against cloud-filled nights of affliction. New and blazing stars of inspiration.

And, so, from an old slaves' cabin of Virginia's hills, Booker T. Washington rose up to be one of America's great leaders. He lit a torch in Alabama, and darkness fled in that setting. Yes, you should know this because it's in your own city.

From a poverty-stricken area of Philadelphia, Pennsylvania, Marian Anderson rose up to be the world's greatest contralto, so that a Toscanini could say that a voice like this comes only once in a century, and Sibelius of Finland could say, "My roof is too low for such a voice."

From the red hills of Gordon County, Georgia, in the arms of a mother who could neither read nor write, Roland Hayes rose up to be one of the world's great singers and carried his melodious voice into the palaces and mansions of kings and queens.

From crippling circumstances there came a George Washington

Carver to carve for himself an imperishable niche in the annals of science.

There was a star in the diplomatic sky. And then came Ralph Bunche, the grandson of a slave preacher, and he reached up and grabbed it and allowed it to shine in his life with all of its scintillating beauty. There was a star in the athletic sky, and then came Jackie Robinson in his day and Willie Mays in his day, with their powerful bats and their calm spirits. Then came Jesse Owens, with his fleeting, dashing feet. Then came Joe Louis and Muhammad Ali, with their educated fists. All of them came to tell us that we can be somebody. And to justify the conviction of the poet:

> *Fleecy locks and black complexion*
> *Cannot forfeit nature's claim;*
> *Skins may differ, but affection*
> *Dwells in white and black the same.*

> *And if I were so tall as to reach the pole*
> *Or to grasp at the ocean at a span,*
> *I must be measured by my soul*
> *The mind is the standard of the man.*[1]

And finally, and finally, in your life's blueprint, must be a commitment to the eternal principles of beauty, love, and justice. Don't allow anybody to pull you so low as to make you hate them. Don't allow anybody to cause you to lose your self-respect to the point that you do not struggle for justice. However young you are, you have a responsibility to seek to make your nation a better nation in which to live. You have a responsibility to seek to make life better for everybody. And so you must be involved in the struggle for freedom and justice.

Now, in this struggle for freedom and justice, there are many constructive things that we all can do and that we all must do. And we must not give ourselves to those things which will not solve our problems. You've heard the word "nonviolent" and you've heard the word "violent." I happen to believe in nonviolence. We struggle with this method with young people and adults alike, all over the South, and we have won some significant victories. And we've got to struggle with it all over the North, because the problems are as serious in the North as they are in the South.

But I believe as we struggle with these problems, we've got to struggle with them with a method that can be militant but at the same time does not destroy life or property. And so our slogan must not be "Burn, baby, burn." It must be, "Build, baby, build." "Organize, baby, organize." Yes, our slogan must be "Learn, baby, learn," so that we can earn, baby, earn.

And with a powerful commitment, I believe that we can transform dark yesterdays of injustice into bright tomorrows of justice and humanity. Let us keep going toward the goal of selfhood, toward the realization of the dream of brotherhood, and toward the realization of the dream of understanding good will. Let nobody stop us.

I close by quoting once more the man that the young lady quoted, that magnificent black bard who has now passed on, Langston Hughes. One day he wrote a poem entitled "Mother to Son." The mother didn't always have her grammar right, but she uttered words of great symbolic profundity:

Well, son, I'll tell you:
Life for me ain't been no crystal stair.
It's had tacks in it,
[And splinters,]
And boards torn up,
places with no carpet on the floor—
Bare.
But all the time
I'se been a-climbin' on,
And reachin' landin's,
And turnin' corners,
And sometimes goin' in the dark
Where there ain't been no light.
So boy, don't you stop now.
Don't you set down on the steps

'Cause you finds it's kinder hard.
For I'se still goin', boy,
I'se still climbin',
And life for me ain't been no crystal stair.

Well, life for none of us has been a crystal stair. But we must keep moving. We must keep going. If you can't fly, run. If you can't run, walk. If you can't walk, crawl. But by all means, keep moving.

Delivered at Barratt Junior High School,
Philadelphia, Pennsylvania, October 26, 1967.

PART TWO

PROPHETIC VISION

GLOBAL ANALYSIS AND LOCAL PRAXIS

Dr. Martin Luther King, Jr., reading The Gandhi Reader, *circa 1960.*

RADICAL LOVE goes hand in hand with radical analysis—of global capitalist forces, nation-states, civic institutions, and individual psyches. Radical analysis looks at the world through the lens of the least of these—the wretched of the earth. It tries to explain why and describe how powers operate in the economy, government, and society. King's final analysis, captured in "The World House," is his most prophetic vision of justice and freedom, where he highlights escalating global interdependence and social misery. His conception of globalization does not focus on the mobility of capital or the movement of stock markets. Instead, he focuses on the catastrophes of racism, poverty, materialism, and war. He calls for a "true revolution" that shifts from a "thing-oriented" society to a "person-oriented" society.

Like the prophetic Pope Francis in our day, King believes that religious faiths in general and the Christian faith in particular must play a crucial role in a spiritual and moral awakening that unleashes radical love for precious poor and working people. In a world in which market values pervade all—is not everything and everybody for sale?—religious traditions can be a strong source for non-market values like love, trust, and tenderness. Needless to say, market religion looms large in market culture. Yet the radical King looks for that prophetic cloud of witnesses from all religions, as well as secular traditions, who bear witness to peace and justice.

King had a special relation to American Jews. He understood the intimate link between modern black identity and ancient Jewish identity. Hebrew scripture, in English translation, was fundamental to modern black culture and life. And a Palestinian Jew named Jesus has been at the center of millions of black lives, including my own. King also was well aware and grateful for the large Jewish support—in money, expertise, bodies, and deaths—of the black freedom movement. Hence he had no patience for anti-Jewish hatred, sentiment, or prejudice.

The radical King looked at Jews through the lens of precious peoples terrorized, traumatized, and stigmatized for more than two thousand years. His radical love embraced Jews and their fragile predicament—here and abroad. There is no doubt King supported Zionism—the Jewish quest for self-determination—yet he did not live long enough to witness a vicious Israeli occupation that terrorizes, traumatizes, and stigmatizes precious Palestinians. King's commitment to the security of Israel was absolute—and rightly so. If he had lived, his commitment to the dignity of and justice for the Palestinians would be absolute—and rightly so. He would condemn Israeli state terrorism and Palestinian terrorism, and reject both anti-Arab racism and anti-Jewish racism. In fact, the continued courageous witness of Bassem al-Tamimi, leader of the nonviolent resistant movement on the West Bank, exemplifies King's vision. For both of them, a Palestinian baby is just as precious as a Jewish baby.

The radical King put the black South African freedom struggle at the center of his global analysis. Its parallels with US Jim Crow were obvious. And the fact that black Americans were also an African people with deep cultural and spiritual links was significant.

King and Mandela are the two towering public figures in the past fifty years in the world. Both have been Santa-Clausified—tamed, domesticated, sanitized, and sterilized—into nonthreatening and smiling old men with toys in their bags and forgiveness in their hearts. Yet both were radical and revolutionary. They were hunted, hated, and hurt by the powers that be. And both had radical love.

King's tribute to W. E. B. Du Bois is one of the great classics of modern culture. What a moment to have America's supreme organic intellectual reflect on America's greatest twentieth-century public intellectual! This speech deserves to be as well known as his great sermons. King's wholesale acknowledgment of the great contributions of W. E. B. Du Bois, even as a communist, reflects his willingness to embrace radical analysis, even as he remained in the prophetic Christian tradition.

SIX

THE WORLD HOUSE

In 1967, Dr. King isolated himself from the demands of the civil rights movement, rented a house in Jamaica with no telephone, and labored over his final manuscript, *Where Do We Go from Here*. In the concluding chapter, excerpted here, King calls us to transcend race, class, nation, and religion and embrace a vision of the World House to eradicate at home and globally the triple evils of racism, poverty, and militarism; to curb excessive materialism; and to use methods of nonviolence to fight for social justice.

I

Some years ago a famous novelist died. Among his papers was found a list of suggested plots for future stories, the most prominently underscored being this one: "A widely separated family inherits a house in which they have to live together." This is the great new problem of mankind. We have inherited a large house, a great "world house" in which we have to live together—black and white, Easterner and Westerner, Gentile and Jew, Catholic and Protestant, Muslim and Hindu—a family unduly separated in ideas, culture and interest, who, because we can never again live apart, must learn somehow to live with each other in peace.

However deeply American Negroes are caught in the struggle to be at last at home in our homeland of the United States, we cannot ignore the larger world house in which we are also dwellers. Equality with whites will not solve the problems of either whites or Negroes if it means equality in a world society stricken by poverty and in a universe doomed to extinction by war.

All inhabitants of the globe are now neighbors. This worldwide neighborhood has been brought into being largely as a result of the modern scientific and technological revolutions. The world of today is vastly different from the world of just one hundred years ago. A century ago Thomas Edison had not yet invented the incandescent lamp to bring light to many dark places of the earth. The Wright brothers had not yet invented that fascinating mechanical bird that would spread its gigantic wings across the skies and soon dwarf distance and place time in the service of man. Einstein had not yet challenged an axiom and the theory of relativity had not yet been posited.

Human beings, searching a century ago as now for better understanding, had no television, no radios, no telephones and no motion pictures through which to communicate. Medical science had not yet discovered the wonder drugs to end many dread plagues and diseases. One hundred years ago military men had not yet developed the terrifying weapons of warfare that we know today—not the bomber, an airborne fortress raining down death; nor napalm, that burner of all things and flesh in its path. A century ago there were no sky-scraping buildings to kiss the stars and no gargantuan bridges to span the waters. Science had not yet peered into the unfathomable ranges of interstellar space, nor had it penetrated oceanic depths. All these new inventions, these new ideas, these sometimes fascinating and sometimes frightening developments, came later. Most of them have come within the past sixty years, sometimes with agonizing slowness, more characteristically with bewildering speed, but always with enormous significance for our future.

The years ahead will see a continuation of the same dramatic developments. Physical science will carve new highways through the stratosphere. In a few years astronauts and cosmonauts will probably walk comfortably across the uncertain pathways of the moon. In two or three years it will be possible, because of the new supersonic jets, to fly from New York to London in two and one-half hours. In the years ahead medical science will greatly prolong the lives of men by finding a cure for cancer and deadly heart ailments. Automation and cybernation will make it possible for working people to have undreamed-of amounts of leisure time. All this is a dazzling picture of the furniture, the workshop, the spacious rooms, the new decorations and the architectural pattern of the large world house in which we are living.

Along with the scientific and technological revolution, we have also witnessed a worldwide freedom revolution over the last few decades. The present upsurge of the Negro people of the United States grows out of a deep and passionate determination to make freedom and equality a reality "here" and "now." In one sense the civil rights movement in the United States is a special American phenomenon which must be understood in the light of American history and dealt with in terms of the American situation. But on another and more important level, what is happening in the United States today is a significant part of a world development.

We live in a day, said the philosopher Alfred North Whitehead, "when civilization is shifting its basic outlook; a major turning point in history where the pre-suppositions on which society is structured are being analyzed, sharply challenged, and profoundly changed." What we are seeing now is a freedom explosion, the realization of "an idea whose time has come," to use Victor Hugo's phrase. The deep rumbling of discontent that we hear today is the thunder of disinherited masses, rising from dungeons of oppression to the bright hills of freedom. In one majestic chorus the rising masses are singing, in the words of our freedom song, "Ain't gonna let nobody turn us around." All over the world like a fever, freedom is spreading in the widest liberation movement in history. The great masses of people are determined to end the exploitation of their races and lands. They are awake and moving toward their goal like a tidal wave. You can hear them rumbling in every village street, on the docks, in the houses, among the students, in the churches and at political meetings. For several centuries the direction of history flowed from the nations and societies of Western Europe out into the rest of the world in "conquests" of various sorts. That period, the era of colonialism, is at an end. East is moving West. The earth is being redistributed. Yes, we are "shifting our basic outlooks."

These developments should not surprise any student of history. Oppressed people cannot remain oppressed forever. The yearning for freedom eventually manifests itself. The Bible tells the thrilling story of how Moses stood in Pharaoh's court centuries ago and cried, "Let my people go." This was an opening chapter in a continuing story. The present struggle in the United States is a later chapter in the same story. Something within has reminded the Negro of his birthright of freedom, and something without has reminded him that it can be gained. Consciously or unconsciously, he has been caught up by the spirit of the times, and with his black brothers of Africa and his brown and yellow brothers in Asia, South America and the Caribbean, the United States Negro is moving with a sense of great urgency toward the promised land of racial justice.

Nothing could be more tragic than for men to live in these revolutionary times and fail to achieve the new attitudes and the new mental outlooks that the new situation demands. In Washington Irving's familiar story of Rip Van Winkle, the one thing that we usually remember is that Rip slept twenty years. There is another important point, however, that is almost always overlooked. It was the sign on the inn in the little town on the Hudson from which Rip departed and scaled the mountain for his long sleep. When he went up, the sign had a picture of King George III of England. When he came down, twenty years later, the sign had a picture of George Washington. As he looked at the picture of the first President of the United States, Rip was confused, flustered and lost. He knew not who Washington was. The most striking thing about this story is not that Rip slept twenty years, but that he slept through a revolution that would alter the course of human history.

One of the great liabilities of history is that all too many people fail to remain awake through great periods of social change. Every society has its protectors of the status quo and its fraternities of the indifferent who are notorious for sleeping through revolutions. But today our very survival depends on our ability to stay awake, to adjust to new ideas, to remain vigilant and to face the challenge of change. The large house in which we live demands that we transform this world-wide neighborhood into a worldwide brotherhood. Together we must learn to live as brothers or together we will be forced to perish as fools.

We must work passionately and indefatigably to bridge the gulf between our scientific progress and our moral progress. One of the great problems of mankind is that we suffer from a poverty of the spirit which stands in glaring contrast to our scientific and technological abundance. The richer we have become materially, the poorer we have become morally and spiritually.

Every man lives in two realms, the internal and the external. The internal is that realm of spiritual ends expressed in art, literature, morals and religion. The external is that complex of devices, techniques, mechanisms and instrumentalities by means of which we live. Our problem today is that we have allowed the internal to become lost in the external. We have allowed the means by which we live to outdistance the ends for which we live. So much of modern life can be summarized in that suggestive phrase of Thoreau: "Improved means to an unimproved end." This is the serious predicament, the deep and haunting problem, confronting modern man. Enlarged material powers spell enlarged peril if there is not proportionate growth of the soul. When the external of man's nature subjugates the internal, dark storm clouds begin to form.

Western civilization is particularly vulnerable at this moment, for our material abundance has brought us neither peace of mind nor serenity of spirit. An Asian writer has portrayed our dilemma in candid terms:

> You call your thousand material devices "labor-saving machinery," yet you are forever "busy." With the multiplying of your machinery you grow increasingly fatigued, anxious, nervous, dissatisfied. Whatever you have, you want more; and wherever you are you want to go somewhere else . . . your devices are neither time-saving nor soul-saving machinery. They are so many sharp spurs which urge you on to invent more machinery and to do more business.[1]

This tells us something about our civilization that cannot be cast aside as a prejudiced charge by an Eastern thinker who is jealous of Western prosperity. We cannot escape the indictment.

This does not mean that we must turn back the clock of scientific progress. No one can overlook the wonders that science has wrought for our lives. The automobile will not abdicate in favor of the horse and buggy, or the train in favor of the stagecoach, or the tractor in favor of the hand plow, or the scientific method in favor of ignorance and superstition. But our moral and spiritual "lag" must be redeemed. When scientific power outruns moral power, we end up with guided missiles and misguided men. When we foolishly minimize the internal of our lives and maximize the external, we sign the warrant for our own day of doom.

Our hope for creative living in this world house that we have inherited lies in our ability to reestablish the moral ends of our lives in personal character and social justice. Without this spiritual and moral reawakening we shall destroy ourselves in the misuse of our own instruments.

II

Among the moral imperatives of our time, we are challenged to work all over the world with unshakable determination to wipe out the last vestiges of racism. As early as 1906 W. E. B. Du Bois prophesied that "the problem of the twentieth century will be the problem of the color line." Now as we stand two-thirds into this exciting period of history we know full well that racism is still that hound of hell which dogs the tracks of our civilization.

Racism is no mere American phenomenon. Its vicious grasp knows no geographical boundaries. In fact, racism and its perennial ally—economic exploitation—provide the key to understanding most of the international complications of this generation.

The classic example of organized and institutionalized racism is the Union of South Africa. Its national policy and practice are the incarnation of the doctrine of white supremacy in the midst of a population which is overwhelmingly black. But the tragedy of South Africa is not simply in its own policy; it is the fact that the racist government of South Africa is virtually made possible by the economic policies of the United States and Great Britain, two countries which profess to be the moral bastions of our Western world.

In country after country we see white men building empires on the sweat and suffering of colored people. Portugal continues its practices of slave labor and subjugation in Angola; the Ian Smith government in Rhodesia continues to enjoy the support of British-based industry and private capital, despite the stated opposition of British government policy. Even in the case of the little country of South West Africa we find the powerful nations of the world incapable of taking a moral position against South Africa, though the smaller country is under the trusteeship of the United Nations. Its policies are controlled by South Africa and its manpower is lured into the mines under slave-labor conditions.

During the Kennedy administration there was some awareness of the problems that breed in the racist and exploitative conditions throughout the colored world, and a temporary concern emerged to free the United States from its complicity though the effort was only on a diplomatic level. Through our ambassador to the United Nations, Adlai Stevenson, there emerged the beginnings of an intelligent approach to the colored peoples of the world. However, there remained little or no attempt to deal with the economic aspects of racist exploitation. We have been notoriously silent about the more than $700 million of American capital which props up the system of apartheid, not to mention the billions of dollars in trade and the military alliances which are maintained under the pretext of fighting Communism in Africa.

Nothing provides the Communists with a better climate for expansion and infiltration than the continued alliance of our nation with racism and exploitation throughout the world. And if we are not diligent in our determination to root out the last vestiges of racism in our dealings with the rest of the world, we may soon see the sins of our fathers visited upon ours and succeeding generations. For the conditions which are so classically represented in Africa are present also in Asia and in our own back yard in Latin America.

Everywhere in Latin America one finds a tremendous resentment of the United States, and that resentment is always strongest among the poorer and darker peoples of the continent. The life and destiny of Latin America are in the hands of United States corporations. The decisions affecting the lives of South Americans are ostensibly made by their government, but there are almost no legitimate democracies alive in the whole continent. The other governments are dominated by huge and exploitative cartels that rob Latin America of her resources while turning over a small rebate to a few members of a corrupt aristocracy, which in turn invests not in its own country for its own people's welfare but in the banks of Switzerland and the playgrounds of the world.

Here we see racism in its more sophisticated form: neo-colonialism. The Bible and the annals of history are replete with tragic stories of one brother robbing another of his birthright and thereby insuring generations of strife and enmity. We can hardly escape such a judgment in Latin America, any more than we have been able to escape the harvest of hate sown in Vietnam by a century of French exploitation.

There is the convenient temptation to attribute the current turmoil and bitterness throughout the world to the presence of a Communist conspiracy to undermine Europe and America, but the potential explosiveness of our world situation is much more attributable to disillusionment with the promises of Christianity and technology.

The revolutionary leaders of Africa, Asia and Latin America have virtually all received their education in the capitals of the West. Their earliest training often occurred in Christian missionary schools. Here their sense of dignity was established and they learned that all men were sons of God. In recent years their countries have been invaded by automobiles, Coca-Cola and Hollywood, so that even remote villages have become aware of the wonders and blessings available to God's white children.

Once the aspirations and appetites of the world have been whetted by the marvels of Western technology and the self-image of a people awakened by religion, one cannot hope to keep people locked out of the earthly kingdom of wealth, health and happiness. Either they share in the blessings of the world or they organize to break down and overthrow those structures or governments which stand in the way of their goals.

Former generations could not conceive of such luxury, but their children now take this vision and demand that it become a reality. And when they look around and see that the only people who do not share in the abundance of Western technology are colored people, it is an almost inescapable conclusion that their condition and their exploitation are somehow related to their color and the racism of the white Western world.

This is a treacherous foundation for a world house. Racism can well be that corrosive evil that will bring down the curtain on Western civilization. Arnold Toynbee has said that some twenty-six civilizations have risen upon the face of the earth. Almost all of them have descended into the junk heaps of destruction. The decline and fall of these civilizations, according to Toynbee, was not caused by external invasions but by internal decay. They failed to respond creatively to the challenges impinging upon them. If Western civilization does not now respond constructively to the challenge to banish racism, some future historian will have to say that a great civilization died because it lacked the soul and commitment to make justice a reality for all men.

Another grave problem that must be solved if we are to live creatively in our world house is that of poverty on an international scale. Like a monstrous octopus, it stretches its choking, prehensile tentacles into lands and villages all over the world. Two-thirds of the peoples of the world go to bed hungry at night. They are undernourished, ill-housed and shabbily clad. Many of them have no houses or beds to sleep in. Their only beds are the sidewalks of the cities and the dusty roads of the villages. Most of these poverty-stricken children of God have never seen a physician or a dentist.

There is nothing new about poverty. What is new, however, is that we now have the resources to get rid of it. Not too many years ago, Dr. Kirtley Mather, a Harvard geologist, wrote a book entitled *Enough and to Spare*.[2] He set forth the basic theme that famine is wholly unnecessary in the modern world. Today, therefore, the question on the agenda must read: why should there be hunger and privation in any land, in any city, at any table, when man has the resources and the scientific know-how to provide all mankind with the basic necessities of life? Even deserts can be irrigated and topsoil can be replaced. We cannot complain of a lack of land, for there are 25 million square miles of tillable land on earth, of which we are using less than seven million. We have amazing knowledge of vitamins, nutrition, the chemistry of food and the versatility of atoms. There is no deficit in human resources; the deficit is in human will.

This does not mean that we can overlook the enormous acceleration in the rate of growth of the world's population. The population explosion is very real, and it must be faced squarely if we are to avoid, in centuries ahead, a "standing room only" situation on these earthly shores. Most of the large undeveloped nations in the world today are confronted with the problem of excess population in relation to resources. But even this problem will be greatly diminished by wiping out poverty. When people see more opportunities for better education and greater economic security, they begin to consider whether a smaller family might not be better for themselves and for their children. In other words, I doubt that there can be a stabilization of the population without a prior stabilization of economic resources.

The time has come for an all-out world war against poverty. The rich nations must use their vast resources of wealth to develop the underdeveloped, school the unschooled and feed the unfed. The well-off and the secure have too often become indifferent and oblivious to the poverty and deprivation in their midst. The poor in our countries have been shut out of our minds, and driven from the mainstream of our societies, because we have allowed them to become invisible. Ultimately a great nation is a compassionate nation. No individual or nation can be great if it does not have a concern for "the least of these."

The first step in the worldwide war against poverty is passionate commitment. All the wealthy nations—America, Britain, Russia, Canada, Australia, and those of Western Europe—must see it as a moral obligation to provide capital and technical assistance to the underdeveloped areas. These rich nations have only scratched the surface in their commitment. There is need now for a general strategy of support. Sketchy aid here and there will not suffice, nor will it sustain economic growth. There must be a sustained effort extending through many years. The wealthy nations of the world must promptly initiate a massive, sustained Marshall Plan for Asia, Africa and South America. If they would allocate just 2 percent of their gross national product annually for a period of ten or twenty years for the development of the underdeveloped nations, mankind would go a long way toward conquering the ancient enemy, poverty.

The aid program that I am suggesting must not be used by the wealthy nations as a surreptitious means to control the poor nations. Such an approach would lead to a new form of paternalism and a neocolonialism which no self-respecting nation could accept. Ultimately, foreign aid programs must be motivated by a compassionate and committed effort to wipe poverty, ignorance and disease from the face of the earth. Money devoid of genuine empathy is like salt devoid of savor, good for nothing except to be trodden under foot of men.

The West must enter into the program with humility and penitence and a sober realization that everything will not always "go our way." It cannot be forgotten that the Western powers were but yesterday the colonial masters. The house of the West is far from in order, and its hands are far from clean.

We must have patience. We must be willing to understand why many of the young nations will have to pass through the same extremism, revolution and aggression that formed our own history. Every new government confronts overwhelming problems. During the days when they were struggling to remove the yoke of colonialism, there was a kind of preexistent unity of purpose that kept things moving in one solid direction. But as soon as independence emerges, all the grim problems of life confront them with stark realism: the lack of capital, the strangulating poverty, the uncontrollable birth rates and, above all, the high aspirational level of their own people. The postcolonial period is more difficult and precarious than the colonial struggle itself.

The West must also understand that its economic growth took place under rather propitious circumstances. Most of the Western nations were relatively underpopulated when they surged forward economically, and they were greatly endowed with the iron ore and coal that were needed for launching industry. Most of the young governments of the world today have come into being without these advantages, and, above all, they confront staggering problems of over-population. There is no possible way for them to make it without aid and assistance.

A genuine program on the part of the wealthy nations to make prosperity a reality for the poor nations will in the final analysis enlarge the prosperity of all. One of the best proofs that reality hinges on moral foundations is the fact that when men and governments work devotedly for the good of others, they achieve their own enrichment in the process.

From time immemorial men have lived by the principle that "self-preservation is the first law of life." But this is a false assumption. I would say that other-preservation is the first law of life. It is the first law of life precisely because we cannot preserve self without being concerned about preserving other selves. The universe is so structured that things go awry if men are not diligent in their cultivation of the other-regarding dimension. "I" cannot reach fulfillment without "thou." The self cannot be self without other selves. Self-concern without other-concern is like a tributary that has no outward flow to the ocean. Stagnant, still and stale, it lacks both life and freshness. Nothing would be more disastrous and out of harmony with our self-interest than for the developed nations to travel a dead-end road of inordinate selfishness. We are in the fortunate position of having our deepest sense of morality coalesce with our self-interest.

But the real reason that we must use our resources to outlaw poverty goes beyond material concerns to the quality of our mind and spirit. Deeply woven into the fiber of our religious tradition is the conviction that men are made in the image of God, and that they are souls of infinite metaphysical value. If we accept this as a profound moral fact, we cannot be content to see men hungry, to see men victimized with ill-health, when we have the means to help them. In the final analysis, the rich must not ignore the poor because both rich and poor are tied together. They entered the same mysterious gateway of human birth, into the same adventure of mortal life.

All men are interdependent. Every nation is an heir of a vast treasury of ideas and labor to which both the living and the dead of all nations have contributed. Whether we realize it or not, each of us lives eternally "in the red." We are everlasting debtors to known and unknown men and women. When we arise in the morning, we go into the bathroom where we reach for a sponge which is provided for us by a Pacific Islander. We reach for soap that is created for us by a European. Then at the table we drink coffee which is provided for us by a South American, or tea by a Chinese or cocoa by a West African. Before we leave for our jobs we are already beholden to more than half of the world.

In a real sense, all life is interrelated. The agony of the poor impoverishes the rich; the betterment of the poor enriches the rich. We are inevitably our brother's keeper because we are our brother's brother. Whatever affects one directly affects all indirectly.

A final problem that mankind must solve in order to survive in the world house that we have inherited is finding an alternative to war and human destruction. Recent events have vividly reminded us that nations are not reducing but rather increasing their arsenals of weapons of mass destruction. The best brains in the highly developed nations of the world are devoted to military technology. The proliferation of nuclear weapons has not been halted, in spite of the limited-test-ban treaty.

In this day of man's highest technical achievement, in this day of dazzling discovery, of novel opportunities, loftier dignities and fuller freedoms for all, there is no excuse for the kind of blind craving for power and resources that provoked the wars of previous generations.

There is no need to fight for food and land. Science has provided us with adequate means of survival and transportation, which make it possible to enjoy the fullness of this great earth. The question now is, do we have the morality and courage required to live together as brothers and not be afraid?

One of the most persistent ambiguities we face is that everybody talks about peace as a goal, but among the wielders of power peace is practically nobody's business. Many men cry "Peace! Peace!" but they refuse to do the things that make for peace.

The large power blocs talk passionately of pursuing peace while expanding defense budgets that already bulge, enlarging already awesome armies and devising ever more devastating weapons. Call the roll of those who sing the glad tidings of peace and one's ears will be surprised by the responding sounds. The heads of all the nations issue clarion calls for peace, yet they come to the peace table accompanied by bands of brigands each bearing unsheathed swords.

The stages of history are replete with the chants and choruses of the conquerors of old who came killing in pursuit of peace. Alexander, Genghis Khan, Julius Caesar, Charlemagne and Napoleon were akin in seeking a peaceful world order, a world fashioned after their selfish conceptions of an ideal existence. Each sought a world at peace which would personify his egotistic dreams. Even within the life span of most of us, another megalomaniac strode across the world stage. He sent his blitzkrieg-bent legions blazing across Europe, bringing havoc and holocaust in his wake. There is grave irony in the fact that Hitler could come forth, following nakedly aggressive expansionist theories, and do it all in the name of peace.

So when in this day I see the leaders of nations again talking peace while preparing for war, I take fearful pause. When I see our country today intervening in what is basically a civil war, mutilating hundreds of thousands of Vietnamese children with napalm, burning villages and rice fields at random, painting the valleys of that small Asian country red with human blood, leaving broken bodies in countless ditches and sending home half-men, mutilated mentally and physically; when I see the unwillingness of our government to create the atmosphere for a negotiated settlement of this awful conflict by halting bombings in the North and agreeing unequivocally to talk with the Vietcong—and all this in the name of pursuing the goal of peace—I tremble for our world. I do so not only from dire recall of the nightmares wreaked in the wars of yesterday, but also from dreadful realization of today's possible nuclear destructiveness and tomorrow's even more calamitous prospects.

Before it is too late, we must narrow the gaping chasm between our proclamations of peace and our lowly deeds which precipitate and perpetuate war. We are called upon to look up from the quagmire of military programs and defense commitments and read the warnings on history's signposts.

One day we must come to see that peace is not merely a distant goal that we seek but a means by which we arrive at that goal. We must pursue peaceful ends through peaceful means. How much longer must we play at deadly war games before we heed the plaintive pleas of the unnumbered dead and maimed of past wars?

President John F. Kennedy said on one occasion, "Mankind must put an end to war or war will put an end to mankind." Wisdom born of experience should tell us that war is obsolete. There may have been a time when war served as a negative good by preventing the spread and growth of an evil force, but the destructive power of modern weapons eliminates even the possibility that war may serve any good at all. If we assume that life is worth living and that man has a right to survive, then we must find an alternative to war. In a day when vehicles hurtle through outer space and guided ballistic missiles carve highways of death through the stratosphere, no nation can claim victory in war. A so-called limited war will leave little more than a calamitous legacy of human suffering, political turmoil and spiritual disillusionment. A world war will leave only smoldering ashes as mute testimony of a human race whose folly led inexorably to ultimate death. If modern man continues to flirt unhesitatingly with war, he will transform his earthly habitat into an inferno such as even the mind of Dante could not imagine.

Therefore I suggest that the philosophy and strategy of nonviolence become immediately a subject for study and for serious experimentation in every field of human conflict, by no means excluding the relations between nations. It is, after all, nation-states which make war, which have produced the weapons that threaten the survival of mankind and which are both genocidal and suicidal in character.

We have ancient habits to deal with, vast structures of power, indescribably complicated problems to solve. But unless we abdicate our humanity altogether and succumb to fear and impotence in the presence of the weapons we have ourselves created, it is as possible and as urgent to put an end to war and violence between nations as it is to put an end to poverty and racial injustice.

The United Nations is a gesture in the direction of nonviolence on a world scale. There, at least, states that oppose one another have sought to do so with words instead of with weapons. But true nonviolence is more than the absence of violence. It is the persistent and determined application of peaceable power to offenses against the community—in this case the world community. As the United Nations moves ahead with the giant tasks confronting it, I would hope that it would earnestly examine the uses of nonviolent direct action.

I do not minimize the complexity of the problems that need to be faced in achieving disarmament and peace. But I am convinced that we shall not have the will, the courage and the insight to deal with such matters unless in this field we are prepared to undergo a mental and spiritual re-evaluation, a change of focus which will enable us to see that the things that seem most real and powerful are indeed now unreal and have come under sentence of death. We need to make a supreme effort to generate the readiness, indeed the eagerness, to enter into the new world which is now possible, "the city which hath foundation, whose Building and Maker is God."

It is not enough to say, "We must not wage war." It is necessary to love peace and sacrifice for it. We must concentrate not merely on the eradication of war but on the affirmation of peace. A fascinating story about Ulysses and the Sirens is preserved for us in Greek literature. The Sirens had the ability to sing so sweetly that sailors could not resist steering toward their island. Many ships were lured upon the rocks, and men forgot home, duty and honor as they flung themselves into the sea to be embraced by arms that drew them down to death. Ulysses, determined not to succumb to the Sirens, first decided to tie himself tightly to the mast of his boat and his crew stuffed their ears with wax. But finally he and his crew learned a better way to save themselves: they took on board the beautiful singer Orpheus, whose melodies were sweeter than the music of the Sirens. When Orpheus sang, who would bother to listen to the Sirens?

So we must see that peace represents a sweeter music, a cosmic melody that is far superior to the discords of war. Somehow we must transform the dynamics of the world power struggle from the nuclear arms race, which no one can win, to a creative contest to harness man's genius for the purpose of making peace and prosperity a reality for all the nations of the world. In short, we must shift the arms race into a "peace race." If we have the will and determination to mount such a peace offensive, we will unlock hitherto tightly sealed doors of hope and bring new light into the dark chambers of pessimism.

III

The stability of the large world house which is ours will involve a revolution of values to accompany the scientific and freedom revolutions engulfing the earth. We must rapidly begin the shift from a "thing"-oriented society to a "person"-oriented society. When machines and computers, profit motives and property rights are considered more important than people, the giant triplets of racism, materialism and militarism are incapable of being conquered. A civilization can flounder as readily in the face of moral and spiritual bankruptcy as it can through financial bankruptcy.

This revolution of values must go beyond traditional capitalism and Communism. We must honestly admit that capitalism has often left a gulf between superfluous wealth and abject poverty, has created conditions permitting necessities to be taken from the many to give luxuries to the few, and has encouraged smallhearted men to become cold and conscienceless so that, like Dives before Lazarus, they are unmoved by suffering, poverty-stricken humanity. The profit motive, when it is the sole basis of an economic system, encourages a cutthroat competition and selfish ambition that inspire men to be more I-centered than thou-centered. Equally, Communism reduces men to a cog in the wheel of the state. The Communist may object, saying that in Marxian theory the state is an "interim reality" that will "wither away" when the classless society emerges. True—in theory; but it is also true that, while the state lasts, it is an end in itself. Man is a means to that end. He has no inalienable rights. His only rights are derived from, and conferred by, the state. Under such a system the fountain of freedom runs dry. Restricted are man's liberties of press and assembly, his freedom to vote and his freedom to listen and to read.

Truth is found neither in traditional capitalism nor in classical Communism. Each represents a partial truth. Capitalism fails to see the truth in collectivism. Communism fails to see the truth in individualism. Capitalism fails to realize that life is social. Communism fails to realize that life is personal. The good and just society is neither the thesis of capitalism nor the antithesis of Communism, but a socially conscious democracy which reconciles the truths of individualism and collectivism.

We have seen some moves in this direction. The Soviet Union has gradually moved away from its rigid Communism and begun to concern itself with consumer products, art and a general increase in benefits to the individual citizen. At the same time, through constant social reforms, we have seen many modifications in laissez-faire capitalism. The problems we now face must take us beyond slogans for their solution. In the final analysis, the right-wing slogans on "government control" and "creeping socialism" are as meaningless and adolescent as the Chinese Red Guard slogans against "bourgeois revisionism." An intelligent approach to the problems of poverty and racism will cause us to see that the words of the Psalmist—"The earth is the Lord's and the fullness thereof"—are still a judgment upon our use and abuse of the wealth and resources with which we have been endowed.

A true revolution of values will soon cause us to question the fairness and justice of many of our past and present policies. We are called to play the Good Samaritan on life's roadside; but that will be only an initial act. One day the whole Jericho Road must be transformed so that men and women will not be beaten and robbed as they make their journey through life. True compassion is more than flinging a coin to a beggar; it understands that an edifice which produces beggars needs restructuring.

A true revolution of values will soon look uneasily on the glaring contrast of poverty and wealth. With righteous indignation, it will look at thousands of working people displaced from their jobs with reduced incomes as a result of automation while the profits of the employers remain intact, and say: "This is not just." It will look across the oceans and see individual capitalists of the West investing huge sums of money in Asia, Africa and South America, only to take the profits out with no concern for the social betterment of the countries, and say: "This is not just." It will look at our alliance with the landed gentry of Latin America and say: "This is not just." The Western arrogance of feeling that it has everything to teach others and nothing to learn from them is not just. A true revolution of values will lay hands on the world order and say of war: "This way of settling differences is not just." This business of burning human beings with napalm, of filling our nation's homes with orphans and widows, of injecting poisonous drugs of hate into the veins of peoples normally humane, of sending men home from dark and bloody battlefields physically handicapped and psychologically deranged cannot be reconciled with wisdom, justice and love. A nation that continues year after year to spend more money on military defense than on programs of social uplift is approaching spiritual death.

America, the richest and most powerful nation in the world, can well lead the way in this revolution of values. There is nothing to prevent us from paying adequate wages to schoolteachers, social workers and other servants of the public to insure that we have the best available personnel in these positions which are charged with the responsibility of guiding our future generations. There is nothing but a lack of social vision to prevent us from paying an adequate wage to every American citizen whether he be a hospital worker, laundry worker, maid or day laborer. There is nothing except shortsightedness to prevent us from guaranteeing an annual minimum—and *livable*—income for every American family. There is nothing, except a tragic death wish, to prevent us from reordering our priorities, so that the pursuit of peace will take precedence over the pursuit of war. There is nothing to keep us from remolding a recalcitrant status quo with bruised hands until we have fashioned it into a brotherhood.

This kind of positive revolution of values is our best defense against Communism. War is not the answer. Communism will never be defeated by the use of atomic bombs or nuclear weapons. Let us not join those who shout war and who through their misguided passions urge the United States to relinquish its participation in the United Nations. These are days which demand wise restraint and calm reasonableness. We must not call everyone a Communist or an appeaser who advocates the seating of Red China in the United Nations, or who recognizes that hate and hysteria are not the final answers to the problems of these turbulent days. We must not engage in a negative anti-Communism, but rather in a positive thrust for democracy, realizing that our greatest defense against Communism is to take offensive action on behalf of justice. We must with affirmative action seek to remove those conditions of poverty, insecurity and injustice which are the fertile soil in which the seed of Communism grows and develops.

These are revolutionary times. All over the globe men are revolting against old systems of exploitation and oppression, and out of the wombs of a frail world new systems of justice and equality are being born. The shirtless and barefoot people of the earth are rising up as never before. "The people who sat in darkness have seen a great light." We in the West must support these revolutions. It is a sad fact that, because of comfort, complacency, a morbid fear of Communism and our proneness to adjust to injustice, the Western nations that initiated so much of the revolutionary spirit of the modern world have now become the arch antirevolutionaries. This has driven many to feel that only Marxism has the revolutionary spirit. Communism is a judgment on our failure to make democracy real and to follow through on the revolutions that we initiated. Our only hope today lies in our ability to recapture the revolutionary spirit and go out into a sometimes hostile world declaring eternal opposition to poverty, racism and militarism. With this powerful commitment we shall boldly challenge the status quo and unjust mores and thereby speed the day when "every valley shall be exalted, and every mountain and hill shall be made low: and the crooked shall be made straight and the rough places plain."

A genuine revolution of values means in the final analysis that our loyalties must become ecumenical rather than sectional. Every nation must now develop an overriding loyalty to mankind as a whole in order to preserve the best in their individual societies.

This call for a worldwide fellowship that lifts neighborly concern beyond one's tribe, race, class and nation is in reality a call for an all-embracing and unconditional love for all men. This often misunderstood and misinterpreted concept has now become an absolute necessity for the survival of man. When I speak of love, I am speaking of that force which all the great religions have seen as the supreme unifying principle of life. Love is the key that unlocks the door which leads to ultimate reality. This Hindu-Muslim-Christian-Jewish-Buddhist belief about ultimate reality is beautifully summed up in the First Epistle of Saint John:

> Let us love one another: for love is of God: and every one that loveth is born of God, and knoweth God. He that loveth not knoweth not God; for God is love. . . . If we love one another, God dwelleth in us, and his love is perfected in us.

Let us hope that this spirit will become the order of the day. We can no longer afford to worship the God of hate or bow before the altar of retaliation. The oceans of history are made turbulent by the ever-rising tides of hate. History is cluttered with the wreckage of nations and individuals who pursued this self-defeating path of hate. As Arnold Toynbee once said in a speech: "Love is the ultimate force that makes for the saving choice of life and good against the damning choice of death and evil. Therefore the first hope in our inventory must be the hope that love is going to have the last word."

We are now faced with the fact that tomorrow is today. We are confronted with the fierce urgency of *now*. In this unfolding conundrum of life and history there is such a thing as being too late. Procrastination is still the thief of time. Life often leaves us standing bare, naked and dejected with a lost opportunity. The "tide in the affairs of men" does not remain at the flood; it ebbs. We may cry out desperately for time to pause in her passage, but time is deaf to every plea and rushes on. Over the bleached bones and jumbled residues of numerous civilizations are written the pathetic words: "Too late." There is an invisible book of life that faithfully records our vigilance or our neglect. "The moving finger writes, and having writ moves on. . . ." We still have a choice today: nonviolent coexistence or violent coannihilation. This may well be mankind's last chance to choose between chaos and community.

From *Where Do We Go from Here: Chaos or Community?*
(Harper & Row, 1967, reprinted by Beacon Press, 2010).

SEVEN

ALL THE GREAT RELIGIONS OF THE WORLD

Dr. King prepared this extensive statement for *Redbook* magazine on how Christianity, Judaism, Islam, Buddhism, and Hinduism might be effective in promoting peace and goodwill. It was published on November 5, 1964.

What evidence is there that religion has ever been, or in the future could be, effective in promoting peace and goodwill among men? Or do you feel that peace depends primarily on new social and political institutions?

Religion at its best has always sought to promote peace and good will among men. This is true of all of the great religions of the world. In their ethical systems, we find the love ethic standing at the center. This is true of Judaism, this is true of Christianity, this is true of Islam, of Hinduism and Buddhism, and if we go right through all the great religions of the world we find this central message of love and this idea of the need for peace, the need for understanding and the need for good will among men. Now the problem has been that these noble creeds and ethical insights of the great religions have not been followed by the adherents of the particular religions, and we must face the shameful fact that all too many religious people have been religious in their creeds but not enough in their deeds. I have felt all along that if religion—and this includes all religions—would take a real stand against war and go all-out for peace and brotherhood, then we would be further along the way in making these into reality. I think the two are tied together. I don't think there can be peace without brotherhood, and I don't think you can have brotherhood without peace. To put it another way, I don't think there can be justice without peace, and I don't think there can be peace without justice. If religious institutions had really been true to their creeds all along, to the demand for justice, the demand for peace, then we would have peace and justice. Now even though there has been a great deal of negligence and even though the religions of the world have not done enough to inspire their followers to work passionately and unrelentingly for peace, I think that in the present and the future religion *can* play a great role. If brotherhood is to become a reality, religion must somehow get into the thick of the battle for peace and reaffirm the fact that, as the Old Testament says, men must beat their swords into plowshares and their spears into pruning hooks, and nations must not rise up against nations; neither must they study war any more. If we are to have a just and lasting peace, religion will have to do more to influence the minds of men and women and be true to their ethical insights. Now I don't say that political institutions don't have a great role to play, and I'm not unmindful of the fact that there are millions of people under political systems that would deny any claim to religion as we know it because they are basically atheistic systems. Still I don't want to go so far as to say that in these systems there can't be a longing for peace. I firmly believe that religion or even God is that which concerns man *ultimately*. When we deal with the ultimate concerns, we are dealing with individuals who whether they know it or not have some form of religion. So I think that even in those situations there can be a longing for peace. But I am sure that if the religions of the world are to bring about the peace that I am talking about and create the climate for it, they've got to rise to the level of not fighting among themselves. Some of the most tragic wars in the world have been religious wars. There is a need for individual religions to realize that God has revealed Himself to all religions and there is some truth in all. And no religion can permit itself to be so arrogant that it fails to see that God has not left Himself without a witness, even though it may be in another religion.

Statement prepared for *Redbook* magazine,
November 5, 1964.

EIGHT

MY JEWISH BROTHER!

Dr. King wrote this article on the evils of anti-Semitism for *New York Amsterdam News*—a black-owned newspaper—on February 26, 1966.

Recently, I was saddened—as I am sure many other Americans were—to read that one of the leaders of a fine and militant civil rights group had made an anti-Semitic remark.

In the heat of a controversy over school desegregation, this individual, who is a Negro, shouted to his audience, which included a number of Jewish people, a statement to the effect that Hitler had not killed enough Jews.

Actually, I do not view this horrible outburst as anti-Jewish. I see it as anti-man and anti-God. It would be a statement to harshly condemn, coming from anyone. It is singularly despicable, coming from the lips of a black man.

For, black people, who have been torturously burned in the crucible of hatred for centuries, should have become so purified of hate in those scorching flames as to be instinctively intolerant of intolerance. In the struggle for human rights, as well as in the struggle for the upward march of our civilization, we have deep need for the partnership, fellowship and courage of our Jewish Brother. History will attest that the Hebrew prophets belong to all people.

For, it has been their concepts of justice and equality which have become ideals for all races and civilizations.

Today, we particularly need the Hebrew prophets because they taught that to love God was to love justice; that each human being has an inescapable obligation to denounce evil where he sees it and to defy a ruler who commands him to break the covenant.

The Hebrew prophets are needed today because decent people must be imbued with the courage to speak the truth, to realize that silence may temporarily preserve status or security but that to live with a lie is a gross affront to God.

It is scarcely a secret that many congressmen, educators, clergymen and leaders of national affairs are gravely disturbed by our foreign policy.

A war in which children are incinerated by napalm, in which American soldiers die in mounting numbers while other American soldiers, according to press accounts, in unrestrained hatred shoot the wounded enemy as he lies upon the ground, is a war that mutilates the conscience. Yet, important leaders keep their silence.

I know this to be true because so many have confided in me that they shared my opinions, but not my willingness to state them in public.

The Hebrew prophets are needed today because we need their flaming courage. We need them because the thunder of their fearless voices is the only sound stronger than the blasts of bombs and the clamour of war hysteria.

The Hebrew prophets are needed today because Amos said, in words that echo across the centuries: "Let justice roll down like the waters and righteousness as a mighty stream." We need them because Micah said, in words lifted to cosmic proportions, "They shall beat their swords into plowshares and their spears into pruning hooks. Nation shall not lift up sword against nation. Neither shall they learn war anymore."

We need them because Isaiah said: "Yes, when ye make many prayers, I will not hear. Your hands are full of blood. Wash you. Make you clean. Put away the evil of your doings from before mine eyes. Cease to do evil."

I think the Hebrew prophets are among us today because, although there are many pulpits that are empty while ministers physically occupy them, there are others from which the passion for justice and compassion for man is still heard.

In the days to come, as the voices of sanity multiply, we will know that, across thousands of years of time, the prophet's message of truth and decency, brotherhood and peace, survives; that they are living in our time, to give hope to a tortured world that their promise of the Kingdom of God has not been lost to mankind.

Originally published in *New York Amsterdam News,*
New York, New York, February 26, 1966.

NINE

THE MIDDLE EAST QUESTION

This statement was made by Dr. King and the Southern Christian Leadership Conference (SCLC) in Chicago in September 1967.

Serious distortions by the press have created an impression that SCLC was part of a group at the Chicago Conference of New Politics which introduced a resolution condemning Israel and unqualifiedly endorsing all the policies of the Arab powers. The facts are as follows:

1. The staff members of SCLC who attended the conference (not as official delegates) were the most vigorous and articulate opponents of the simplistic resolution on the Middle East question. As a result of this opposition the Black caucus modified its stand and the convention voted to eliminate references to Zionism and referred to the executive board the matter of final wording. This change was the direct result of the spirited opposition on the floor by Hosea Williams, Southern Director of SCLC.

2. SCLC and Dr. King have repeatedly stated that the Middle East problem embodies the related questions of security and development. *Israel's right to exist as a state in security is incontestable. At the same time the great powers have the obligation to recognize that the Arab world is in a state of imposed*

poverty and backwardness that must threaten peace and har-mony. Until a concerted and democratic program of assistance is affected, tensions cannot be relieved. Neither Israel nor its neighbors can live in peace without an underlying basis of economic and social development.

At the heart of the problem are oil interests. As the American Jewish Congress has stated, "American policies in the Middle East have been motivated in no small measure by the desire to protect the $2,500,000,000 stake which U.S. oil companies have invested in the area." Some Arab feudal rulers are no less concerned for oil wealth and neglect the plight of their own peoples. The solution will have to be found in statesmanship by Israel and progressive Arab forces who in concert with the great powers recognize that fair and peaceful solutions are the concern of all of humanity and must be found.

Neither military measures nor a stubborn effort to reverse history can provide a permanent solution for peoples who need and deserve both development and security.

3. SCLC and Dr. King have expressly, frequently and vigorously denounced anti-Semitism and will continue to do so. It is not only that anti-Semitism is immoral—though that alone is enough. It is used to divide Negro and Jew, who have effectively collaborated in the struggle for justice. It injures Negroes because it upholds the doctrine of racism which they have the greatest stake in destroying. The individual Jew or gentile who may be an exploiter acts out of his greed as an individual, not his religious precepts—just as a criminal—Negro or white—is expressing his anti-social tendencies—not the ethical values of his race.

SCLC will continue tirelessly to denounce racism, whether its form is white supremacy or anti-Semitism.

Statement by Dr. King and the Southern Christian Leadership Conference, Chicago, Illinois, September 1967.

TEN

LET MY PEOPLE GO

These remarks were made by Dr. King on Human Rights Day at a benefit speech for South Africa on December 10, 1965, at Hunter College in New York. It was his second and most detailed speech on South Africa and called for an international alliance in opposition to apartheid.

Africa has been depicted for more than a century as the home of black cannibals and ignorant primitives. Despite volumes of facts contradicting this picture the stereotype persists in books, motion pictures, and other media of communication.

Africa does have spectacular savages and brutes today, but they are not black. They are the sophisticated white rulers of South Africa who profess to be cultured, religious and civilised, but whose conduct and philosophy stamp them unmistakably as modern-day barbarians.

We are in an era in which the issue of human rights is the central question confronting all nations. In this complex struggle an obvious but little-appreciated fact has gained attention—the large majority of the human race is non-white, yet it is that large majority that lives in hideous poverty. While millions enjoy an unexampled opulence in developed nations 10,000 people die of hunger each and every day of the year in the undeveloped world. To assert white supremacy, to invoke white economic and military power to maintain the *status quo* is to foster the danger of international race war. Already the largest nation on earth, Red China, plays seriously with the concept of colour conflict. What does the South African Government contribute to this tense situation? These are the incendiary words of the South African philosophy spoken by its Prime Minister Dr. Verwoerd:

> We want to keep South Africa white. Keeping it white can only mean one thing, namely white domination, not "leadership," not "guidance," but control, supremacy.

The South African Government to make the white supreme has had to reach into the past and revive the nightmarish ideology and practices of Nazism. We are witnessing a recrudescence of that barbarism which murdered more humans than any war in history. In South Africa today all opposition to white supremacy is condemned as communism, and in its name, due process is destroyed, a medieval segregation is organised with twentieth century efficiency and drive, a sophisticated form of slavery is imposed by a minority upon a majority who are kept in grinding poverty, the dignity of human personality is defiled and world opinion is arrogantly defied.

Once more we read of tortures in jails with electric devices, suicides among prisoners, forced confessions, while in the outside community ruthless persecution of editors, religious leaders and political opponents suppresses free speech and a free press.

South Africa says to the world, "We have become a powerful industrial economy, we are too strong to be defeated by paper resolutions of world tribunals, we are immune to protest and to economic reprisals. We are invulnerable to opposition from within or without; if our evil offends you, you will have to learn to live with it."

Increasingly in recent months this conclusion has been echoed by sober commentators of other countries who disapprove, but nevertheless assert that there can be no remedy against this formidable adversary of human rights.

Do we too acknowledge defeat? Have we tried everything and failed? In examining this question as Americans we are immediately struck by the fact that the United States moved with strikingly different energy when it reached a dubious conclusion that our interests were threatened in the Dominican Republic. We inundated that small nation with overwhelming force shocking the world with our zealousness and naked power. With respect to South Africa however, our protest is so muted and peripheral it merely mildly disturbs the sensibilities of the segregationists, while our trade and investments substantially stimulate their economy to greater heights. We pat them on the wrist in permitting racially mixed receptions in our embassy, and by exhibiting films depicting Negro artists. But we give them massive support through American investments in motor and rubber industries, by extending some forty million dollars in loans through our most distinguished banking and financial institutions, by purchasing gold and other minerals mined by black slave labour, by giving them a sugar quota, by maintaining three tracking stations there and by providing them with the prestige of a nuclear reactor built with our technical cooperation and fueled with refined uranium supplied by us.

When it is realised that Great Britain, France and other democratic powers also prop up the economy of South Africa and when to all of this is added the fact that the U.S.S.R. has indicated its willingness to participate in a boycott it is proper to wonder how South Africa can so confidently defy the civilised world. The conclusion is inescapable that it is less sure of its own power, but more sure that the great nations will not sacrifice trade and profit to effectively oppose them. The shame of our nation is that it is objectively an ally of this monstrous government in its grim war with its own black people.

Our default is all the more grievous because one of the blackest pages of our history was our participation in the infamous African slave trade of the 17th century. The rape of Africa was conducted substantially for our benefit to facilitate the growth of our nation and to enhance its commerce. There are few parallels in human history of the period in which Africans were seized and branded like animals, packed into ships' holds like cargo and transported into chattel slavery. Millions suffered agonising death in the middle passage in a holocaust reminiscent of the Nazi slaughter of Jews, Poles and others. We have an obligation of atonement that is not cancelled by the passage of time. Indeed the slave trade in one sense was more understandable than our contemporary policy. There was less sense of humanity in the world three hundred years ago. The slave trade was widely approved by the major powers of the world. The economies of England, Spain and the United States rested heavily on the profits derived from it. Today in our opulent society our reliance on trade with South Africa is infinitesimal in significance. No real national interest impels us to be cautious, gentle, or a good customer of a nation that offends the world's conscience.

Have we the power to be more than peevish with South Africa, but yet refrain from acts of war? To list the extensive economic relations of the great powers with South Africa is to suggest a potent non-violent path. The international potential of non-violence has never been employed. Non-violence has been practised within national borders in India, the United States and in regions of Africa with spectacular success. The time has come fully to utilise non-violence through a massive international boycott which would involve the U.S.S.R., Great Britain, France, the United States, Germany and Japan. Millions of people can personally give expression to their abhorrence of the world's worst racism through such a far flung boycott. No nation professing a concern for man's dignity could avoid assuming its obligations if people of all states and races adopted a firm stand. Nor need we confine an international boycott to South Africa. Rhodesia has earned a place as a target, as has Portugal, colonial master of Angola and Mozambique. The time has come for an international alliance of peoples of all nations against racism.

For the American Negro there is a special relationship with Africa. It is the land of his origin. It was despoiled by invaders, its culture was arrested and concealed to justify white supremacy. The American Negro's ancestors were not only driven into slavery, but their links with their past were severed so that their servitude might be psychological as well as physical. In this period when the American Negro is giving moral leadership and inspiration to his own nation, he must find the resources to aid his suffering brothers in his ancestral homeland. Nor is this aid a one-way street. The civil rights movement in the United States has derived immense inspiration from the successful struggles of those Africans who have attained freedom in their own nations. The fact that black men govern states, are building democratic institutions, sit in world tribunals, and participate in global decision making gives every Negro a needed sense of dignity.

In this effort the American Negro will not be alone. As this meeting testifies there are many white people who know that liberty is indivisible. Even more inspiring is the fact that in South Africa itself incredibly brave white people are risking their careers, their homes and their lives in the cause of human justice. Nor is this a plea to Negroes to fight on two fronts. The struggle for freedom forms one long front crossing oceans and mountains. The brotherhood of man is not confined within a narrow, limited circle of select people. It is felt everywhere in the world, it is an international sentiment of surpassing strength and because this is true when men of good will finally unite they will be invincible.

Through recent anthropological discoveries science has substantially established that the cradle of humanity is Africa. The earliest creatures who passed the divide between animal and man seem to have first emerged in East and South Africa. Professor Raymond Dart described this historical epoch as the moment when man "trembled on the brink of humanity." A million years later in the same place some men of South Africa are again "trembling on the brink of humanity," but instead of advancing from pre-human to human they are reversing the process and are travelling backward in time from human to pre-human.

Civilization has come a long way, it has far still to go and it cannot afford to be set back by resolute wicked men. Negroes were dispersed over thousands of miles and over many continents yet today they have found each other again. Negro and white have been separated for centuries by evil men and evil myths. But they have found each other.

The powerful unity of Negro with Negro and white with Negro is stronger than the most potent and entrenched racism. The whole human race will benefit when it ends the abomination that has diminished the stature of man for too long. This is the task to which we are called by the suffering in South Africa and our response should be swift and unstinting. Out of this struggle will come the glorious reality of the family of man.

South Africa benefit speech, Hunter College,
New York, New York, December 10, 1965.

ELEVEN

HONORING DR. DU BOIS

This essay by Dr. King was originally published by the editors of *Freedomways* in a collection of writings by and about W. E. B. Du Bois titled *Black Titan. Freedomways*, a quarterly review of the freedom movement, was a leading, provocative journal edited by black Americans from the 1960s to the 1980s.

Tonight we assemble here to pay tribute to one of the most remarkable men of our time.

Dr. Du Bois was not only an intellectual giant exploring the frontiers of knowledge, he was in the first place a teacher. He would have wanted his life to teach us something about our tasks of emancipation.

One idea he insistently taught was that Black people have been kept in oppression and deprivation by a poisonous fog of lies that depicted them as inferior, born deficient, and deservedly doomed to servitude to the grave. So assiduously has this poison been injected into the mind of America that its disease has infected not only whites but many Negroes. So long as the lie was believed the brutality and criminality of conduct toward the Negro was easy for the conscience to bear. The twisted logic ran: if the black man was inferior he was not oppressed—his place in society was appropriate to his meager talent and intellect.

Dr. Du Bois recognized that the keystone in the arch of oppression was the myth of inferiority and he dedicated his brilliant talents to demolish it.

There could scarcely be a more suitable person for such a monumental task. First of all he was himself unsurpassed as an intellect and he was a Negro. But beyond this he was passionately proud to be black and finally he had not only genius and pride but he had the indomitable fighting spirit of the valiant.

To pursue his mission, Dr. Du Bois gave up the substantial privileges a highly educated Negro enjoyed living in the North. Though he held degrees from Harvard and the University of Berlin, though he had more academic credentials than most Americans, black or white, he moved south where a majority of Negroes then lived. He deliberately chose to share their daily abuse and humiliation. He could have offered himself to the white rulers and exacted substantial tribute for selling his genius. There were few like him, Negro or white. He could have amassed riches and honors and lived in material splendor and applause from the powerful and important men of his time. Instead, he lived part of his creative life in the South—most of it in modest means and some of it in poverty and he died in exile, praised sparingly and in many circles ignored.

But he was an exile only to the land of his birth. He died at home in Africa among his cherished ancestors and he was ignored by a pathetically ignorant America but not by history.

History cannot ignore W. E. B. Du Bois. Because history has to reflect truth and Dr. Du Bois was a tireless explorer and a gifted discoverer of social truths. His singular greatness lay in his quest for truth about his own people. There were very few scholars who concerned themselves with honest study of the black man and he sought to fill this immense void. The degree to which he succeeded discloses the great dimensions of the man.

Yet he had more than a void to fill. He had to deal with the army of white propagandists—the myth-makers of Negro history. Dr. Du Bois took them all on in battle. It would be impossible to sketch the whole range of his intellectual contributions. Back in the nineteenth century he laid out a program of a hundred years of study of problems affecting American Negroes and worked tirelessly to implement it.

Long before sociology was a science he was pioneering in the field of social study of Negro life and completed works on health, education, employment, urban conditions, and religion. This was at a time when scientific inquiry of Negro life was so unbelievably neglected that only a single university in the entire nation had such a program and it was funded with $5,000 for a year's work.

Against such odds Dr. Du Bois produced two enduring classics before the twentieth century. His *Suppression of the African Slave Trade* written in 1896 is Volume I in the Harvard Historical Studies. His study, *The Philadelphia Negro*, completed in 1899, is still used today. Illustrating the painstaking quality of his scientific method, to do this work Dr. Du Bois personally visited and interviewed five thousand people.

He soon realized that studies would never adequately be pursued nor changes realized without the mass involvement of Negroes. The scholar then became an organizer and with others founded the NAACP. At the same time he became aware that the expansion of imperialism was a threat to the emergence of Africa.

He recognized the importance of the bonds between American Negroes and the land of their ancestors and he extended his activities to African affairs. After World War I he called Pan-African Congresses in 1919, 1921, and 1923, alarming imperialists in all countries and disconcerting Negro moderates in America who were afraid of this restless, militant, black genius.

Returning to the United States from abroad he found his pioneering agitation for Negro studies was bearing fruit and a beginning was made to broaden Negro higher education. He threw himself into the task of raising the intellectual level of this work. Much later in 1940 he participated in the establishment of the first Negro scholarly publication, *Phylon*. At the same time he stimulated Negro colleges to collaborate through annual conferences to increase their effectiveness and elevate the quality of their academic studies.

But these activities, enough to be the life work for ten men, were far from the sum of his achievements. In the six years between 1935 and 1941 he produced the monumental seven-hundred-page volume on *Black Reconstruction in America*, and at the same time writing many articles and essays. *Black Reconstruction* was six years in writing but was thirty-three years in preparation. On its publication, one critic said: "It crowns the long, unselfish, and brilliant career of Dr. Du Bois. It is comparable in clarity, originality, and importance to the Beards' *Rise of American Civilization.*" The *New York Times* said, "It is beyond question the most painstaking and thorough study ever made of the Negroes' part in Reconstruction," and the *New York Herald Tribune* proclaimed it "a solid history of the period, an economic treatise, a philosophical discussion, a poem, a work of art all rolled into one."

To understand why his study of the Reconstruction was a monumental achievement it is necessary to see it in context. White historians had for a century crudely distorted the Negro's role in the Reconstruction years. It was a conscious and deliberate manipulation of history and the stakes were high. The Reconstruction was a period in which black men had a small measure of freedom of action. If, as white historians tell it, Negroes wallowed in corruption, opportunism, displayed spectacular stupidity, were wanton, evil, and ignorant, their case was made. They would have proved that freedom was dangerous in the hands of inferior beings. One generation after another of Americans were assiduously taught these falsehoods and the collective mind of America became poisoned with racism and stunted with myths.

Dr. Du Bois confronted this powerful structure of historical distortion and dismantled it. He virtually, before anyone else and more than anyone else, demolished the lies about Negroes in their most important and creative period of history. The truths he revealed are not yet the property of all Americans but they have been recorded and arm us for our contemporary battles.

In *Black Reconstruction* Dr. Du Bois dealt with the almost universally accepted concept that civilization virtually collapsed in the South during Reconstruction because Negroes had a measure of political power. Dr. Du Bois marshalled irrefutable evidence that far from collapsing, the Southern economy was recovering in these years. Within five years the cotton crop had been restored and in the succeeding five years had exceeded prewar levels. At the same time other economic activity had ascended so rapidly the rebirth of the South was almost completed.

Beyond this he restored to light the most luminous achievement of the Reconstruction—it brought free public education into existence not only for the benefit of the Negro but it opened school doors to the poor whites. He documented the substantial body of legislation that was socially so useful it was retained into the twentieth century even though the Negroes who helped to write it were brutally disenfranchised and driven from political life. He revealed that far from being the tragic era white historians described, it was the only period in which democracy existed in the South. This stunning fact was the reason the history books had to lie because to tell the truth would have acknowledged the Negroes' capacity to govern and fitness to build a finer nation in a creative relationship with poor whites.

With the completion of his book *Black Reconstruction*, despite its towering contributions, despite his advanced age, Dr. Du Bois was still not ready to accept a deserved rest in peaceful retirement. His dedication to freedom drove him on as relentlessly in his seventies as it did in his twenties. He had already encompassed three careers. Beginning as a pioneer sociologist he had become an activist to further mass organization. The activist had then transformed himself into a historian. By the middle of the twentieth century when imperialism and war arose once more to imperil humanity he became a peace leader. He served as chairman of the Peace Information Bureau and like the Rev. William Sloane Coffin and Dr. Benjamin Spock of today he found himself indicted by the Government and harried by reactionaries. Undaunted by obstacles and repression, with his characteristic fortitude he fought on. Finally in 1961, with Ghana's independence established, an opportunity opened to begin the writing of an African Encyclopedia and in his ninety-third year he emigrated to Ghana to begin new intellectual labors. In 1963 death finally came to this most remarkable man.

It is axiomatic that he will be remembered for his scholarly contributions and organizational attainments. These monuments are imperishable. But there were human qualities less immediately visible that are no less imperishable.

Dr. Du Bois was a man possessed of priceless dedication to his people. The vast accumulation of achievement and public recognition were not for him pathways to personal affluence and a diffusion of identity. Whatever else he was, with his multitude of careers and professional titles, he was first and always a black man. He used his richness of talent as a trust for his people. He saw that Negroes were robbed of so many things decisive to their existence that the theft of their history seemed only a small part of their losses. But Dr. Du Bois knew that to lose one's history is to lose one's self-understanding and with it the roots for pride. This drove him to become a historian of Negro life and the combination of his unique zeal and intellect rescued for all of us a heritage whose loss would have profoundly impoverished us.

Dr. Du Bois *the man* needs to be remembered today when despair is all too prevalent. In the years he lived and fought there was far more justification for frustration and hopelessness and yet his faith in his people never wavered. His love and faith in Negroes permeate every sentence of his writings and every act of his life. Without these deeply rooted emotions his work would have been arid and abstract. With them his deeds were a passionate storm that swept the filth of falsehood from the pages of established history.

He symbolized in his being his pride in the black man. He did not apologize for being black and because of it, handicapped. Instead he attacked the oppressor for the crime of stunting black men. He confronted the Establishment as a model of militant manhood and integrity. He defied them and though they heaped venom and scorn on him his powerful voice was never stilled.

And yet, with all his pride and spirit he did not make a mystique out of blackness. He was proud of his people, not because their color endowed them with some vague greatness but because their concrete achievements in struggle had advanced humanity and he saw and loved progressive humanity in all its hues, black, white, yellow, red, and brown.

Above all he did not content himself with hurling invectives for emotional release and then to retire into smug passive satisfaction. History had taught him it is not enough for people to be angry—the supreme task is to organize and unite people so that their anger becomes a transforming force. It was never possible to know where the scholar Du Bois ended and the organizer Du Bois began. The two qualities in him were a single unified force.

This life style of Dr. Du Bois is the most important quality this generation of Negroes needs to emulate. The educated Negro who is not really part of us, and the angry militant who fails to organize us, have nothing in common with Dr. Du Bois. He exemplified black power in achievement and he organized black power in action. It was no abstract slogan to him.

We cannot talk of Dr. Du Bois without recognizing that he was a radical all of his life. Some people would like to ignore the fact that he was a communist in his later years. It is worth noting that Abraham Lincoln warmly welcomed the support of Karl Marx during the Civil War and corresponded with him freely. In contemporary life the English-speaking world has no difficulty with the fact that Sean O'Casey was a literary giant of the twentieth century and a communist or that Pablo Neruda is generally considered the greatest living poet though he also served in the Chilean Senate as a communist. It is time to cease muting the fact that Dr. Du Bois was a genius and chose to be a communist. Our irrational obsessive anti-communism has led us into too many quagmires to be retained as if it were a mode of scientific thinking.

In closing it would be well to remind white America of its debt to Dr. Du Bois. When they corrupted Negro history they distorted American history because Negroes are too big a part of the building of this nation to be written out of it without destroying scientific history. White America, drenched with lies about Negroes, has lived too long in a fog of ignorance. Dr. Du Bois gave them a gift of truth for which they should eternally be indebted to him.

Negroes have heavy tasks today. We were partially liberated and then re-enslaved. We have to fight again on old battlefields but our confidence is greater, our vision is clearer and our ultimate victory surer because of the contributions a militant, passionate black giant left behind him.

Dr. Du Bois has left us but he has not died. The spirit of freedom is not buried in the grave of the valiant. He will be with us when we go to Washington in April to demand our right to life, liberty, and the pursuit of happiness.

We have to go to Washington because they have declared an armistice in the war on poverty while squandering billions to expand a senseless, cruel, unjust war in Vietnam. We will go there, we will demand to be heard, and we will stay until the Administration responds. If this means forcible repression of our movement, we will confront it, for we have done this before. If this means scorn or ridicule, we will embrace it for that is what America's poor now receive. If it means jail we accept it willingly, for the millions of poor already are imprisoned by exploitation and discrimination.

Dr. Du Bois would be in the front ranks of the peace movement today. He would readily see the parallel between American support of the corrupt and despised Thieu-Ky regime and Northern support to the Southern Slavemasters in 1876. The CIA scarcely exaggerates, indeed it is surprisingly honest, when it calculates for Congress that the war in Vietnam can persist for a hundred years. People deprived of their freedom do not give up—Negroes have been fighting more than a hundred years and even if the date of full emancipation is uncertain, what is explicitly certain is that the struggle for it will endure.

In conclusion let me say that Dr. Du Bois' greatest virtue was his committed empathy with all the oppressed and his divine dissatisfaction with all forms of injustice. Today we are still challenged to be dissatisfied. Let us be dissatisfied until every man can have food and material necessities for his body, culture and education for his mind, freedom and human dignity for his spirit. Let us be dissatisfied until rat-infested, vermin-filled slums will be a thing of a dark past and every family will have a decent sanitary house in which to live. Let us be dissatisfied until the empty stomachs of Mississippi are filled and the idle industries of Appalachia are revitalized. Let us be dissatisfied until brotherhood is no longer a meaningless word at the end of a prayer but the first order of business on every legislative agenda. Let us be dissatisfied until our brother of the Third World—Asia, Africa, and Latin America—will no longer be the victim of imperialist exploitation, but will be lifted from the long night of poverty, illiteracy, and disease. Let us be dissatisfied until this pending cosmic elegy will be transformed into a creative psalm of peace and "justice will roll down like waters from a mighty stream."

From John Henrik Clarke, Esther Jackson, Ernest Kaiser, and J. H. O'Dell, *Black Titan: W. E. B. Du Bois* (Beacon Press, 1970).

PART THREE

THE REVOLUTION OF NONVIOLENT RESISTANCE

AGAINST EMPIRE AND WHITE SUPREMACY

Dr. Martin Luther King, Jr., is arrested for loitering outside a courtroom where his friend Ralph Abernathy is appearing for a trial, Montgomery, Alabama, 1958.

THE RADICAL KING has a dark side. History may be a nightmare—an endless cycle of violence and oppression. Old victims of domination soon became new perpetrators of domination. We have seen this cycle over and over again: American revolutionaries dominating Indigenous peoples and defending slavery, anti-colonial heroes becoming dictators, anti-racists supporting patriarchy and homophobia, liberals crusading for imperial invasion and occupation. Such a nightmare radically calls into question the power of radical love in human history. For King, if we accept such a nightmare, then only self-destruction awaits us. To dream is to hold death at arm's length. To love is to really be alive in history. Without radical love, nihilism triumphs—"power without compassion, might without morality, and strength without sight."[1]

The revolution of nonviolent resistance is radical love in public action. King's revolutionary method requires more internal moral discipline than that of Marxist or anarchist revolutionaries because one has to accept suffering without retaliation, to receive blows without striking back. For King, this is not cowardice but courage, not fear but fortitude. Revolutionary nonviolent resistance is directed at the forces of evil rather than against persons who commit the evil. The enemy is injustice and oppression, not those who perpetuate the injustice and oppression.

This kind of radical love goes against our common instincts and moral intuitions. In this sense, the application of radical love in public action requires not only tremendous moral discipline and fortitude but also profound trust in the redemptive power of love and in the salvific plan of God. This trust assumes that the unearned suffering of love-motivated nonviolent resisters can educate, transform, and even convert one's opponents. The aim is not simply to rely on the moral sense or conscience of the adversary but, if need be, to force the adversary to develop such a sense or conscience. If one concludes that no such development is possible, the dark side of the radical King springs forth: Ecological catastrophe looms large. Nuclear catastrophe lurks around the corner. Imperial, economic, moral, and spiritual catastrophes are our constant companions.

Yet from the cell of a Jim Crow Birmingham jail, King's love letter to his fellow clergymen is a flickering candle against the darkness. His monumental speech in Riverside Church exactly one year before his death rings with analytical power, righteous indignation, and prophetic vision. Radical love requires a radical leap of faith. The radical King is like the biblical eagle (or Walter Benjamin's angel), who mounts his wings to fly in the catastrophic storms of history. And like all those who bear witness, a Cross awaits him. In his church they often sang, "Must Jesus bear the Cross alone, and all the world go free? / No, there's a Cross for everyone, and there's a Cross for me."

For King, the scandal of the Cross—the human crushing of unarmed truth and unconditional love in history—is the way of the world. For those who pursue radical love, the Cross may be the only dwelling place. As King noted, "When I took up the Cross, I recognized its meaning. . . . The Cross is something that you bear, and ultimately that you die on."[2] To be a revolutionary Christian is to take up one's Cross, deny one's self, and find joy in fighting for justice even as that Cross leaves its wounds upon us and "redeems us to that more excellent way which comes only through suffering."[3] Radical love is the affirmation of life even within the consciousness of impotence. The gift of Grace leaves the Cross untenanted; we feel either abandoned by the death of God (Good Friday) or refreshed by the Resurrection (Easter). The revolutionary Christian lives in the dark shadows of Holy Saturday with radical love the "evidence" of Easter.

The revolution of nonviolent resistance is a David against the Goliath of empire and white supremacy. In his brief anti-colonial letters and anti-imperial speeches, the radical King becomes paradoxically more desperate and determined, more confident that he is right and more doubtful that much can be done about it. King enters and inhabits the space of Chekhov—deeply melancholic though decidedly melioristic. Yet, he is too much an activist to be a spectator and too much a Christian to be stuck forever on Holy Saturday. For the radical King, subversive remembrance and militant reverence yield revolutionary nonviolent resistance—always against overwhelming odds!

TWELVE

LETTER FROM BIRMINGHAM JAIL

On April 12, 1963, Dr. King and some of his followers were arrested in Birmingham, Alabama, for violating a city order against public protest, and King was placed in solitary confinement. Here, in one of his most famous pieces of writing, King defends nonviolent resistance as necessary to the freedom movement. Though the letter was never sent to the eight ministers it was intended for, it was published and distributed in a variety of formats, such as newspapers, magazines, and pamphlets, before King revised it a year later and included it in his memoir of the Birmingham campaign, *Why We Can't Wait.*[1]

April 16, 1963

My dear fellow clergymen:

While confined here in the Birmingham city jail, I came across your recent statement calling my present activities "unwise and untimely." Seldom do I pause to answer criticism of my work and ideas. If I sought to answer all the criticisms that cross my desk, my secretaries would have little time for anything other than such correspondence in the course of the day, and I would have no time for constructive work. But since I feel that you are men of genuine good will and that your criticisms are sincerely set forth, I want to try to answer your statement in what I hope will be patient and reasonable terms.

I think I should indicate why I am here in Birmingham, since you have been influenced by the view which argues against "outsiders coming in." I have the honor of serving as president of the Southern Christian Leadership Conference, an organization operating in every southern state, with headquarters in Atlanta, Georgia. We have some eighty-five affiliated organizations across the South, and one of them is the Alabama Christian Movement for Human Rights. Frequently we share staff, educational and financial resources with our affiliates. Several months ago the affiliate here in Birmingham asked us to be on call to engage in a nonviolent direct-action program if such were deemed necessary. We readily consented, and when the hour came we lived up to our promise. So I, along with several members of my staff, am here because I was invited here. I am here because I have organizational ties here.

But more basically, I am in Birmingham because injustice is here. Just as the prophets of the eighth century B.C. left their villages and carried their "thus saith the Lord" far beyond the boundaries of their home towns, and just as the Apostle Paul left his village of Tarsus and carried the gospel of Jesus Christ to the far corners of the Greco-Roman world, so am I compelled to carry the gospel of freedom beyond my own home town. Like Paul, I must constantly respond to the Macedonian call for aid.

Moreover, I am cognizant of the interrelatedness of all communities and states. I cannot sit idly by in Atlanta and not be concerned about what happens in Birmingham. Injustice anywhere is a threat to justice everywhere. We are caught in an inescapable network of mutuality, tied in a single garment of destiny. Whatever affects one directly, affects all indirectly. Never again can we afford to live with the narrow, provincial "outside agitator" idea. Anyone who lives inside the United States can never be considered an outsider anywhere within its bounds.

You deplore the demonstrations taking place in Birmingham. But your statement, I am sorry to say, fails to express a similar concern for the conditions that brought about the demonstrations. I am sure that none of you would want to rest content with the superficial kind of social analysis that deals merely with effects and does not grapple with underlying causes. It is unfortunate that demonstrations are taking place in Birmingham, but it is even more unfortunate that the city's white power structure left the Negro community with no alternative.

In any nonviolent campaign there are four basic steps: collection of the facts to determine whether injustices exist; negotiation; self-purification; and direct action. We have gone through all these steps in Birmingham. There can be no gainsaying the fact that racial injustice engulfs this community. Birmingham is probably the most thoroughly segregated city in the United States. Its ugly record of brutality is widely known. Negroes have experienced grossly unjust treatment in the courts. There have been more unsolved bombings of Negro homes and churches in Birmingham than in any other city in the nation. These are the hard, brutal facts of the case. On the basis of these conditions, Negro leaders sought to negotiate with the city fathers. But the latter consistently refused to engage in good-faith negotiation.

Then, last September, came the opportunity to talk with leaders of Birmingham's economic community. In the course of the negotiations, certain promises were made by the merchants—for example, to remove the stores' humiliating racial signs. On the basis of these promises, the Reverend Fred Shuttlesworth and the leaders of the Alabama Christian Movement for Human Rights agreed to a moratorium on all demonstrations. As the weeks and months went by, we realized that we were the victims of a broken promise. A few signs, briefly removed, returned; the others remained.

As in so many past experiences, our hopes had been blasted, and the shadow of deep disappointment settled upon us. We had no alternative except to prepare for direct action, whereby we would present our very bodies as a means of laying our case before the conscience of the local and the national community. Mindful of the difficulties involved, we decided to undertake a process of self-purification. We began a series of workshops on nonviolence, and we repeatedly asked ourselves: "Are you able to accept blows without retaliating?" "Are you able to endure the ordeal of jail?" We decided to schedule our direct-action program for the Easter season, realizing that except for Christmas, this is the main shopping period of the year. Knowing that a strong economic-withdrawal program would be the by-product of direct action, we felt that this would be the best time to bring pressure to bear on the merchants for the needed change.

Then it occurred to us that Birmingham's mayoralty election was coming up in March, and we speedily decided to postpone action until after election day. When we discovered that the Commissioner of Public Safety, Eugene "Bull" Connor, had piled up enough votes to be in the run-off, we decided again to postpone action until the day after the run-off so that the demonstrations could not be used to cloud the issues. Like many others, we waited to see Mr. Connor defeated, and to this end we endured postponement after postponement. Having aided in this community need, we felt that our direct-action program could be delayed no longer.

You may well ask: "Why direct action? Why sit-ins, marches and so forth? Isn't negotiation a better path?" You are quite right in calling for negotiation. Indeed, this is the very purpose of direct action. Nonviolent direct action seeks to create such a crisis and foster such a tension that a community which has constantly refused to negotiate is forced to confront the issue. It seeks so to dramatize the issue that it can no longer be ignored. My citing the creation of tension as part of the work of the nonviolent-resister may sound rather shocking. But I must confess that I am not afraid of the word "tension." I have earnestly opposed violent tension, but there is a type of constructive, nonviolent tension which is necessary for growth. Just as Socrates felt that it was necessary to create a tension in the mind so that individuals could rise from the bondage of myths and half-truths to the unfettered realm of creative analysis and objective appraisal, so must we see the need for nonviolent gadflies to create the kind of tension in society that will help men rise from the dark depths of prejudice and racism to the majestic heights of understanding and brotherhood.

The purpose of our direct-action program is to create a situation so crisis-packed that it will inevitably open the door to negotiation. I therefore concur with you in your call for negotiation. Too long has our beloved Southland been bogged down in a tragic effort to live in monologue rather than dialogue.

One of the basic points in your statement is that the action that I and my associates have taken in Birmingham is untimely. Some have asked: "Why didn't you give the new city administration time to act?" The only answer that I can give to this query is that the new Birmingham administration must be prodded about as much as the outgoing one, before it will act. We are sadly mistaken if we feel that the election of Albert Boutwell as mayor will bring the millennium to Birmingham. While Mr. Boutwell is a much more gentle person than Mr. Connor, they are both segregationists, dedicated to maintenance of the status quo. I have hope that Mr. Boutwell will be reasonable enough to see the futility of massive resistance to desegregation. But he will not see this without pressure from devotees of civil rights. My friends, I must say to you that we have not made a single gain in civil rights without determined legal and nonviolent pressure. Lamentably, it is an historical fact that privileged groups seldom give up their privileges voluntarily. Individuals may see the moral light and voluntarily give up their unjust posture; but, as Reinhold Niebuhr has reminded us, groups tend to be more immoral than individuals.

We know through painful experience that freedom is never voluntarily given by the oppressor; it must be demanded by the oppressed. Frankly, I have yet to engage in a direct-action campaign that was "well timed" in the view of those who have not suffered unduly from the disease of segregation. For years now I have heard the word "Wait!" It rings in the ear of every Negro with piercing familiarity. This "Wait" has almost always meant "Never." We must come to see, with one of our distinguished jurists, that "justice too long delayed is justice denied."

We have waited for more than 340 years for our constitutional and God-given rights. The nations of Asia and Africa are moving with jet-like speed toward gaining political independence, but we still creep at horse-and-buggy pace toward gaining a cup of coffee at a lunch counter. Perhaps it is easy for those who have never felt the stinging darts of segregation to say, "Wait." But when you have seen vicious mobs lynch your mothers and fathers at will and drown your sisters and brothers at whim; when you have seen hate-filled policemen curse, kick and even kill your black brothers and sisters; when you see the vast majority of your twenty million Negro brothers smothering in an airtight cage of poverty in the midst of an affluent society; when you suddenly find your tongue twisted and your speech stammering as you seek to explain to your six-year-old daughter why she can't go to the public amusement park that has just been advertised on television, and see tears welling up in her eyes when she is told that Funtown is closed to colored children, and see ominous clouds of inferiority beginning to form in her little mental sky, and see her beginning to distort her personality by developing an unconscious bitterness toward white people; when you have to concoct an answer for a five-year-old son who is asking: "Daddy, why do white people treat colored people so mean?"; when you take a cross-country drive and find it necessary to sleep night after night in the uncomfortable corners of your automobile because no motel will accept you; when you are humiliated day in and day out by nagging signs reading "white" and "colored"; when your first name becomes "nigger," your middle name becomes "boy" (however old you are) and your last name becomes "John," and your wife and mother are never given the respected title "Mrs."; when you are harried by day and haunted by night by the fact that you are a Negro, living constantly at tiptoe stance, never quite knowing what to expect next, and are plagued with inner fears and outer resentments; when you are forever fighting a degenerating sense of "nobodiness"— then you will understand why we find it difficult to wait. There comes a time when the cup of endurance runs over, and men are no longer willing to be plunged into the abyss of despair. I hope, sirs, you can understand our legitimate and unavoidable impatience.

You express a great deal of anxiety over our willingness to break laws. This is certainly a legitimate concern. Since we so diligently urge people to obey the Supreme Court's decision of 1954 outlawing segregation in the public schools, at first glance it may seem rather paradoxical for us consciously to break laws. One may well ask: "How can you advocate breaking some laws and obeying others?" The answer lies in the fact that there are two types of laws: just and unjust. I would be the first to advocate obeying just laws. One has not only a legal but a moral responsibility to obey just laws. Conversely, one has a moral responsibility to disobey unjust laws. I would agree with St. Augustine that "an unjust law is no law at all."

Now, what is the difference between the two? How does one determine whether a law is just or unjust? A just law is a man-made code that squares with the moral law or the law of God. An unjust law is a code that is out of harmony with the moral law. To put it in the terms of St. Thomas Aquinas: An unjust law is a human law that is not rooted in eternal law and natural law. Any law that uplifts human personality is just. Any law that degrades human personality is unjust. All segregation statutes are unjust because segregation distorts the soul and damages the personality. It gives the segregator a false sense of superiority and the segregated a false sense of inferiority. Segregation, to use the terminology of the Jewish philosopher Martin Buber, substitutes an "I-it" relationship for an "I-thou" relationship and ends up relegating persons to the status of things. Hence segregation is not only politically, economically and sociologically unsound, it is morally wrong and sinful. Paul Tillich has said that sin is separation. Is not segregation an existential expression of man's tragic separation, his awful estrangement, his terrible sinfulness? Thus it is that I can urge men to obey the 1954 decision of the Supreme Court, for it is morally right; and I can urge them to disobey segregation ordinances, for they are morally wrong.

Let us consider a more concrete example of just and unjust laws. An unjust law is a code that a numerical or power majority group compels a minority group to obey but does not make binding on itself. This is *difference* made legal. By the same token, a just law is a code that a majority compels a minority to follow and that it is willing to follow itself. This is *sameness* made legal.

Let me give another explanation. A law is unjust if it is inflicted on a minority that, as a result of being denied the right to vote, had no part in enacting or devising the law. Who can say that the legislature of Alabama which set up that state's segregation laws was democratically elected? Throughout Alabama all sorts of devious methods are used to prevent Negroes from becoming registered voters, and there are some counties in which, even though Negroes constitute a majority of the population, not a single Negro is registered. Can any law enacted under such circumstances be considered democratically structured?

Sometimes a law is just on its face and unjust in its application. For instance, I have been arrested on a charge of parading without a permit. Now, there is nothing wrong in having an ordinance which requires a permit for a parade. But such an ordinance becomes unjust when it is used to maintain segregation and to deny citizens the First-Amendment privilege of peaceful assembly and protest.

I hope you are able to see the distinction I am trying to point out. In no sense do I advocate evading or defying the law, as would the rabid segregationist. That would lead to anarchy. One who breaks an unjust law must do so openly, lovingly, and with a willingness to accept the penalty. I submit that an individual who breaks a law that conscience tells him is unjust, and who willingly accepts the penalty of imprisonment in order to arouse the conscience of the community over its injustice, is in reality expressing the highest respect for law.

Of course, there is nothing new about this kind of civil disobedience. It was evidenced sublimely in the refusal of Shadrach, Meshach and Abednego to obey the laws of Nebuchadnezzar, on the ground that a higher moral law was at stake. It was practiced superbly by the early Christians, who were willing to face hungry lions and the excruciating pain of chopping blocks rather than submit to certain unjust laws of the Roman Empire. To a degree, academic freedom is a reality today because Socrates practiced civil disobedience. In our own nation, the Boston Tea Party represented a massive act of civil disobedience.

We should never forget that everything Adolf Hitler did in Germany was "legal" and everything the Hungarian freedom fighters did in Hungary was "illegal." It was "illegal" to aid and comfort a Jew in Hitler's Germany. Even so, I am sure that, had I lived in Germany at the time, I would have aided and comforted my Jewish brothers. If today I lived in a Communist country where certain principles dear to the Christian faith are suppressed, I would openly advocate disobeying that country's antireligious laws.

I must make two honest confessions to you, my Christian and Jewish brothers. First, I must confess that over the past few years I have been gravely disappointed with the white moderate. I have almost reached the regrettable conclusion that the Negro's great stumbling block in his stride toward freedom is not the White Citizens' Counciler or the Ku Klux Klanner, but the white moderate, who is more devoted to "order" than to justice; who prefers a negative peace which is the absence of tension to a positive peace which is the presence of justice; who constantly says: "I agree with you in the goal you seek, but I cannot agree with your methods of direct action"; who paternalistically believes he can set the timetable for another man's freedom; who lives by a mythical concept of time and who constantly advises the Negro to wait for a "more convenient season." Shallow understanding from people of good will is more frustrating than absolute misunderstanding from people of ill will. Lukewarm acceptance is much more bewildering than outright rejection.

I had hoped that the white moderate would understand that law and order exist for the purpose of establishing justice and that when they fail in this purpose they become the dangerously structured dams that block the flow of social progress. I had hoped that the white moderate would understand that the present tension in the South is a necessary phase of the transition from an obnoxious negative peace, in which the Negro passively accepted his unjust plight, to a substantive and positive peace, in which all men will respect the dignity and worth of human personality. Actually, we who engage in nonviolent direct action are not the creators of tension. We merely bring to the surface the hidden tension that is already alive. We bring it out in the open, where it can be seen and dealt with. Like a boil that can never be cured so long as it is covered up but must be opened with all its ugliness to the natural medicines of air and light, injustice must be exposed, with all the tension its exposure creates, to the light of human conscience and the air of national opinion before it can be cured.

In your statement you assert that our actions, even though peaceful, must be condemned because they precipitate violence. But is this a logical assertion? Isn't this like condemning a robbed man because his possession of money precipitated the evil act of robbery? Isn't this like condemning Socrates because his unswerving commitment to truth and his philosophical inquiries precipitated the act by the misguided populace in which they made him drink hemlock? Isn't this like condemning Jesus because his unique God-consciousness and never-ceasing devotion to God's will precipitated the evil act of crucifixion? We must come to see that, as the federal courts have consistently affirmed, it is wrong to urge an individual to cease his efforts to gain his basic constitutional rights because the quest may precipitate violence. Society must protect the robbed and punish the robber.

I had also hoped that the white moderate would reject the myth concerning time in relation to the struggle for freedom. I have just received a letter from a white brother in Texas. He writes: "All Christians know that the colored people will receive equal rights eventually, but it is possible that you are in too great a religious hurry. It has taken Christianity almost two thousand years to accomplish what it has. The teachings of Christ take time to come to earth." Such an attitude stems from a tragic misconception of time, from the strangely irrational notion that there is something in the very flow of time that will inevitably cure all ills. Actually, time itself is neutral; it can be used either destructively or constructively. More and more I feel that the people of ill will have used time much more effectively than have the people of good will. We will have to repent in this generation not merely for the hateful words and actions of the bad people but for the appalling silence of the good people. Human progress never rolls in on wheels of inevitability; it comes through the tireless efforts of men willing to be coworkers with God, and without this hard work, time itself becomes an ally of the forces of social stagnation. We must use time creatively, in the knowledge that the time is always ripe to do right. Now is the time to make real the promise of democracy and transform our pending national elegy into a creative psalm of brotherhood. Now is the time to lift our national policy from the quicksand of racial injustice to the solid rock of human dignity.

You speak of our activity in Birmingham as extreme. At first I was rather disappointed that fellow clergymen would see my nonviolent efforts as those of an extremist. I began thinking about the fact that I stand in the middle of two opposing forces in the Negro community. One is a force of complacency, made up in part of Negroes who, as a result of long years of oppression, are so drained of self-respect and a sense of "somebodiness" that they have adjusted to segregation; and in part of a few middle-class Negroes who, because of a degree of academic and economic security and because in some ways they profit by segregation, have become insensitive to the problems of the masses. The other force is one of bitterness and hatred, and it comes perilously close to advocating violence. It is expressed in the various black nationalist groups that are springing up across the nation, the largest and best known being Elijah Muhammad's Muslim movement. Nourished by the Negro's frustration over the continued existence of racial discrimination, this movement is made up of people who have lost faith in America, who have absolutely repudiated Christianity, and who have concluded that the white man is an incorrigible "devil."

I have tried to stand between these two forces, saying that we need emulate neither the "do-nothingism" of the complacent nor the hatred and despair of the black nationalist. For there is the more excellent way of love and nonviolent protest. I am grateful to God that, through the influence of the Negro church, the way of nonviolence became an integral part of our struggle.

If this philosophy had not emerged, by now many streets of the South would, I am convinced, be flowing with blood. And I am further convinced that if our white brothers dismiss as "rabble-rousers" and "outside agitators" those of us who employ nonviolent direct action, and if they refuse to support our nonviolent efforts, millions of Negroes will, out of frustration and despair, seek solace and security in black-nationalist ideologies—a development that would inevitably lead to a frightening racial nightmare.

Oppressed people cannot remain oppressed forever. The yearning for freedom eventually manifests itself, and that is what has happened to the American Negro. Something within has reminded him of his birthright of freedom, and something without has reminded him that it can be gained. Consciously or unconsciously, he has been caught up by the *Zeitgeist*, and with his black brothers of Africa and his brown and yellow brothers of Asia, South America and the Caribbean, the United States Negro is moving with a sense of great urgency toward the promised land of racial justice. If one recognizes this vital urge that has engulfed the Negro community, one should readily understand why public demonstrations are taking place. The Negro has many pent-up resentments and latent frustrations, and he must release them. So let him march; let him make prayer pilgrimages to the city hall; let him go on freedom rides—and try to understand why he must do so. If his repressed emotions are not released in nonviolent ways, they will seek expression through violence; this is not a threat but a fact of history. So I have not said to my people: "Get rid of your discontent." Rather, I have tried to say that this normal and healthy discontent can be channeled into the creative outlet of nonviolent direct action. And now this approach is being termed extremist.

But though I was initially disappointed at being categorized as an extremist, as I continued to think about the matter I gradually gained a measure of satisfaction from the label. Was not Jesus an extremist for love: "Love your enemies, bless them that curse you, do good to them that hate you, and pray for them which despitefully use you, and persecute you." Was not Amos an extremist for justice: "Let justice roll down like waters and righteousness like an ever-flowing stream." Was not Paul an extremist for the Christian gospel: "I bear in my body the marks of the Lord Jesus." Was not Martin Luther an extremist: "Here I stand; I cannot do otherwise, so help me God." And John Bunyan: "I will stay in jail to the end of my days before I make a butchery of my conscience." And Abraham Lincoln: "This nation cannot survive half slave and half free." And Thomas Jefferson: "We hold these truths to be self-evident, that all men are created equal . . ." So the question is not whether we will be extremists, but what kind of extremists we will be. Will we be extremists for hate or for love? Will we be extremists for the preservation of injustice or for the extension of justice? In that dramatic scene on Calvary's hill three men were crucified. We must never forget that all three were crucified for the same crime—the crime of extremism. Two were extremists for immorality, and thus fell below their environment. The other, Jesus Christ, was an extremist for love, truth and goodness, and thereby rose above his environment. Perhaps the South, the nation and the world are in dire need of creative extremists.

I had hoped that the white moderate would see this need. Perhaps I was too optimistic; perhaps I expected too much. I suppose I should have realized that few members of the oppressor race can understand the deep groans and passionate yearnings of the oppressed race, and still fewer have the vision to see that injustice must be rooted out by strong, persistent and determined action. I am thankful, however, that some of our white brothers in the South have grasped the meaning of this social revolution and committed themselves to it. They are still all too few in quantity, but they are big in quality. Some—such as Ralph McGill, Lillian Smith, Harry Golden, James McBride Dabbs, Ann Braden and Sarah Patton Boyle—have written about our struggle in eloquent and prophetic terms. Others have marched with us down nameless streets of the South. They have languished in filthy, roach-infested jails, suffering the abuse and brutality of policemen who view them as "dirty nigger-lovers." Unlike so many of their moderate brothers and sisters, they have recognized the urgency of the moment and sensed the need for powerful "action" antidotes to combat the disease of segregation.

Let me take note of my other major disappointment. I have been so greatly disappointed with the white church and its leadership. Of course, there are some notable exceptions. I am not unmindful of the fact that each of you has taken some significant stands on this issue. I commend you, Reverend Stallings, for your Christian stand on this past Sunday, in welcoming Negroes to your worship service on a nonsegregated basis. I commend the Catholic leaders of this state for integrating Spring Hill College several years ago.

But despite these notable exceptions, I must honestly reiterate that I have been disappointed with the church. I do not say this as one of those negative critics who can always find something wrong with the church. I say this as a minister of the gospel, who loves the church; who was nurtured in its bosom; who has been sustained by its spiritual blessings and who will remain true to it as long as the cord of life shall lengthen.

When I was suddenly catapulted into the leadership of the bus protest in Montgomery, Alabama, a few years ago, I felt we would be supported by the white church. I felt that the white ministers, priests and rabbis of the South would be among our strongest allies. Instead, some have been outright opponents, refusing to understand the freedom movement and misrepresenting its leaders; all too many others have been more cautious than courageous and have remained silent behind the anesthetizing security of stained-glass windows.

In spite of my shattered dreams, I came to Birmingham with the hope that the white religious leadership of this community would see the justice of our cause and, with deep moral concern, would serve as the channel through which our just grievances could reach the power structure. I had hoped that each of you would understand. But again I have been disappointed.

I have heard numerous southern religious leaders admonish their worshipers to comply with a desegregation decision because it is the law, but I have longed to hear white ministers declare: "Follow this decree because integration is morally right and because the Negro is your brother." In the midst of blatant injustices inflicted upon the Negro, I have watched white churchmen stand on the sideline and mouth pious irrelevancies and sanctimonious trivialities. In the midst of a mighty struggle to rid our nation of racial and economic injustice, I have heard many ministers say: "Those are social issues, with which the gospel has no real concern." And I have watched many churches commit themselves to a completely otherworldly religion which makes a strange, un-Biblical distinction between body and soul, between the sacred and the secular.

I have traveled the length and breadth of Alabama, Mississippi and all the other southern states. On sweltering summer days and crisp autumn mornings I have looked at the South's beautiful churches with their lofty spires pointing heavenward. I have beheld the impressive outlines of her massive religious-education buildings. Over and over I have found myself asking: "What kind of people worship here? Who is their God? Where were their voices when the lips of Governor Barnett dripped with words of interposition and nullification? Where were they when Governor Wallace gave a clarion call for defiance and hatred? Where were their voices of support when bruised and weary Negro men and women decided to rise from the dark dungeons of complacency to the bright hills of creative protest?"

Yes, these questions are still in my mind. In deep disappointment I have wept over the laxity of the church. But be assured that my tears have been tears of love. There can be no deep disappointment where there is not deep love. Yes, I love the church. How could I do otherwise? I am in the rather unique position of being the son, the grandson and the great-grandson of preachers. Yes, I see the church as the body of Christ. But, oh! How we have blemished and scarred that body through social neglect and through fear of being non-conformists.

There was a time when the church was very powerful—in the time when the early Christians rejoiced at being deemed worthy to suffer for what they believed. In those days the church was not merely a thermometer that recorded the ideas and principles of popular opinion; it was a thermostat that transformed the mores of society. Whenever the early Christians entered a town, the people in power became disturbed and immediately sought to convict the Christians for being "disturbers of the peace" and "outside agitators." But the Christians pressed on, in the conviction that they were "a colony of heaven," called to obey God rather than man. Small in number, they were big in commitment. They were too God-intoxicated to be "astronomically intimidated." By their effort and example they brought an end to such ancient evils as infanticide and gladiatorial contests.

Things are different now. So often the contemporary church is a weak, ineffectual voice with an uncertain sound. So often it is an archdefender of the status quo. Far from being disturbed by the presence of the church, the power structure of the average community is consoled by the church's silent—and often even vocal—sanction of things as they are.

But the judgment of God is upon the church as never before. If today's church does not recapture the sacrificial spirit of the early church, it will lose its authenticity, forfeit the loyalty of millions, and be dismissed as an irrelevant social club with no meaning for the twentieth century. Every day I meet young people whose disappointment with the church has turned into outright disgust.

Perhaps I have once again been too optimistic. Is organized religion too inextricably bound to the status quo to save our nation and the world? Perhaps I must turn my faith to the inner spiritual church, the church within the church, as the true *ekklesia* and the hope of the world. But again I am thankful to God that some noble souls from the ranks of organized religion have broken loose from the paralyzing chains of conformity and joined us as active partners in the struggle for freedom. They have left their secure congregations and walked the streets of Albany, Georgia, with us. They have gone down the highways of the South on tortuous rides for freedom. Yes, they have gone to jail with us. Some have been dismissed from their churches, have lost the support of their bishops and fellow ministers. But they have acted in the faith that right defeated is stronger than evil triumphant. Their witness has been the spiritual salt that has preserved the true meaning of the gospel in these troubled times. They have carved a tunnel of hope through the dark mountain of disappointment.

I hope the church as a whole will meet the challenge of this decisive hour. But even if the church does not come to the aid of justice, I have no despair about the future. I have no fear about the outcome of our struggle in Birmingham, even if our motives are at present misunderstood. We will reach the goal of freedom in Birmingham and all over the nation, because the goal of America is freedom. Abused and scorned though we may be, our destiny is tied up with America's destiny. Before the pilgrims landed at Plymouth, we were here. Before the pen of Jefferson etched the majestic words of the Declaration of Independence across the pages of history, we were here. For more than two centuries our forebears labored in this country without wages; they made cotton king; they built the homes of their masters while suffering gross injustice and shameful humiliation—and yet out of a bottomless vitality they continued to thrive and develop. If the inexpressible cruelties of slavery could not stop us, the opposition we now face will surely fail. We will win our freedom because the sacred heritage of our nation and the eternal will of God are embodied in our echoing demands.

Before closing I feel impelled to mention one other point in your statement that has troubled me profoundly. You warmly commended the Birmingham police force for keeping "order" and "preventing violence." I doubt that you would have so warmly commended the police force if you had seen its dogs sinking their teeth into unarmed, nonviolent Negroes. I doubt that you would so quickly commend the policemen if you were to observe their ugly and inhumane treatment of Negroes here in the city jail; if you were to watch them push and curse old Negro women and young Negro girls; if you were to see them slap and kick old Negro men and young boys; if you were to observe them, as they did on two occasions, refuse to give us food because we wanted to sing our grace together. I cannot join you in your praise of the Birmingham police department.

It is true that the police have exercised a degree of discipline in handling the demonstrators. In this sense they have conducted themselves rather "nonviolently" in public. But for what purpose? To preserve the evil system of segregation. Over the past few years I have consistently preached that nonviolence demands that the means we use must be as pure as the ends we seek. I have tried to make clear that it is wrong to use immoral means to attain moral ends. But now I must affirm that it is just as wrong, or perhaps even more so, to use moral means to preserve immoral ends. Perhaps Mr. Connor and his policemen have been rather nonviolent in public, as was Chief Pritchett in Albany, Georgia, but they have used the moral means of nonviolence to maintain the immoral end of racial injustice. As T. S. Eliot has said: "The last temptation is the greatest treason: To do the right deed for the wrong reason."

I wish you had commended the Negro sit-inners and demonstrators of Birmingham for their sublime courage, their willingness to suffer and their amazing discipline in the midst of great provocation. One day the South will recognize its real heroes. They will be the James Merediths, with the noble sense of purpose that enables them to face jeering and hostile mobs, and with the agonizing loneliness that characterizes the life of the pioneer. They will be old, oppressed, battered Negro women, symbolized in a seventy-two-year-old woman in Montgomery, Alabama, who rose up with a sense of dignity and with her people decided not to ride segregated buses, and who responded with ungrammatical profundity to one who inquired about her weariness: "My feets is tired, but my soul is at rest." They will be the young high school and college students, the young ministers of the gospel and a host of their elders, courageously and nonviolently sitting in at lunch counters and willingly going to jail for conscience's sake. One day the South will know that when these disinherited children of God sat down at lunch counters, they were in reality standing up for what is best in the American dream and for the most sacred values in our Judaeo-Christian heritage, thereby bringing our nation back to those great wells of democracy which were dug deep by the founding fathers in their formulation of the Constitution and the Declaration of Independence.

Never before have I written so long a letter. I'm afraid it is much too long to take your precious time. I can assure you that it would have been much shorter if I had been writing from a comfortable desk, but what else can one do when he is alone in a narrow jail cell other than write long letters, think long thoughts and pray long prayers?

If I have said anything in this letter that overstates the truth and indicates an unreasonable impatience, I beg you to forgive me. If I have said anything that understates the truth and indicates my having a patience that allows me to settle for anything less than brotherhood, I beg God to forgive me.

I hope this letter finds you strong in the faith. I also hope that circumstances will soon make it possible for me to meet each of you, not as an integrationist or a civil-rights leader but as a fellow clergyman and a Christian brother. Let us all hope that the dark clouds of racial prejudice will soon pass away and the deep fog of misunderstanding will be lifted from our fear-drenched communities, and in some not too distant tomorrow the radiant stars of love and brotherhood will shine over our great nation with all their scintillating beauty.

Yours for the cause of Peace and Brotherhood,

Martin Luther King, Jr.

From *Why We Can't Wait* (Harper & Row, 1963, 1964, reprinted by Beacon Press, 2010).

THIRTEEN
NONVIOLENCE AND SOCIAL CHANGE

In 1967, Dr. King delivered five lectures for the renowned Massey Lecture Series of the Canadian Broadcasting Corporation. Prior to King's assassination, the lectures were published as a book under the title *Conscience for Change* and were republished in 1968 as *The Trumpet of Conscience*. Each oration features a distinct theme related to the African American civil rights struggle, revealing some of King's most introspective and last impressions of the civil rights movement.

There is nothing wrong with a traffic law which says you have to stop for a red light. But when a fire is raging, the fire truck goes right through that red light, and normal traffic had better get out of its way. Or, when a man is bleeding to death, the ambulance goes through those red lights at top speed.

There is a fire raging now for the Negroes and the poor of this society. They are living in tragic conditions because of the terrible economic injustices that keep them locked in as an "underclass," as the sociologists are now calling it. Disinherited people all over the world are bleeding to death from deep social and economic wounds. They need brigades of ambulance drivers who will have to ignore the red lights of the present system until the emergency is solved.

Massive civil disobedience is a strategy for social change which is at least as forceful as an ambulance with its siren on full. In the past ten years, nonviolent civil disobedience has made a great deal of history, especially in the Southern United States. When we and the Southern Christian Leadership Conference went to Birmingham, Alabama, in 1963, we had decided to take action on the matter of integrated public accommodations. We went knowing that the Civil Rights Commission had written powerful documents calling for change, calling for the very rights we were demanding. But nobody did anything about the Commission's report. Nothing was done until we acted on these very issues, and demonstrated before the court of world opinion the urgent need for change. It was the same story with voting rights. The Civil Rights Commission, three years before we went to Selma, had recommended the changes we started marching for, but nothing was done until, in 1965, we created a crisis the nation couldn't ignore. Without violence, we totally disrupted the system, the lifestyle of Birmingham, and then of Selma, with their unjust and unconstitutional laws. Our Birmingham struggle came to its dramatic climax when some 3,500 demonstrators virtually filled every jail in that city and surrounding communities, and some 4,000 more continued to march and demonstrate nonviolently. The city knew then in terms that were crystal clear that Birmingham could no longer continue to function until the demands of the Negro community were met. The same kind of dramatic crisis was created in Selma two years later. The result on the national scene was the Civil Rights Bill and the Voting Rights Act, as President and Congress responded to the drama and the creative tension generated by the carefully planned demonstrations.

Of course, by now it is obvious that new laws are not enough. The emergency we now face is economic, and it is a desperate and worsening situation. For the 35 million poor people in America—not even to mention, just yet, the poor in the other nations—there is a kind of strangulation in the air. In our society it is murder, psychologically, to deprive a man of a job or an income. You are in substance saying to that man that he has no right to exist. You are in a real way depriving him of life, liberty, and the pursuit of happiness, denying in his case the very creed of his society. Now, millions of people are being strangled that way. The problem is international in scope. And it is getting worse, as the gap between the poor and the "affluent society" increases.

The question that now divides the people who want radically to change that situation is: can a program of nonviolence—even if it envisions massive civil disobedience—realistically expect to deal with such an enormous, entrenched evil?

First of all, will nonviolence work, psychologically, after the summer of 1967? Many people feel that nonviolence as a strategy for social change was cremated in the flames of the urban riots of the last two years. They tell us that Negroes have only now begun to find their true manhood in violence; that the riots prove not only that Negroes hate whites, but that, compulsively, they must destroy them.

This bloodlust interpretation ignores one of the most striking features of the city riots. Violent they certainly were. But the violence, to a startling degree, was focused against property rather than against people. There were very few cases of injury to persons, and the vast majority of the rioters were not involved at all in attacking people. The much publicized "death toll" that marked the riots, and the many injuries, were overwhelmingly inflicted on the rioters by the military. It is clear that the riots were exacerbated by police action that was designed to injure or even to kill people. As for the snipers, no account of the riots claims that more than one or two dozen people were involved in sniping. From the facts, an unmistakable pattern emerges: a handful of Negroes used gunfire substantially to intimidate, not to kill; and all of the other participants had a different target—property.

I am aware that there are many who wince at a distinction between property and persons—who hold both sacrosanct. My views are not so rigid. A life is sacred. Property is intended to serve life, and no matter how much we surround it with rights and respect, it has no personal being. It is part of the earth man walks on; it is not man.

The focus on property in the 1967 riots is not accidental. It has a message; it is saying something.

If hostility to whites were ever going to dominate a Negro's attitude and reach murderous proportions, surely it would be during a riot. But this rare opportunity for bloodletting was sublimated into arson, or turned into a kind of stormy carnival of free-merchandise distribution. Why did the rioters avoid personal attacks? The explanation cannot be fear of retribution, because the physical risks incurred in the attacks on property were no less than for personal assaults. The military forces were treating acts of petty larceny as equal to murder. Far more rioters took chances with their own lives, in their attacks on property, than threatened the life of anyone else. Why were they so violent with property then? Because property represents the white power structure, which they were attacking and trying to destroy. A curious proof of the symbolic aspect of the looting for some who took part in it is the fact that, after the riots, police received hundreds of calls from Negroes trying to return merchandise they had taken. Those people wanted the experience of taking, of redressing the power imbalance that property represents. Possession, afterward, was secondary.

A deeper level of hostility came out in arson, which was far more dangerous than the looting. But it, too, was a demonstration and a warning. It was directed against symbols of exploitation, and it was designed to express the depth of anger in the community.

What does this restraint in the summer riots mean for our future strategy?

If one can find a core of nonviolence toward persons, even during the riots when emotions were exploding, it means that nonviolence should not be written off for the future as a force in Negro life. Many people believe that the urban Negro is too angry and too sophisticated to be nonviolent. Those same people dismiss the nonviolent marches in the South and try to describe them as processions of pious, elderly ladies. The fact is that in all the marches we have organized some men of very violent tendencies have been involved. It was routine for us to collect hundreds of knives from our own ranks before the demonstrations, in case of momentary weakness. And in Chicago last year we saw some of the most violent individuals accepting nonviolent discipline. Day after day during those Chicago marches I walked in our lines and I never saw anyone retaliate with violence. There were lots of provocations, not only the screaming white hoodlums lining the sidewalks, but also groups of Negro militants talking about guerrilla warfare. We had some gang leaders and members marching with us. I remember walking with the Blackstone Rangers while bottles were flying from the sidelines, and I saw their noses being broken and blood flowing from their wounds; and I saw them continue and not retaliate, not one of them, with violence. I am convinced that even very violent temperaments can be channeled through nonviolent discipline, if the movement is moving, if they can act constructively and express through an effective channel their very legitimate anger.

But even if nonviolence can be valid, psychologically, for the protesters who want change, is it going to be effective, strategically, against a government and a status quo that have so far resisted this summer's demands on the grounds that "we must not reward the rioters"? Far from rewarding the rioters, far from even giving a hearing to their just and urgent demands, the administration has ignored its responsibility for the causes of the riots, and instead has used the negative aspects of them to justify continued inaction on the underlying issues. The administration's only concrete response was to initiate a study and call for a day of prayer. As a minister, I take prayer too seriously to use it as an excuse for avoiding work and responsibility. When a government commands more wealth and power than has ever been known in the history of the world, and offers no more than this, it is worse than blind, it is provocative. It is paradoxical but fair to say that Negro terrorism is incited less on ghetto street corners than in the halls of Congress.

I intended to show that nonviolence will be effective, but not until it has achieved the massive dimensions, the disciplined planning, and the intense commitment of a sustained, direct-action movement of civil disobedience on the national scale.

The dispossessed of this nation—the poor, both white and Negro —live in a cruelly unjust society. They must organize a revolution against that injustice, not against the lives of the persons who are their fellow citizens, but against the structures through which the society is refusing to take means which have been called for, and which are at hand, to lift the load of poverty.

The only real revolutionary, people say, is a man who has nothing to lose. There are millions of poor people in this country who have very little, or even nothing, to lose. If they can be helped to take action together, they will do so with a freedom and a power that will be a new and unsettling force in our complacent national life. Beginning in the New Year, we will be recruiting three thousand of the poorest citizens from ten different urban and rural areas to initiate and lead a sustained, massive, direct-action movement in Washington. Those who choose to join this initial three thousand, this nonviolent army, this "freedom church" of the poor, will work with us for three months to develop nonviolent action skills. Then we will move on Washington, determined to stay there until the legislative and executive branches of the government take serious and adequate action on jobs and income. A delegation of poor people can walk into a high official's office with a carefully, collectively prepared list of demands. (If you're poor, if you're unemployed anyway, you can choose to stay in Washington as long as the struggle needs you.) And if that official says, "But Congress would have to approve this," or, "But the President would have to be consulted on that," you can say, "All right, we'll wait." And you can settle down in his office for as long a stay as necessary. If you are, let's say, from rural Mississippi, and have never had medical attention, and your children are undernourished and unhealthy, you can take those little children into the Washington hospitals and stay with them there until the medical workers cope with their needs, and in showing it your children you will have shown this country a sight that will make it stop in its busy tracks and think hard about what it has done. The many people who will come and join this three thousand, from all groups in the country's life, will play a supportive role, deciding to be poor for a time along with the dispossessed who are asking for their right to jobs or income—jobs, income, the demolition of slums, and the rebuilding by the people who live there of new communities in their place; in fact, a new economic deal for the poor.

Why camp in Washington to demand these things? Because only the federal Congress and administration can decide to use the billions of dollars we need for a real war on poverty. We need, not a new law, but a massive, new national program. This Congress has done nothing to help such measures, and plenty to hinder them. Why should Congress care about our dying cities? It is still dominated by senior representatives of the rural South, who still unite in an obstructive coalition with unprogressive Northerners to prevent public funds from going where they are socially needed. We broke that coalition in 1963 and 1964, when the Civil Rights and Voting Rights laws were passed. We need to break it again by the size and force of our movement, and the best place to do that is before the eyes and inside the buildings of these same Congressmen. The people of this country, if not the Congressmen, are ready for a serious economic attack on slums and unemployment, as two recent polls by Lou Harris have revealed. So we have to make Congress ready to act on the plight of the poor. We will prod and sensitize the legislators, the administrators, and all the wielders of power until they have faced this utterly imperative need.

I have said that the problem, the crisis we face, is international in scope. In fact, it is inseparable from an international emergency which involves the poor, the dispossessed, and the exploited of the whole world.

Can a nonviolent, direct-action movement find application on the international level, to confront economic and political problems? I believe it can. It is clear to me that the next stage of the movement is to become international. National movements within the developed countries—forces that focus on London, or Paris, or Washington, or Ottawa—must help to make it politically feasible for their governments to undertake the kind of massive aid that the developing countries need if they are to break the chains of poverty. We in the West must bear in mind that the poor countries are poor primarily because we have exploited them through political or economic colonialism. Americans in particular must help their nation repent of her modern economic imperialism.

But movements in our countries alone will not be enough. In Latin America, for example, national reform movements have almost despaired of nonviolent methods; many young men, even many priests, have joined guerrilla movements in the hills. So many of Latin America's problems have roots in the United States of America that we need to form a solid, united movement, nonviolently conceived and carried through, so that pressure can be brought to bear on the capital and government power structures concerned, from both sides of the problem at once. I think that may be the only hope for a nonviolent solution in Latin America today; and one of the most powerful expressions of nonviolence may come out of that international coalition of socially aware forces, operating outside governmental frameworks.

Even entrenched problems like the South African Government and its racial policies could be tackled on this level. If just two countries, Britain and the United States, could be persuaded to end all economic interaction with the South African regime, they could bring that government to its knees in a relatively short time. Theoretically, the British and American governments could make that kind of decision; almost every corporation in both countries has economic ties with its government which it could not afford to do without. In practice, such a decision would represent such a major reordering of priorities that we should not expect that any movement could bring it about in one year or two. Indeed, although it is obvious that nonviolent movements for social change must internationalize, because of the interlocking nature of the problems they all face, and because otherwise those problems will breed war, we have hardly begun to build the skills and the strategy, or even the commitment, to planetize our movement for social justice.

In a world facing the revolt of ragged and hungry masses of God's children; in a world torn between the tensions of East and West, white and colored, individualists and collectivists; in a world whose cultural and spiritual power lags so far behind her technological capabilities that we live each day on the verge of nuclear co-annihilation; in this world, nonviolence is no longer an option for intellectual analysis, it is an imperative for action.

From *The Trumpet of Conscience*
(1968, reprinted by Beacon Press, 2010).

FOURTEEN

MY TALK
WITH BEN BELLA

Originally published by the *New York Amsterdam News* on October 27, 1962, Dr. King's conversation with Premier Ben Bella of the new Algerian Republic illustrates the notion that African Americans and Africans are engaged in a common struggle.

A few days ago I had the good fortune of talking with Premier Ben Bella of the new Algerian Republic. Algeria is one of the most recent African nations to remove the last sanction of colonialism. For almost two hours Mr. Ben Bella and I discussed issues ranging from the efficacy of nonviolence to the Cuban crisis. However, it was on the question of racial injustice that we spent most of our time. As I sat talking with Mr. Ben Bella he displayed again and again an intimate knowledge of the Negro struggle here in America. The details of the Montgomery bus protest were immediately at his fingertips. He understood clearly what the issues were. The "Sit-ins" of 1960 were discussed animatedly and he expressed regret at the violence that accompanied the Freedom Rides. He knew all about Albany, Georgia, too, and Oxford, Mississippi, was currently in the headlines. The significance of our conversation was Ben Bella's complete familiarity with the progression of events in the Negro struggle for full citizenship.

Our nation needs to note this well. All through our talks he repeated or inferred, "We are brothers." For Ben Bella, it was unmistakably clear that there is a close relationship between colonialism and segregation. He perceived that both are immoral systems aimed at the degradation of human personality. The battle of the Algerians against colonialism and the battle of the Negro against segregation is a common struggle. This points up a sobering fact for our nation. The matter of racial segregation in America has international implications. Either we must solve our human relations dilemma occasioned by race and color prejudice—and solve it soon—or we shall lose our moral and political voice in the world community of nations. *Ben Bella said this!* Racism in our nation must go or we will be relegated to a second-rate power in the world. We must face the inescapable fact that the shape of the world today does not afford us the luxury of an anemic democracy. The price that America must pay for the continued oppression of the Negro is the price of its own destruction. I must hasten to say, however, that this is not the only reason that America must solve this cancerous, domestic problem.

It must not be done merely to meet the Communist challenge; it must not be done merely to appeal to Asian and African peoples; in the final analysis, equal opportunity without regard to race must be established in America *because it is right.*

The Mississippi debacle of a few days ago pointed up this sore need in our midst. Somewhere in our ranks of government, education, the church and business, strong, clear voices must be raised to declare that integration in American life is to be effected, not alone because it is the law of the land or to keep our good name, but because it is a moral demand of the universe. Men and women all over America must be reminded over and over again that racial segregation is morally wrong because it relegates persons to the status of things.

Originally published in *New York Amsterdam News,*
New York, New York, October 27, 1962.

FIFTEEN

JAWAHARLAL NEHRU, A LEADER IN THE LONG ANTI-COLONIAL STRUGGLE

Dr. King's article on Jawaharlal Nehru was written as a tribute to the Indian leader after his death and was originally published in the centenary volume *Legacy of Nehru* in 1965.

Jawaharlal Nehru was a man of three extraordinary epochs. He was a leader in the long anti-colonial struggle to free his own land and to inspire a fighting will in other lands under bondage.

He lived to see victory and to move then to another epochal confrontation—the fight for peace after World War II. In this climactic struggle he did not have Gandhi at his side, but he did have the Indian people now free in their own great Republic.

It would be hard to overstate Nehru's and India's contributions in this period. It was a time fraught with the constant threat of a devastating finality for mankind. There was no moment in this period free from the peril of atomic war. In these years Nehru was a towering world force skillfully inserting the peace will of India between the raging antagonisms of the great powers of East and West.

The world needed a mediator and an "honest broker" lest, in its sudden acquisition of overwhelming destructive force, one side or the other might plunge the world into mankind's last war. Nehru had the prestige, the wisdom, and the daring to play the role.

The markedly relaxed tensions of today are Nehru's legacy to us and at the same time they are our monument to him.

It should not be forgotten that the treaty to end nuclear testing accomplished in 1963 was first proposed by Nehru. Let us also remember that the world dissolution of colonialism now speedily unfolding had its essential origins in India's massive victory. And let it also be remembered that Nehru guided into being the "Asian-African Bloc" as a united voice for the billions who were groping toward a modern world. He was the architect of the policy of non-alignment or neutralism which was calculated to give independent expression to the emerging nations while enabling them to play a constructive role in world affairs.

The third epoch of Nehru's work is unfolding after his death. Even though his physical presence is gone his spiritual influence retains a living force. The great powers are not yet in harmonious relationships to each other, but with the help of the non-aligned world they have learned to exercise a wise restraint. In this is the basis for a lasting detente. Beyond this, Nehru's example in daring to believe and act for peaceful co-existence gives mankind its most glowing hope.

In this period my people, the Negroes of the United States have made strides toward freedom beyond all precedent in our history. Our successes directly derive from our employment of the tactics of non-violent direct action and non-cooperation with evil which Nehru effectively employed under Gandhi's inspiration.

The peculiar genius of Imperialism was found in its capacity to delude so much of the world into the belief that it was civilizing primitive cultures even though it was grossly exploiting them.

Satyagraha made the myth transparent as it revealed the oppressed to be the truly civilized party. They rejected violence but maintained resistance, while the oppressor knew nothing but the use of violence.

My people found that Satyagraha applied in the U.S. to our oppressors also clarified who was right and who was wrong. On this foundation of truth an irresistible majority could be organized for just solutions.

Our fight is not yet won, just as the struggle against colonialism is still unfinished, and above all, the achievement of a stable peace still lies ahead of, and not behind us.

In all of these struggles of mankind to rise to a true state of civilization, the towering figure of Nehru sits unseen but felt at all council tables. He is missed by the world, and because he is so wanted, he is a living force in the tremulous world of today.

Originally published in the centenary volume
Legacy of Nehru, Atlanta, Georgia, February 8, 1965.

SIXTEEN

WHERE DO WE GO FROM HERE?

Dr. King delivered this speech at the annual convention of the Southern
Christian Leadership Conference in Atlanta on August 16, 1967.
It was his last and most radical SCLC presidential address.

Dr. Abernathy, our distinguished vice president, fellow delegates to
this, the tenth annual session of the Southern Christian Leadership
Conference, my brothers and sisters from not only all over the South,
but from all over the United States of America: Ten years ago during
the piercing chill of a January day and on the heels of the year-long
Montgomery bus boycott, a group of approximately one hundred
Negro leaders from across the South assembled in this church and
agreed on the need for an organization to be formed that could serve
as a channel through which local protest organizations in the South
could coordinate their protest activities. It was this meeting that gave
birth to the Southern Christian Leadership Conference.

And when our organization was formed ten years ago, racial segregation was still a structured part of the architecture of southern society. Negroes with the pangs of hunger and the anguish of thirst were
denied access to the average lunch counter. The downtown restau-
rants were still off-limits for the black man. Negroes, burdened with

the fatigue of travel, were still barred from the motels of the highways and the hotels of the cities. Negro boys and girls in dire need of recreational activities were not allowed to inhale the fresh air of the big city parks. Negroes in desperate need of allowing their mental buckets to sink deep into the wells of knowledge were confronted with a firm no when they sought to use the city libraries. Ten years ago, legislative halls of the South were still ringing loud with such words as "interposition" and "nullification." All types of conniving methods were still being used to keep the Negro from becoming a registered voter. A decade ago, not a single Negro entered the legislative chambers of the South except as a porter or a chauffeur. Ten years ago, all too many Negroes were still harried by day and haunted by night by a corroding sense of fear and a nagging sense of nobody-ness.

But things are different now. In assault after assault, we caused the sagging walls of segregation to come tumbling down. And during this era the entire edifice of segregation was profoundly shaken. This is an accomplishment whose consequences are deeply felt by every southern Negro in his daily life. It is no longer possible to count the number of public establishments that are open to Negroes. Ten years ago, Negroes seemed almost invisible to the larger society, and the facts of their harsh lives were unknown to the majority of the nation. But today, civil rights is a dominating issue in every state, crowding the pages of the press and the daily conversation of white Americans. In this decade of change, the Negro stood up and confronted his oppressor. He faced the bullies and the guns, the dogs and the tear gas. He put himself squarely before the vicious mobs and moved with strength and dignity toward them and decisively defeated them. And the courage with which he confronted enraged mobs dissolved the stereotype of the grinning, submissive Uncle Tom. He came out of his struggle integrated only slightly in the external society, but powerfully integrated within. This was a victory that had to precede all other gains.

In short, over the last ten years the Negro decided to straighten his back up, realizing that a man cannot ride your back unless it is bent. We made our government write new laws to alter some of the cruelest injustices that affected us. We made an indifferent and unconcerned nation rise from lethargy and subpoenaed its conscience to appear before the judgment seat of morality on the whole question of civil rights. We gained manhood in the nation that had always called us "boy." It would be hypocritical indeed if I allowed modesty to forbid my saying that SCLC stood at the forefront of all of the watershed movements that brought these monumental changes in the South. For this, we can feel a legitimate pride. But in spite of a decade of significant progress, the problem is far from solved. The deep rumbling of discontent in our cities is indicative of the fact that the plant of freedom has grown only a bud and not yet a flower.

Before discussing the awesome responsibilities that we face in the days ahead, let us take an inventory of our programmatic action and activities over the past year. Last year as we met in Jackson, Mississippi, we were painfully aware of the struggle of our brothers in Grenada, Mississippi. After living for a hundred or more years under the yoke of total segregation, the Negro citizens of this northern Delta hamlet banded together in nonviolent warfare against racial discrimination under the leadership of our affiliate chapter and organization there. The fact of this nondestructive rebellion was as spectacular as its results. In a few short weeks the Grenada County Movement challenged every aspect of the society's exploitive life. Stores which denied employment were boycotted; voter registration increased by thousands. We can never forget the courageous action of the people of Grenada who moved our nation and its federal courts to powerful action on behalf of school integration, giving Grenada one of the most integrated school systems in America. The battle is far from over, but the black people of Grenada have achieved forty of fifty-three demands through their persistent nonviolent efforts.

Slowly but surely, our southern affiliates continued their building and organizing. Seventy-nine counties conducted voter registration drives, while double that number carried on political education and get-out-the-vote efforts. In spite of press opinions, our staff is still overwhelmingly a southern-based staff. One hundred and five persons have worked across the South under the direction of Hosea Williams. What used to be primarily a voter registration staff is actually a multifaceted program dealing with the total life of the community, from farm cooperatives, business development, tutorials, credit unions, et cetera. Especially to be commended are those ninety-nine communities and their staffs which maintain regular mass meetings throughout the year.

Our Citizenship Education Program continues to lay the solid foundation of adult education and community organization upon which all social change must ultimately rest. This year, five hundred local leaders received training at Dorchester and ten community centers through our Citizenship Education Program. And they were trained in literacy, consumer education, planned parenthood, and many other things. And this program, so ably directed by Mrs. Dorothy Cotton, Mrs. Septima Clark, and their staff of eight persons, continues to cover ten southern states. Our auxiliary feature of C.E.P. is the aid which they have given to poor communities, poor counties, in receiving and establishing O.E.O. [Office of Economic Opportunity] projects. With the competent professional guidance of our marvelous staff member Miss Mew Soong-Li, Lowndes and Wilcox counties in Alabama have pioneered in developing outstanding poverty programs totally controlled and operated by residents of the area.

Perhaps the area of greatest concentration of my efforts has been in the cities of Chicago and Cleveland. Chicago has been a wonderful proving ground for our work in the North. There have been no earth-shaking victories, but neither has there been failure. Our open housing marches, which finally brought about an agreement which actually calls the power structure of Chicago to capitulate to the Civil Rights Movement, these marches and the agreement have finally begun to pay off. After the season of delay around election periods, the Leadership Conference, organized to meet our demands for an open city, has finally begun to implement the programs agreed to last summer.

But this is not the most important aspect of our work. As a result of our tenant union organizing, we have begun a four-million-dollar rehabilitation project which will renovate deteriorating buildings and allow their tenants the opportunity to own their own homes. This pilot project was the inspiration for the new home ownership bill, which Senator Percy introduced in Congress only recently.

The most dramatic success in Chicago has been Operation Breadbasket. Through Operation Breadbasket we have now achieved for the Negro community of Chicago more than twenty-two hundred new jobs with an income of approximately eighteen million dollars a year, new income to the Negro community. But not only have we gotten jobs through Operation Breadbasket in Chicago; there was another area through this economic program, and that was the development of financial institutions which were controlled by Negroes and which were sensitive to problems of economic deprivation of the Negro community. The two banks in Chicago that were interested in helping Negro businessmen were largely unable to loan much because of limited assets. Hi-Lo, one of the chain stores in Chicago, agreed to maintain substantial accounts in the two banks, thus increasing their ability to serve the needs of the Negro community. And I can say to you today that as a result of Operation Breadbasket in Chicago, both of these Negro-operated banks have now more than double their assets, and this has been done in less than a year by the work of Operation Breadbasket.

In addition, the ministers learned that Negro scavengers had been deprived of significant accounts in the ghetto. Whites controlled even the garbage of Negroes. Consequently, the chain stores agreed to contract with Negro scavengers to service at least the stores in Negro areas. Negro insect and rodent exterminators as well as janitorial services were likewise excluded from major contracts with chain stores. The chain stores also agreed to utilize these services. It also became apparent that chain stores advertised only rarely in Negro-owned community newspapers. This area of neglect was also negotiated, giving community newspapers regular, substantial accounts. And finally, the ministers found that Negro contractors, from painters to masons, from electricians to excavators, had also been forced to remain small by the monopolies of white contractors. Breadbasket negotiated agreements on new construction and rehabilitation work for the chain stores. These several interrelated aspects of economic development, all based on the power of organized consumers, hold great possibilities for dealing with the problems of Negroes in other northern cities. The kinds of requests made by Breadbasket in Chicago can be made not only of chain stores, but of almost any major industry in any city in the country.

And so Operation Breadbasket has a very simple program, but a powerful one. It simply says, "If you respect my dollar, you must respect my person." It simply says that we will no longer spend our money where we can not get substantial jobs.

In Cleveland, Ohio, a group of ministers have formed an Operation Breadbasket through our program there and have moved against a major dairy company. Their requests include jobs, advertising in Negro newspapers, and depositing funds in Negro financial institutions. This effort resulted in something marvelous. I went to Cleveland just last week to sign the agreement with Sealtest. We went to get the facts about their employment. We discovered that they had 442 employees and only forty-three were Negroes, yet the Negro population of Cleveland is 35 percent of the total population. They refused to give us all of the information that we requested, and we said in substance: "Mr. Sealtest, we're sorry. We aren't going to burn your store down. We aren't going to throw any bricks in the window. But we are going to put picket signs around and we are going to put leaflets out and we are going to our pulpits and tell them not to sell Sealtest products, and not to purchase Sealtest products."

We did that. We went through the churches. Reverend Doctor Hoover, who pastors the largest church in Cleveland, who's here today, and all of the ministers got together and got behind this program. We went to every store in the ghetto and said: "You must take Sealtest products off of your counters. If not, we're going to boycott your whole store." A&P refused. We put picket lines around A&P; they have a hundred and some stores in Cleveland, and we picketed A&P and closed down eighteen of them in one day. Nobody went in A&P. The next day Mr. A&P was calling on us, and Bob Brown, who is here on our board and who is a public relations man representing a number of firms, came in. They called him in because he works for A&P also; and they didn't know he worked for us, too. Bob Brown sat down with A&P, and he said, they said, "Now, Mr. Brown, what would you advise us to do?" He said, "I would advise you to take Sealtest products off of all of your counters." A&P agreed next day not only to take Sealtest products off of the counters in the ghetto, but off of the counters of every store, A&P store in Cleveland, and they said to Sealtest, "If you don't reach an agreement with SCLC and Operation Breadbasket, we will take Sealtest products off of every A&P store in the state of Ohio."

The next day, the next day the Sealtest people were talking nice, they were very humble. And I am proud to say that I went to Cleveland just last Tuesday, and I sat down with the Sealtest people and some seventy ministers from Cleveland, and we signed the agreement. This effort resulted in a number of jobs, which will bring almost $500,000 of new income to the Negro community a year. We also said to Sealtest: "The problem that we face is that the ghetto is a domestic colony that's constantly drained without being replenished. And you are always telling us to lift ourselves by our own bootstraps, and yet we are being robbed every day. Put something back in the ghetto." So along with our demand for jobs, we said, "We also demand that you put money in the Negro savings and loan association and that you take ads, advertise, in the Cleveland *Call & Post*, the Negro newspaper." So along with the new jobs, Sealtest has now deposited thousands of dollars in the Negro bank of Cleveland and has already started taking ads in the Negro newspaper in that city. This is the power of Operation Breadbasket.

Now for fear you may feel that it's limited to Chicago and Cleveland, let me say to you that we've gotten even more than that, in Atlanta, Georgia. Breadbasket has been equally successful in the South. Here the emphasis has been divided between governmental employment and private industry. And while I do not have time to go into the details, I want to commend the men who have been working with it here: the Reverend Bennette, the Reverend Joe Boone, the Reverend J. C. Ward, Reverend Dorsey, Reverend Greer, and I could go on down the line. And they have stood up along with all of the other ministers. But here is the story that's not printed in the newspapers in Atlanta: As a result of Operation Breadbasket, over the last three years, we have added about twenty-five million dollars of new income to the Negro community every year. Now, as you know, Operation Bread-basket has now gone national in the sense that we had a national conference in Chicago and agreed to launch a nationwide program, which you will hear more about.

Finally, SCLC has entered the field of housing. Under the leadership of attorney James Robinson, we have already contracted to build 152 units of low-income housing with apartments for the elderly on a choice downtown Atlanta site under the sponsorship of Ebenezer Baptist Church. This is the first project, this is the first project of a proposed south-wide Housing Development Corporation which we hope to develop in conjunction with SCLC, and through this corporation we hope to build housing from Mississippi to North Carolina using Negro workmen, Negro architects, Negro attorneys, and Negro financial institutions throughout. And it is our feeling that in the next two or three years, we can build right here in the South forty million dollars' worth of new housing for Negroes, and with millions and millions of dollars in income coming to the Negro community. Now there are many other things that I could tell you, but time is passing. This, in short, is an account of SCLC's work over the last year. It is a record of which we can all be proud.

With all the struggle and all the achievements, we must face the fact, however, that the Negro still lives in the basement of the Great Society. He is still at the bottom, despite the few who have penetrated to slightly higher levels. Even where the door has been forced partially open, mobility for the Negro is still sharply restricted. There is often no bottom at which to start, and when there is there's almost no room at the top. In consequence, Negroes are still impoverished aliens in an affluent society. They are too poor even to rise with the society, too impoverished by the ages to be able to ascend by using their own resources. And the Negro did not do this himself; it was done to him. For more than half of his American history, he was enslaved. Yet he built the spanning bridges, the grand mansions, the sturdy docks, and stout factories of the South. His unpaid labor made cotton king and established America as a significant nation in international commerce. Even after his release from chattel slavery, the nation grew over him, submerging him. It became the richest, most powerful society in the history of man, but it left the Negro far behind.

And so we still have a long, long way to go before we reach the promised land of freedom. Yes, we have left the dusty soils of Egypt, and we have crossed a Red Sea that had for years been hardened by a long and piercing winter of massive resistance, but before we reach the majestic shores of the Promised Land, there will still be gigantic mountains of opposition ahead and prodigious hilltops of injustice. We still need some Paul Revere of conscience to alert every hamlet and every village of America that revolution is still at hand. Yes, we need a chart; we need a compass; indeed, we need some North Star to guide us into a future shrouded with impenetrable uncertainties.

Now in order to answer the question, "Where do we go from here?" which is our theme, we must first honestly recognize where we are now. When the Constitution was written, a strange formula to determine taxes and representation declared that the Negro was 60 percent of a person. Today another curious formula seems to declare he is 50 percent of a person. Of the good things in life, the Negro has approximately one half those of whites. Of the bad things of life, he has twice those of whites. Thus, half of all Negroes live in substandard housing. And Negroes have half the income of whites. When we turn to the negative experiences of life, the Negro has a double share: There are twice as many unemployed; the rate of infant mortality among Negroes is double that of whites; and there are twice as many Negroes dying in Vietnam as whites in proportion to their size in the population.

In other spheres, the figures are equally alarming. In elementary schools, Negroes lag one to three years behind whites, and their segregated schools receive substantially less money per student than the white schools. One-twentieth as many Negroes as whites attend college. Of employed Negroes, 75 percent hold menial jobs. This is where we are.

Where do we go from here? First, we must massively assert our dignity and worth. We must stand up amid a system that still oppresses us and develop an unassailable and majestic sense of values. We must no longer be ashamed of being black. The job of arousing manhood within a people that have been taught for so many centuries that they are nobody is not easy.

Even semantics have conspired to make that which is black seem ugly and degrading. In Roget's *Thesaurus* there are some 120 synonyms for blackness and at least sixty of them are offensive, such words as blot, soot, grim, devil, and foul. And there are some 134 synonyms for whiteness and all are favorable, expressed in such words as purity, cleanliness, chastity, and innocence. A white lie is better than a black lie. The most degenerate member of a family is the "black sheep." Ossie Davis has suggested that maybe the English language should be reconstructed so that teachers will not be forced to teach the Negro child sixty ways to despise himself and thereby perpetuate his false sense of inferiority, and the white child 134 ways to adore himself and thereby perpetuate his false sense of superiority. The tendency to ignore the Negro's contribution to American life and strip him of his personhood is as old as the earliest history books and as contemporary as the morning's newspaper.

To offset this cultural homicide, the Negro must rise up with an affirmation of his own Olympian manhood. Any movement for the Negro's freedom that overlooks this necessity is only waiting to be buried. As long as the mind is enslaved, the body can never be free. Psychological freedom, a firm sense of self-esteem, is the most powerful weapon against the long night of physical slavery. No Lincolnian Emancipation Proclamation, no Johnsonian civil rights bill can totally bring this kind of freedom. The Negro will only be free when he reaches down to the inner depths of his own being and signs with the pen and ink of assertive manhood his own emancipation proclamation. And with a spirit straining toward true self-esteem, the Negro must boldly throw off the manacles of self-abnegation and say to himself and to the world, "I am somebody. I am a person. I am a man with dignity and honor. I have a rich and noble history, however painful and exploited that history has been. Yes, I was a slave through my foreparents, and now I'm not ashamed of that. I'm ashamed of the people who were so sinful to make me a slave." Yes, yes, we must stand up and say, "I'm black, but I'm black and beautiful." This, this self-affirmation is the black man's need, made compelling by the white man's crimes against him.

Now another basic challenge is to discover how to organize our strength into economic and political power. No one can deny that the Negro is in dire need of this kind of legitimate power. Indeed, one of the great problems that the Negro confronts is his lack of power. From the old plantations of the South to the newer ghettos of the North, the Negro has been confined to a life of voicelessness and powerlessness. Stripped of the right to make decisions concerning his life and destiny, he has been subject to the authoritarian and sometimes whimsical decisions of the white power structure. The plantation and the ghetto were created by those who had power, both to confine those who had no power and to perpetuate their powerlessness. Now the problem of transforming the ghetto, therefore, is a problem of power, a confrontation between the forces of power demanding change and the forces of power dedicated to the preserving of the status quo. Now, power properly understood is nothing but the ability to achieve purpose. It is the strength required to bring about social, political, and economic change. Walter Reuther defined power one day. He said, "Power is the ability of a labor union like UAW to make the most powerful corporation in the world, General Motors, say 'Yes' when it wants to say 'No.' That's power."

Now a lot of us are preachers, and all of us have our moral convictions and concerns, and so often we have problems with power. There is nothing wrong with power if power is used correctly. You see, what happened is that some of our philosophers got off base. And one of the great problems of history is that the concepts of love and power have usually been contrasted as opposites, polar opposites, so that love is identified with a resignation of power, and power with a denial of love. It was this misinterpretation that caused the philosopher Nietzsche, who was a philosopher of the will to power, to reject the Christian concept of love. It was this same misinterpretation which induced Christian theologians to reject Nietzsche's philosophy of the will to power in the name of the Christian idea of love.

Now we got to get this thing right. What is needed is a realization that power without love is reckless and abusive, and that love without power is sentimental and anemic. Power at its best, power at its best is love implementing the demands of justice, and justice at its best is love correcting everything that stands against love. And this is what we must see as we move on.

Now what has happened is that we've had it wrong and mixed up in our country, and this has led Negro Americans in the past to seek their goals through love and moral suasion devoid of power, and white Americans to seek their goals through power devoid of love and conscience. It is leading a few extremists today to advocate for Negroes the same destructive and conscienceless power that they have justly abhorred in whites. It is precisely this collision of immoral power with powerless morality which constitutes the major crisis of our times.

Now we must develop progress, or rather, a program—and I can't stay on this long—that will drive the nation to a guaranteed annual income. Now early in the century this proposal would have been greeted with ridicule and denunciation as destructive of initiative and responsibility. At that time economic status was considered the measure of the individual's abilities and talents. And in the thinking of that day, the absence of worldly goods indicated a want of industrious habits and moral fiber. We've come a long way in our understanding of human motivation and of the blind operation of our economic system. Now we realize that dislocations in the market operation of our economy and the prevalence of discrimination thrust people into idleness and bind them in constant or frequent unemployment against their will. The poor are less often dismissed, I hope, from our conscience today by being branded as inferior and incompetent. We also know that no matter how dynamically the economy develops and expands, it does not eliminate all poverty.

The problem indicates that our emphasis must be twofold: We must create full employment, or we must create incomes. People must be made consumers by one method or the other. Once they are placed in this position, we need to be concerned that the potential of the individual is not wasted. New forms of work that enhance the social good will have to be devised for those for whom traditional jobs are not available. In 1879 Henry George anticipated this state of affairs when he wrote in *Progress and Poverty*:

> The fact is that the work which improves the condition of mankind, the work which extends knowledge and increases power and enriches literature and elevates thought, is not done to secure a living. It is not the work of slaves driven to their tasks either by the task of that of a taskmaster or by animal necessities. It is the work of men who somehow find a form of work that brings a security for its own sake and a state of society where want is abolished.

Work of this sort could be enormously increased, and we are likely to find that the problem of housing, education, instead of preceding the elimination of poverty, will themselves be affected if poverty is first abolished. The poor, transformed into purchasers, will do a great deal on their own to alter housing decay. Negroes, who have a double disability, will have a greater effect on discrimination when they have the additional weapon of cash to use in their struggle.

Beyond these advantages, a host of positive psychological changes inevitably will result from widespread economic security. The dignity of the individual will flourish when the decisions concerning his life are in his own hands, when he has the assurance that his income is stable and certain, and when he knows that he has the means to seek self-improvement. Personal conflicts between husband, wife, and children will diminish when the unjust measurement of human worth on a scale of dollars is eliminated.

Now our country can do this. John Kenneth Galbraith said that a guaranteed annual income could be done for about twenty billion dollars a year. And I say to you today, that if our nation can spend thirty-five billion dollars a year to fight an unjust, evil war in Vietnam, and twenty billion dollars to put a man on the moon, it can spend billions of dollars to put God's children on their own two feet right here on earth.

Now let me rush on to say we must reaffirm our commitment to nonviolence. And I want to stress this. The futility of violence in the struggle for racial justice has been tragically etched in all the recent Negro riots. Now yesterday, I tried to analyze the riots and deal with the causes for them. Today I want to give the other side. There is something painfully sad about a riot. One sees screaming youngsters and angry adults fighting hopelessly and aimlessly against impossible odds. Deep down within them, you perceive a desire for self-destruction, a kind of suicidal longing.

Occasionally, Negroes contend that the 1965 Watts riot and the other riots in various cities represented effective civil rights action. But those who express this view always end up with stumbling words when asked what concrete gains have been won as a result. At best the riots have produced a little additional anti-poverty money allotted by frightened government officials, and a few water sprinklers to cool the children of the ghettos. It is something like improving the food in the prison while the people remain securely incarcerated behind bars. Nowhere have the riots won any concrete improvement such as have the organized protest demonstrations.

And when one tries to pin down advocates of violence as to what acts would be effective, the answers are blatantly illogical. Sometimes they talk of over-throwing racist state and local governments and they talk about guerrilla warfare. They fail to see that no internal revolution has ever succeeded in overthrowing a government by violence unless the government had already lost the allegiance and effective control of its armed forces. Anyone in his right mind knows that this will not happen in the United States. In a violent racial situation, the power structure has the local police, the state troopers, the National Guard, and finally, the Army to call on, all of which are predominantly white. Furthermore, few, if any, violent revolutions have been successful unless the violent minority had the sympathy and support of the non-resisting majority. Castro may have had only a few Cubans actually fighting with him and up in the hills, but he would have never overthrown the Batista regime unless he had the sympathy of the vast majority of Cuban people. It is perfectly clear that a violent revolution on the part of American blacks would find no sympathy and support from the white population and very little from the majority of the Negroes themselves.

This is no time for romantic illusions and empty philosophical debates about freedom. This is a time for action. What is needed is a strategy for change, a tactical program that will bring the Negro into the mainstream of American life as quickly as possible. So far, this has only been offered by the nonviolent movement. Without recognizing this we will end up with solutions that don't solve, answers that don't answer, and explanations that don't explain.

And so I say to you today that I still stand by nonviolence. And I am still convinced, and I'm still convinced that it is the most potent weapon available to the Negro in his struggle for justice in this country.

And the other thing is, I'm concerned about a better world. I'm concerned about justice; I'm concerned about brotherhood; I'm concerned about truth. And when one is concerned about that, he can never advocate violence. For through violence you may murder a murderer, but you can't murder murder. Through violence you may murder a liar, but you can't establish truth. Through violence you may murder a hater, but you can't murder hate through violence. Darkness cannot put out darkness; only light can do that.

And I say to you, I have also decided to stick with love, for I know that love is ultimately the only answer to mankind's problems. And I'm going to talk about it everywhere I go. I know it isn't popular to talk about it in some circles today. And I'm not talking about emotional bosh when I talk about love; I'm talking about a strong, demanding love. For I have seen too much hate. I've seen too much hate on the faces of sheriffs in the South. I've seen hate on the faces of too many Klansmen and too many White Citizens' Councilors in the South to want to hate, myself, because every time I see it, I know that it does something to their faces and their personalities, and I say to myself that hate is too great a burden to bear. I have decided to love. If you are seeking the highest good, I think you can find it through love. And the beautiful thing is that we aren't moving wrong when we do it, because John was right, God is love. He who hates does not know God, but he who loves has the key that unlocks the door to the meaning of ultimate reality.

And so I say to you today, my friends, that you may be able to speak with the tongues of men and angels, you may have the eloquence of articulate speech; but if you have not love, it means nothing. Yes, you may have the gift of prophecy, you may have the gift of scientific prediction and understand the behavior of molecules, you may break into the storehouse of nature and bring forth many new insights; yes, you may ascend to the heights of academic achievement so that you have all knowledge, and you may boast of your great institutions of learning and the boundless extent of your degrees; but if you have not love, all of these mean absolutely nothing. You may even give your goods to feed the poor, you may bestow great gifts to charity, and you may tower high in philanthropy; but if you have not love, your charity means nothing. You may even give your body to be burned and die the death of a martyr, and your spilt blood may be a symbol of honor for generations yet unborn, and thousands may praise you as one of history's greatest heroes; but if you have not love, your blood was spilt in vain. What I'm trying to get you to see this morning is that a man may be self-centered in his self-denial and self-righteous in his self-sacrifice. His generosity may feed his ego, and his piety may feed his pride. So without love, benevolence becomes egotism, and martyrdom becomes spiritual pride.

I want to say to you as I move to my conclusion, as we talk about "Where do we go from here?" that we must honestly face the fact that the movement must address itself to the question of restructuring the whole of American society. There are forty million poor people here, and one day we must ask the question, "Why are there forty million poor people in America?" And when you begin to ask that question, you are raising a question about the economic system, about a broader distribution of wealth. When you ask that question, you begin to question the capitalistic economy. And I'm simply saying that more and more, we've got to begin to ask questions about the whole society. We are called upon to help the discouraged beggars in life's marketplace. But one day we must come to see that an edifice which produces beggars needs restructuring. It means that questions must be raised. And you see, my friends, when you deal with this you begin to ask the question, "Who owns the oil?" You begin to ask the question, "Who owns the iron ore?" You begin to ask the question, "Why is it that people have to pay water bills in a world that's two-thirds water?" These are words that must be said.

Now don't think you have me in a bind today. I'm not talking about communism. What I'm talking about is far beyond communism. My inspiration didn't come from Karl Marx; my inspiration didn't come from Engels; my inspiration didn't come from Trotsky; my inspiration didn't come from Lenin. Yes, I read *Communist Manifesto* and *Das Kapital* a long time ago, and I saw that maybe Marx didn't follow Hegel enough. He took his dialectics, but he left out his idealism and his spiritualism. And he went over to a German philosopher by the name of Feuerbach, and took his materialism and made it into a system that he called "dialectical materialism." I have to reject that.

What I'm saying to you this morning is communism forgets that life is individual. Capitalism forgets that life is social. And the kingdom of brotherhood is found neither in the thesis of communism nor the antithesis of capitalism, but in a higher synthesis. It is found in a higher synthesis that combines the truths of both. Now when I say questioning the whole society, it means ultimately coming to see that the problem of racism, the problem of economic exploitation, and the problem of war are all tied together. These are the triple evils that are interrelated.

And if you will let me be a preacher just a little bit. One day, one night, a juror came to Jesus and he wanted to know what he could do to be saved. Jesus didn't get bogged down on the kind of isolated approach of what you shouldn't do. Jesus didn't say, "Now, Nicodemus, you must stop lying." He didn't say, "Nicodemus, now you must not commit adultery." He didn't say, "Now, Nicodemus, you must stop cheating if you are doing that." He didn't say, "Nicodemus, you must stop drinking liquor if you are doing that excessively." He said something altogether different, because Jesus realized something basic: that if a man will lie, he will steal. And if a man will steal, he will kill.

So instead of just getting bogged down on one thing, Jesus looked at him and said, "Nicodemus, you must be born again."

In other words, "Your whole structure must be changed." A nation that will keep people in slavery for 244 years will "thingify" them and make them things. And therefore, they will exploit them and poor people generally economically. And a nation that will exploit economically will have to have foreign investments and everything else, and it will have to use its military might to protect them. All of these problems are tied together.

What I'm saying today is that we must go from this convention and say, "America, you must be born again!"

And so I conclude by saying today that we have a task, and let us go out with a divine dissatisfaction.

Let us be dissatisfied until America will no longer have a high blood pressure of creeds and an anemia of deeds.

Let us be dissatisfied until the tragic walls that separate the outer city of wealth and comfort from the inner city of poverty and despair shall be crushed by the battering rams of the forces of justice.

Let us be dissatisfied until those who live on the outskirts of hope are brought into the metropolis of daily security.

Let us be dissatisfied until slums are cast into the junk heaps of history, and every family will live in a decent, sanitary home.

Let us be dissatisfied until the dark yesterdays of segregated schools will be transformed into bright tomorrows of quality integrated education.

Let us be dissatisfied until integration is not seen as a problem but as an opportunity to participate in the beauty of diversity.

Let us be dissatisfied until men and women, however black they may be, will be judged on the basis of the content of their character, not on the basis of the color of their skin. Let us be dissatisfied.

Let us be dissatisfied until every state capitol will be housed by a governor who will do justly, who will love mercy, and who will walk humbly with his God.

Let us be dissatisfied until from every city hall, justice will roll down like waters, and righteousness like a mighty stream.

Let us be dissatisfied until that day when the lion and the lamb shall lie down together, and every man will sit under his own vine and fig tree, and none shall be afraid.

Let us be dissatisfied, until men will recognize that out of one blood God made all men to dwell upon the face of the earth.

Let us be dissatisfied until that day when nobody will shout, "White Power!" when nobody will shout, "Black Power!" but everybody will talk about God's power and human power.

And I must confess, my friends, that the road ahead will not always be smooth. There will still be rocky places of frustration and meandering points of bewilderment. There will be inevitable setbacks here and there. And there will be those moments when the buoyancy of hope will be transformed into the fatigue of despair. Our dreams will sometimes be shattered and our ethereal hopes blasted. We may again, with tear-drenched eyes, have to stand before the bier of some courageous civil rights worker whose life will be snuffed out by the dastardly acts of bloodthirsty mobs. But difficult and painful as it is, we must walk on in the days ahead with an audacious faith in the future. And as we continue our charted course, we may gain consolation from the words so nobly left by that great black bard, who was also a great freedom fighter of yesterday, James Weldon Johnson:

> Stony the road we trod,
> Bitter the chastening rod
> Felt in the days
> When hope unborn had died.
>
> Yet with a steady beat,
> Have not our weary feet
> Come to the place
> For which our fathers sighed?
>
> We have come over a way
> That with tears has been watered.
> We have come treading our paths
> Through the blood of the slaughtered.

Out from the gloomy past,
Till now we stand at last
Where the bright gleam
Of our bright star is cast.

Let this affirmation be our ringing cry. It will give us the courage to face the uncertainties of the future. It will give our tired feet new strength as we continue our forward stride toward the city of freedom. When our days become dreary with low-hovering clouds of despair, and when our nights become darker than a thousand midnights, let us remember that there is a creative force in this universe working to pull down the gigantic mountains of evil, a power that is able to make a way out of no way and transform dark yesterdays into bright tomorrows.

Let us realize that the arc of the moral universe is long, but it bends toward justice. Let us realize that William Cullen Bryant is right: "Truth, crushed to earth, will rise again." Let us go out realizing that the Bible is right: "Be not deceived. God is not mocked. Whatsoever a man soweth, that shall he also reap." This is our hope for the future, and with this faith we will be able to sing in some not too distant tomorrow, with a cosmic past tense: "We have overcome! We have overcome! Deep in my heart, I *did* believe we would overcome."

Delivered at the annual convention of the Southern Christian Leadership Conference, Atlanta, Georgia, August 16, 1967.

SEVENTEEN

BLACK POWER

Dr. King embraced the essential sociopolitical agenda of black power advocates, but he fiercely opposed violence and black separatism. The following excerpt is from the last book written by King, *Where Do We Go from Here* (1967), his final statement and analysis on the state of American race relations and the movement after a decade of US civil rights struggles.

I

"James Meredith has been shot!"

It was about three o'clock in the afternoon on a Monday in June 1966, and I was presiding over the regular staff meeting of the Southern Christian Leadership Conference in our Atlanta headquarters. When we heard that Meredith had been shot in the back only a day after he had begun his Freedom March through Mississippi, there was a momentary hush of anger and dismay throughout the room. Our horror was compounded by the fact that the early reports announced that Meredith was dead. Soon the silence was broken, and from every corner of the room came expressions of outrage. The business of the meeting was forgotten in the shock of this latest evidence that a Negro's life is still worthless in many parts of his own country.

When order was finally restored, our executive staff immediately agreed that the march must continue. After all, we reasoned, Meredith had begun his lonely journey as a pilgrimage against fear. Wouldn't failure to continue only intensify the fears of the oppressed and deprived Negroes of Mississippi? Would this not be a setback for the whole civil rights movement and a blow to nonviolent discipline?

After several calls between Atlanta and Memphis, we learned that the earlier reports of Meredith's death were false and that he would recover. This news brought relief, but it did not alter our feeling that the civil rights movement had a moral obligation to continue along the path that Meredith had begun.

The next morning I was off to Memphis along with several members of my staff. Floyd McKissick, national director of CORE [Congress of Racial Equality], flew in from New York and joined us on the flight from Atlanta to Memphis. After landing we went directly to the Municipal Hospital to visit Meredith. We were happy to find him resting well. After expressing our sympathy and gratitude for his courageous witness, Floyd and I shared our conviction with him that the march should continue in order to demonstrate to the nation and the world that Negroes would never again be intimidated by the terror of extremist white violence. Realizing that Meredith was often a loner and that he probably wanted to continue the march without a large group, we felt that it would take a great deal of persuasion to convince him that the issue involved the whole civil rights movement. Fortunately, he soon saw this and agreed that we should continue without him. We spent some time discussing the character and logistics of the march, and agreed that we would consult with him daily on every decision.

As we prepared to leave, the nurse came to the door and said, "Mr. Meredith, there is a Mr. Carmichael in the lobby who would like to see you and Dr. King. Should I give him permission to come in?" Meredith consented. Stokely Carmichael entered with his associate, Cleveland Sellers, and immediately reached out for Meredith's hand. He expressed his concern and admiration and brought messages of sympathy from his colleagues in the Student Nonviolent Coordinating Committee. After a brief conversation we all agreed that James should get some rest and that we should not burden him with any additional talk. We left the room assuring him that we would conduct the march in his spirit and would seek as never before to expose the ugly racism that pervaded Mississippi and to arouse a new sense of dignity and manhood in every Negro who inhabited that bastion of man's inhumanity to man.

In a brief conference Floyd, Stokely and I agreed that the march would be jointly sponsored by CORE, SNCC [Student Nonviolent Coordinating Committee] and SCLC [Southern Christian Leadership Conference], with the understanding that all other civil rights organizations would be invited to join. It was also agreed that we would issue a national call for support and participation.

One hour later, after making staff assignments and setting up headquarters at the Rev. James Lawson's church in Memphis, a group of us packed into four automobiles and made our way to that desolate spot on Highway 51 where James Meredith had been shot the day before. So began the second stage of the Meredith Mississippi Freedom March.

As we walked down the meandering highway in the sweltering heat, there was much talk and many questions were raised.

"I'm not for that nonviolence stuff any more," shouted one of the younger activists.

"If one of these damn white Mississippi crackers touches me, I'm gonna knock the hell out of him," shouted another.

Later on a discussion of the composition of the march came up.

"This should be an all-black march," said one marcher. "We don't need any more white phonies and liberals invading our movement. This is our march."

Once during the afternoon we stopped to sing "We Shall Overcome." The voices rang out with all the traditional fervor, the glad thunder and gentle strength that had always characterized the singing of this noble song. But when we came to the stanza which speaks of "black and white together," the voices of a few of the marchers were muted. I asked them later why they refused to sing that verse. The retort was:

"This is a new day, we don't sing those words any more. In fact, the whole song should be discarded. Not 'We Shall Overcome,' but 'We Shall Overrun.'"

As I listened to all these comments, the words fell on my ears like strange music from a foreign land. My hearing was not attuned to the sound of such bitterness. I guess I should not have been surprised. I should have known that in an atmosphere where false promises are daily realities, where deferred dreams are nightly facts, where acts of unpunished violence toward Negroes are a way of life, nonviolence would eventually be seriously questioned. I should have been re-minded that disappointment produces despair and despair produces bitterness, and that the one thing certain about bitterness is its blind-ness. Bitterness has not the capacity to make the distinction between some and *all*. When some members of the dominant group, particu-larly those in power, are racist in attitude and practice, bitterness ac-cuses the whole group.

At the end of the march that first day we all went back to Mem-phis and spent the night in a Negro motel, since we had not yet se-cured the tents that would serve as shelter each of the following nights on our journey. The discussion continued at the motel. I decided that I would plead patiently with my brothers to remain true to the time-honored principles of our movement. I began with a plea for nonviolence. This immediately aroused some of our friends from the Deacons for Defense, who contended that self-defense was essential and that therefore nonviolence should not be a prerequisite for par-ticipation in the march. They were joined in this view by some of the activists from CORE and SNCC.

I tried to make it clear that besides opposing violence on principle, I could imagine nothing more impractical and disastrous than for any of us, through misguided judgment, to precipitate a violent confron-tation in Mississippi. We had neither the resources nor the techniques to win. Furthermore, I asserted, many Mississippi whites, from the government on down, would enjoy nothing more than for us to turn to violence in order to use this as an excuse to wipe out scores of Ne-groes in and out of the march. Finally, I contended that the debate over the question of self-defense was unnecessary since few people suggested that Negroes should not defend themselves as individuals when attacked. The question was not whether one should use his gun when his home was attacked, but whether it was tactically wise to use a gun while participating in an organized demonstration. If they lowered the banner of nonviolence, I said, Mississippi injustice would not be exposed and the moral issues would be obscured.

Next the question of the participation of whites was raised. Stokely Carmichael contended that the inclusion of whites in the march should be de-emphasized and that the dominant appeal should be made for black participation. Others in the room agreed. As I listened to Stokely, I thought about the years that we had worked together in communities all across the South, and how joyously we had then welcomed and accepted our white allies in the movement. What accounted for this reversal in Stokely's philosophy?

I surmised that much of the change had its psychological roots in the experience of SNCC in Mississippi during the summer of 1964, when a large number of Northern white students had come down to help in that racially torn state. What the SNCC workers saw was the most articulate, powerful and self-assured young white people coming to work with the poorest of the Negro people—and simply overwhelming them. That summer Stokely and others in SNCC had probably unconsciously concluded that this was no good for Negroes, for it simply increased their sense of their own inadequacies. Of course, the answer to this dilemma was not to give up, not to conclude that blacks must work with blacks in order for Negroes to gain a sense of their own meaning. The answer was only to be found in persistent trying, perpetual experimentation, persevering togetherness.

Like life, racial understanding is not something that we find but something that we must create. What we find when we enter these mortal plains is existence; but existence is the raw material out of which all life must be created. A productive and happy life is not something that you find; it is something that you make. And so the ability of Negroes and whites to work together, to understand each other, will not be found ready-made; it must be created by the fact of contact.

Along these lines, I implored everyone in the room to see the morality of making the march completely interracial. Consciences must be enlisted in our movement, I said, not merely racial groups. I reminded them of the dedicated whites who had suffered, bled and died in the cause of racial justice, and suggested that to reject white participation now would be a shameful repudiation of all for which they had sacrificed.

Finally, I said that the formidable foe we now faced demanded more unity than ever before and that I would stretch every point to maintain this unity, but that I could not in good conscience agree to continue my personal involvement and that of SCLC in the march if it were not publicly affirmed that it was based on nonviolence and the participation of both black and white. After a few more minutes of discussion Floyd and Stokely agreed that we could unite around these principles as far as the march was concerned. The next morning we had a joint press conference affirming that the march was nonviolent and that whites were welcomed.

As the days progressed, debates and discussions continued, but they were usually pushed to the background by the onrush of enthusiasm engendered by the large crowds that turned out to greet us in every town. We had been marching for about ten days when we passed through Grenada on the way to Greenwood. Stokely did not conceal his growing eagerness to reach Greenwood. This was SNCC territory, in the sense that the organization had worked courageously there during that turbulent summer of 1964.

As we approached the city, large crowds of old friends and new turned out to welcome us. At a huge mass meeting that night, which was held in a city park, Stokely mounted the platform and after arousing the audience with a powerful attack on Mississippi justice, he proclaimed: "What we need is black power." Willie Ricks, the fiery orator of SNCC, leaped to the platform and shouted, "What do you want?" The crowd roared, "Black Power." Again and again Ricks cried, "What do you want?" and the response "Black Power" grew louder and louder, until it had reached fever pitch.

So Greenwood turned out to be the arena for the birth of the Black Power slogan in the civil rights movement. The phrase had been used long before by Richard Wright and others, but never until that night had it been used as a slogan in the civil rights movement. For people who had been crushed so long by white power and who had been taught that black was degrading, it had a ready appeal.

Immediately, however, I had reservations about its use. I had the deep feeling that it was an unfortunate choice of words for a slogan. Moreover, I saw it bringing about division within the ranks of the marchers. For a day or two there was fierce competition between those who were wedded to the Black Power slogan and those wedded to Freedom Now. Speakers on each side sought desperately to get the crowds to chant their slogan the loudest.

Sensing this widening split in our ranks, I asked Stokely and Floyd to join me in a frank discussion of the problem. We met the next morning, along with members of each of our staffs, in a small Catholic parish house in Yazoo City. For five long hours I pleaded with the group to abandon the Black Power slogan. It was my contention that a leader has to be concerned about the problem of semantics. Each word, I said, has a denotative meaning—its explicit and recognized sense—and a connotative meaning—its suggestive sense. While the concept of legitimate Black Power might be denotatively sound, the slogan "Black Power" carried the wrong connotations. I mentioned the implications of violence that the press had already attached to the phrase. And I went on to say that some of the rash statements on the part of a few marchers only reinforced this impression.

Stokely replied by saying that the question of violence versus non-violence was irrelevant. The real question was the need for black people to consolidate their political and economic resources to achieve power. "Power," he said, "is the only thing respected in this world, and we must get it at any cost." Then he looked me squarely in the eye and said, "Martin, you know as well as I do that practically every other ethnic group in America has done just this. The Jews, the Irish and the Italians did it, why can't we?"

"That is just the point," I answered. "No one has ever heard the Jews publicly chant a slogan of Jewish power, but they have power. Through group unity, determination and creative endeavor, they have gained it. The same thing is true of the Irish and Italians. Neither group has used a slogan of Irish or Italian power, but they have worked hard to achieve it. This is exactly what we must do," I said. "We must use every constructive means to amass economic and political power. This is the kind of legitimate power we need. We must work to build racial pride and refute the notion that black is evil and ugly. But this must come through a program, not merely through a slogan."

Stokely and Floyd insisted that the slogan itself was important. "How can you arouse people to unite around a program without a slogan as a rallying cry? Didn't the labor movement have slogans? Haven't we had slogans all along in the freedom movement? What we need is a new slogan with 'black' in it."

I conceded the fact that we must have slogans. But why have one that would confuse our allies, isolate the Negro community and give many prejudiced whites, who might otherwise be ashamed of their anti-Negro feeling, a ready excuse for self-justification?

"Why not use the slogan 'black consciousness' or 'black equality'?" I suggested. "These phrases would be less vulnerable and would more accurately describe what we are about. The words 'black' and 'power' together give the impression that we are talking about black domination rather than black equality."

Stokely responded that neither would have the ready appeal and persuasive force of Black Power. Throughout the lengthy discussion, Stokely and Floyd remained adamant, and Stokely concluded by saying, with candor, "Martin, I deliberately decided to raise this issue on the march in order to give it a national forum, and force you to take a stand for Black Power."

I laughed. "I have been used before," I said to Stokely. "One more time won't hurt."

The meeting ended with the SCLC staff members still agreeing with me that the slogan was unfortunate and would only divert attention from the evils of Mississippi, while most CORE and SNCC staff members joined Stokely and Floyd in insisting that it should be projected nationally. In a final attempt to maintain unity I suggested that we compromise by not chanting either "Black Power" or "Freedom Now" for the rest of the march. In this way neither the people nor the press would be confused by the apparent conflict, and staff members would not appear to be at loggerheads. They all agreed with this compromise.

But while the chant died out, the press kept the debate going. News stories now centered, not on the injustices of Mississippi, but on the apparent ideological division in the civil rights movement. Every revolutionary movement has its peaks of united activity and its valleys of debate and internal confusion. This debate might well have been little more than a healthy internal difference of opinion, but the press loves the sensational and it could not allow the issue to remain within the private domain of the movement. In every drama there has to be an antagonist and a protagonist, and if the antagonist is not there the press will find and build one.

II

So Black Power is now a part of the nomenclature of the national community. To some it is abhorrent, to others dynamic; to some it is repugnant, to others exhilarating; to some it is destructive, to others it is useful. Since Black Power means different things to different people and indeed, being essentially an emotional concept, can mean different things to the same person on differing occasions, it is impossible to attribute its ultimate meaning to any single individual or organization. One must look beyond personal styles, verbal flourishes and the hysteria of the mass media to assess its values, its assets and liabilities honestly.

First, it is necessary to understand that Black Power is a cry of disappointment. The Black Power slogan did not spring full grown from the head of some philosophical Zeus. It was born from the wounds of despair and disappointment. It is a cry of daily hurt and persistent pain. For centuries the Negro has been caught in the tentacles of white power. Many Negroes have given up faith in the white majority because "white power" with total control has left them empty-handed. So in reality the call for Black Power is a reaction to the failure of white power.

It is no accident that the birth of this slogan in the civil rights movement took place in Mississippi—the state symbolizing the most blatant abuse of white power. In Mississippi the murder of civil rights workers is still a popular pastime. In that state more than forty Negroes and whites have either been lynched or murdered over the last three years, and not a single man has been punished for these crimes. More than fifty Negro churches have been burned or bombed in Mississippi in the last two years, yet the bombers still walk the streets surrounded by the halo of adoration.[1] This is white power in its most brutal, cold-blooded and vicious form.

Many of the young people proclaiming Black Power today were but yesterday the devotees of black-white cooperation and nonviolent direct action. With great sacrifice and dedication and a radiant faith in the future they labored courageously in the rural areas of the South; with idealism they accepted blows without retaliating; with dignity they allowed themselves to be plunged into filthy, stinking jail cells; with a majestic scorn for risk and danger they nonviolently confronted the Jim Clarks and the Bull Connors of the South, and exposed the disease of racism in the body politic. If they are America's angry children today, this anger is not congenital. It is a response to the feeling that a real solution is hopelessly distant because of the inconsistencies, resistance and faintheartedness of those in power. If Stokely Carmichael now says that nonviolence is irrelevant, it is because he, as a dedicated veteran of many battles, has seen with his own eyes the most brutal white violence against Negroes and white civil rights workers, and he has seen it go unpunished.

Their frustration is further fed by the fact that even when blacks and whites die together in the cause of justice, the death of the white person gets more attention and concern than the death of the black person. Stokely and his colleagues from SNCC were with us in Alabama when Jimmy Lee Jackson, a brave young Negro man, was killed and when James Reeb, a committed Unitarian white minister, was fatally clubbed to the ground. They remembered how President Johnson sent flowers to the gallant Mrs. Reeb, and in his eloquent "We Shall Overcome" speech paused to mention that one person, James

Reeb, had already died in the struggle. Somehow the President forgot to mention Jimmy, who died first. The parents and sister of Jimmy received no flowers from the President. The students felt this keenly. Not that they felt that the death of James Reeb was less than tragic, but because they felt that the failure to mention Jimmy Jackson only reinforced the impression that to white America the life of a Negro is insignificant and meaningless.

There is also great disappointment with the federal government and its timidity in implementing the civil rights laws on its statute books. The gap between promise and fulfillment is distressingly wide. Millions of Negroes are frustrated and angered because extravagant promises made little more than a year ago are a mockery today. When the 1965 Voting Rights Law was signed, it was proclaimed as the dawn of freedom and the open door to opportunity. What was minimally required under the law was the appointment of hundreds of registrars and thousands of federal marshals to inhibit Southern terror. Instead, fewer than sixty registrars were appointed and not a single federal law officer capable of making arrests was sent into the South. As a consequence the old way of life—economic coercion, terrorism, murder and inhuman contempt—has continued unabated. This gulf between the laws and their enforcement is one of the basic reasons why Black Power advocates express contempt for the legislative process.

The disappointment mounts as they turn their eyes to the North. In the Northern ghettos, unemployment, housing discrimination and slum schools mock the Negro who tries to hope. There have been accomplishments and some material gain, but these beginnings have revealed how far we have yet to go. The economic plight of the masses of Negroes has worsened. The gap between the wages of the Negro worker and those of the white worker has widened. Slums are worse and Negroes attend more thoroughly segregated schools today than in 1954.

The Black Power advocates are disenchanted with the inconsistencies in the militaristic posture of our government. Over the last decade they have seen America applauding nonviolence whenever the Negroes have practiced it. They have watched it being praised in the sit-in movements of 1960, in the Freedom Rides of 1961, in the Albany movement of 1962, in the Birmingham movement of 1963 and in the Selma movement of 1965. But then these same black young men and women have watched as America sends black young men to burn Vietnamese with napalm, to slaughter men, women and children; and they wonder what kind of nation it is that applauds nonviolence whenever Negroes face white people in the streets of the United States but then applauds violence and burning and death when these same Negroes are sent to the fields of Vietnam.

All of this represents disappointment lifted to astronomical proportions. It is disappointment with timid white moderates who feel that they can set the timetable for the Negro's freedom. It is disappointment with a federal administration that seems to be more concerned about winning an ill-considered war in Vietnam than about winning the war against poverty here at home. It is disappointment with white legislators who pass laws on behalf of Negro rights that they never intended to implement. It is disappointment with the Christian church that appears to be more white than Christian, and with many white clergymen who prefer to remain silent behind the security of stained-glass windows. It is disappointment with some Negro clergymen who are more concerned about the size of the wheel base on their automobiles than about the quality of their service to the Negro community. It is disappointment with the Negro middle class that has sailed or struggled out of the muddy ponds into the relatively fresh-flowing waters of the mainstream, and in the process has forgotten the stench of the backwaters where their brothers are still drowning.

Second, Black Power, in its broad and positive meaning, is a call to black people to amass the political and economic strength to achieve their legitimate goals. No one can deny that the Negro is in dire need of this kind of legitimate power. Indeed, one of the great problems that the Negro confronts is his lack of power. From the old plantations of the South to the newer ghettos of the North, the Negro has been confined to a life of voicelessness and powerlessness. Stripped of the right to make decisions concerning his life and destiny, he has been subject to the authoritarian and sometimes whimsical decisions of the white power structure. The plantation and the ghetto were created by those who had power both to confine those who had no power and to perpetuate their powerlessness. The problem of transforming the ghetto is, therefore, a problem of power—a confrontation between the forces of power demanding change and the forces of power dedicated to preserving the status quo.

Power, properly understood, is the ability to achieve purpose. It is the strength required to bring about social, political or economic changes. In this sense power is not only desirable but necessary in order to implement the demands of love and justice. One of the greatest problems of history is that the concepts of love and power are usually contrasted as polar opposites. Love is identified with a resignation of power and power with a denial of love. It was this misinterpretation that caused Nietzsche, the philosopher of the "will to power," to reject the Christian concept of love. It was this same misinterpretation which induced Christian theologians to reject Nietzsche's philosophy of the "will to power" in the name of the Christian idea of love. What is needed is a realization that power without love is reckless and abusive and that love without power is sentimental and anemic. Power at its best is love implementing the demands of justice. Justice at its best is love correcting everything that stands against love.

There is nothing essentially wrong with power. The problem is that in America power is unequally distributed. This has led Negro Americans in the past to seek their goals through love and moral suasion devoid of power and white Americans to seek their goals through power devoid of love and conscience. It is leading a few extremists today to advocate for Negroes the same destructive and conscienceless power that they have justly abhorred in whites. It is precisely this collision of immoral power with powerless morality which constitutes the major crisis of our times.

In his struggle for racial justice, the Negro must seek to transform his condition of powerlessness into creative and positive power. One of the most obvious sources of this power is political. In *Why We Can't Wait*[2] I wrote at length of the need for Negroes to unite for political action in order to compel the majority to listen. I urged the development of political awareness and strength in the Negro community, the election of blacks to key positions, and the use of the bloc vote to liberalize the political climate and achieve our just aspirations for freedom and human dignity. To the extent that Black Power advocates these goals, it is a positive and legitimate call to action that we in the civil rights movement have sought to follow all along and which we must intensify in the future.

Black Power is also a call for the pooling of black financial resources to achieve economic security. While the ultimate answer to the Negroes' economic dilemma will be found in a massive federal program for all the poor along the lines of A. Philip Randolph's Freedom Budget, a kind of Marshall Plan for the disadvantaged, there is something that the Negro himself can do to throw off the shackles of poverty. Although the Negro is still at the bottom of the economic ladder, his collective annual income is upwards of $30 billion. This gives him a considerable buying power that can make the difference between profit and loss in many businesses.

Through the pooling of such resources and the development of habits of thrift and techniques of wise investment, the Negro will be doing his share to grapple with his problem of economic deprivation. If Black Power means the development of this kind of strength within the Negro community, then it is a quest for basic, necessary, legitimate power.

Finally, Black Power is a psychological call to manhood. For years the Negro has been taught that he is nobody, that his color is a sign of his biological depravity, that his being has been stamped with an indelible imprint of inferiority, that his whole history has been soiled with the filth of worthlessness. All too few people realize how slavery and racial segregation have scarred the soul and wounded the spirit of the black man. The whole dirty business of slavery was based on the premise that the Negro was a thing to be used, not a person to be respected.

The historian Kenneth Stampp, in his remarkable book *The Peculiar Institution*,[3] has a fascinating section on the psychological indoctrination that was necessary from the master's viewpoint to make a good slave. He gathered the material for this section primarily from the manuals and other documents which were produced by slave-owners on the subject of training slaves. Stampp notes five recurring aspects of this training.

First, those who managed the slaves had to maintain strict discipline. One master said, "Unconditional submission is the only footing upon which slavery should be placed." Another said, "The slave must know that his master is to govern absolutely and he is to obey implicitly, that he is never, for a moment, to exercise either his will or judgment in opposition to a positive order." Second, the masters felt that they had to implant in the bondsman a consciousness of personal inferiority. This sense of inferiority was deliberately extended to his past. The slaveowners were convinced that in order to control the Negroes, the slaves "had to feel that African ancestry tainted them, that their color was a badge of degradation." The third step in the training process was to awe the slaves with a sense of the masters' enormous power. It was necessary, various owners said, "to make them stand in fear." The fourth aspect was the attempt to "persuade the bondsman to take an interest in the master's enterprise and to accept his standards of good conduct." Thus the master's criteria of what was good and true and beautiful were to be accepted unquestioningly by the slaves. The final step, according to Stampp's documents, was "to impress Negroes with their helplessness: to create in them a habit of perfect dependence upon their masters."

Here, then, was the way to produce a perfect slave. Accustom him to rigid discipline, demand from him unconditional submission, impress upon him a sense of his innate inferiority, develop in him a paralyzing fear of white men, train him to adopt the master's code of good behavior, and instill in him a sense of complete dependence.

Out of the soil of slavery came the psychological roots of the Black Power cry. Anyone familiar with the Black Power movement recognizes that defiance of white authority and white power is a constant theme; the defiance almost becomes a kind of taunt. Underneath it, however, there is a legitimate concern that the Negro break away from "unconditional submission" and thereby assert his own selfhood.

Another obvious reaction of Black Power to the American system of slavery is the determination to glory in blackness and to resurrect joyously the African past. In response to the emphasis on their masters' "enormous power," Black Power advocates contend that the Negro must develop his own sense of strength. No longer are "fear, awe and obedience" to rule. This accounts for, though it does not justify, some Black Power advocates who encourage contempt and even uncivil disobedience as alternatives to the old patterns of slavery. Black Power assumes that Negroes will be slaves unless there is a new power to counter the force of the men who are still determined to be masters rather than brothers.

It is in the context of the slave tradition that some of the ideologues of the Black Power movement call for the need to develop new and indigenous codes of justice for the ghettos, so that blacks may move entirely away from their former masters' "standards of good conduct." Those in the Black Power movement who contend that blacks should cut themselves off from every level of dependence upon whites for advice, money or other help are obviously reacting against the slave pattern of "perfect dependence" upon the masters.

Black Power is a psychological reaction to the psychological indoctrination that led to the creation of the perfect slave. While this reaction has often led to negative and unrealistic responses and has frequently brought about intemperate words and actions, one must not overlook the positive value in calling the Negro to a new sense of manhood, to a deep feeling of racial pride and to an audacious appreciation of his heritage. The Negro must be grasped by a new realization of his dignity and worth. He must stand up amid a system that still oppresses him and develop an unassailable and majestic sense of his own value. He must no longer be ashamed of being black.

The job of arousing manhood within a people that have been taught for so many centuries that they are nobody is not easy. Even semantics have conspired to make that which is black seem ugly and degrading. In *Roget's Thesaurus* there are some 120 synonyms for "blackness" and at least 60 of them are offensive—such words as "blot," "soot," "grime," "devil" and "foul." There are some 134 synonyms for "whiteness," and all are favorable, expressed in such words as "purity," "cleanliness," "chastity" and "innocence." A white lie is better than a black lie. The most degenerate member of a family is the "black sheep," not the "white sheep." Ossie Davis has suggested that maybe the English language should be "reconstructed" so that teachers will not be forced to teach the Negro child 60 ways to despise himself and thereby perpetuate his false sense of inferiority and the white child 134 ways to adore himself and thereby perpetuate his false sense of superiority.

The history books, which have almost completely ignored the contribution of the Negro in American history, have only served to intensify the Negroes' sense of worthlessness and to augment the anachronistic doctrine of white supremacy. All too many Negroes and whites are unaware of the fact that the first American to shed blood in the revolution which freed this country from British oppression was a black seaman named Crispus Attucks. Negroes and whites are almost totally oblivious of the fact that it was a Negro physician, Dr. Daniel Hale Williams, who performed the first successful operation on the heart in America, and that another Negro physician, Dr. Charles Drew, was largely responsible for developing the method of separating blood plasma and storing it on a large scale, a process that saved thousands of lives in World War II and has made possible many of the important advances in postwar medicine. History books have virtually overlooked the many Negro scientists and inventors who have enriched American life. Although a few refer to George Washington Carver, whose research in agricultural products helped to revive the economy of the South when the throne of King Cotton began to totter, they ignore the contribution of Norbert Rillieux, whose invention of an evaporating pan revolutionized the process of sugar refining. How many people know that the multimillion-dollar United Shoe Machinery Company developed from the shoe-lasting machine invented in the last century by a Negro from Dutch Guiana, Jan Matzeliger; or that Granville T. Woods, an expert in electric motors, whose many patents speeded the growth and improvement of the railroads at the beginning of this century, was a Negro?

Even the Negroes' contribution to the music of America is some-times overlooked in astonishing ways. Two years ago my oldest son and daughter entered an integrated school in Atlanta. A few months later my wife and I were invited to attend a program entitled "Mu-sic That Has Made America Great." As the evening unfolded, we lis-tened to the folk songs and melodies of the various immigrant groups. We were certain that the program would end with the most original of all American music, the Negro spiritual. But we were mistaken. Instead, all the students, including our children, ended the program by singing "Dixie."

As we rose to leave the hall, my wife and I looked at each other with a combination of indignation and amazement. All the students, black and white, all the parents present that night, and all the faculty members had been victimized by just another expression of America's penchant for ignoring the Negro, making him invisible and making his contributions insignificant. I wept within that night. I wept for my children and all black children who have been denied a knowl-edge of their heritage; I wept for all white children, who, through daily miseducation, are taught that the Negro is an irrelevant entity in American society; I wept for all the white parents and teachers who are forced to overlook the fact that the wealth of cultural and technological progress in America is a result of the commonwealth of inpouring contributions.

The tendency to ignore the Negro's contribution to American life and strip him of his personhood is as old as the earliest history books and as contemporary as the morning's newspaper. To offset this cul-tural homicide, the Negro must rise up with an affirmation of his own Olympian manhood. Any movement for the Negro's freedom that overlooks this necessity is only waiting to be buried. As long as the mind is enslaved the body can never be free. Psychological freedom, a firm sense of self-esteem, is the most powerful weapon against the long night of physical slavery. No Lincolnian Emancipation Proclamation or Kennedyan or Johnsonian civil rights bill can totally bring this kind of freedom. The Negro will only be truly free when he reaches down to the inner depths of his own being and signs with the pen and ink of assertive selfhood his own emancipation proclamation. With a spirit straining toward true self-esteem, the Negro must boldly throw off the manacles of self-abnegation and say to himself and the world: "I am somebody. I am a person. I am a man with dignity and honor. I have a rich and noble history, however painful and exploited that history has been. I am black and comely." This self-affirmation is the black man's need made compelling by the white man's crimes against him. This is positive and necessary power for black people.

From *Where Do We Go from Here: Chaos or Community?*
(Harper & Row, 1967, reprinted by Beacon Press, 2010).

EIGHTEEN

BEYOND VIETNAM: A TIME TO BREAK SILENCE

Dr. King delivered the following speech on April 4, 1967, to an audience of about three thousand at Riverside Church in New York City. King drafted it with the help of advisors including Vincent Harding and John Maguire. Though many politicians and civil rights leaders criticized King's stance against the Vietnam War, he was undeterred and continued to speak out against the war until his death.

I come to this magnificent house of worship tonight because my conscience leaves me no other choice. I join you in this meeting because I am in deepest agreement with the aims and work of the organization which has brought us together: Clergy and [Laity] Concerned About Vietnam. The recent statement of your executive committee are the sentiments of my own heart and I found myself in full accord when I read its opening lines: "A time comes when silence is betrayal." That time has come for us in relation to Vietnam.

The truth of these words is beyond doubt, but the mission to which they call us is a most difficult one. Even when pressed by the demands of inner truth, men do not easily assume the task of opposing their government's policy, especially in time of war. Nor does the human spirit move without great difficulty against all the apathy of conformist thought within one's own bosom and in the surrounding world. Moreover when the issues at hand seem as perplexing as they often do in the case of this dreadful conflict we are always on the verge of being mesmerized by uncertainty: but we must move on.

Some of us who have already begun to break the silence of the night have found that the calling to speak is often a vocation of agony, but we must speak. We must speak with all the humility that is appropriate to our limited vision, but we must speak. And we must rejoice as well, for surely this is the first time in our nation's history that a significant number of its religious leaders have chosen to move beyond the prophesying of smooth patriotism to the high grounds of a firm dissent based upon the mandates of conscience and the reading of history. Perhaps a new spirit is rising among us. If it is, let us trace its movements well and pray that our own inner being may be sensitive to its guidance, for we are deeply in need of a new way beyond the darkness that seems so close around us.

Over the past two years, as I have moved to break the betrayal of my own silences and to speak from the burnings of my own heart, as I have called for radical departures from the destruction of Vietnam, many persons have questioned me about the wisdom of my path. At the heart of their concerns this query has often loomed large and loud: Why are *you* speaking about the war, Dr. King? Why are *you* joining the voices of dissent? Peace and civil rights don't mix, they say. Aren't you hurting the cause of your people, they ask? And when I hear them, though I often understand the sources of their concern, I am nevertheless greatly saddened, for such questions mean that the inquirers have not really known me, my commitment or my calling. Indeed, their questions suggest that they do not know the world in which they live.

In the light of such tragic misunderstanding, I deem it of signal importance to try to state clearly, and I trust concisely, why I believe that the path from Dexter Avenue Baptist Church—the church in Montgomery, Alabama, where I began my pastorate—leads clearly to this sanctuary tonight.

I come to this platform tonight to make a passionate plea to my beloved nation. This speech is not addressed to Hanoi or to the National Liberation Front. It is not addressed to China or to Russia.

Nor is it an attempt to overlook the ambiguity of the total situation and the need for a collective solution to the tragedy of Vietnam. Neither is it an attempt to make North Vietnam or the National Liberation Front paragons of virtue, nor to overlook the role they can play in a successful resolution of the problem. While they both may have justifiable reason to be suspicious of the good faith of the United States, life and history give eloquent testimony to the fact that conflicts are never resolved without trustful give and take on both sides.

Tonight, however, I wish not to speak with Hanoi and the NLF, but rather to my fellow Americans who, with me, bear the greatest responsibility in ending a conflict that has exacted a heavy price on both continents.

Since I am a preacher by trade, I suppose it is not surprising that I have several reasons for bringing Vietnam into the field of my moral vision. There is at the outset a very obvious and almost facile connection between the war in Vietnam and the struggle I, and others, have been waging in America. A few years ago there was a shining moment in that struggle. It seemed as if there was a real promise of hope for the poor—both black and white—through the Poverty Program. There were experiments, hopes, new beginnings. Then came the build-up in Vietnam and I watched the program broken and eviscerated as if it were some idle political plaything of a society gone mad on war, and I knew that America would never invest the necessary funds or energies in rehabilitation of its poor so long as adventures like Vietnam continued to draw men and skills and money like some demoniacal destructive suction tube. So I was increasingly compelled to see the war as an enemy of the poor and to attack it as such.

Perhaps the more tragic recognition of reality took place when it became clear to me that the war was doing far more than devastating the hopes of the poor at home. It was sending their sons and their brothers and their husbands to fight and to die in extraordinarily high proportions relative to the rest of the population. We were taking the black young men who had been crippled by our society and sending them 8,000 miles away to guarantee liberties in Southeast Asia which they had not found in Southwest Georgia and East Harlem. So we have been repeatedly faced with the cruel irony of watching Negro and white boys on TV screens as they kill and die together for a nation that has been unable to seat them together in the same schools. So we watch them in brutal solidarity burning the huts of a poor village but we realize that they would never live on the same block in Detroit. I could not be silent in the face of such cruel manipulation of the poor.

My third reason moves to an even deeper level of awareness, for it grows out of my experience in the ghettos of the north over the last three years—especially the last three summers. As I have walked among the desperate, rejected and angry young men I have told them that Molotov cocktails and rifles would not solve their problems. I have tried to offer them my deepest compassion while maintaining my conviction that social change comes most meaningfully through non-violent action. But they asked—and rightly so—what about Vietnam? They asked if our own nation wasn't using massive doses of violence to solve its problems, to bring about the changes it wanted. Their questions hit home, and I knew that I could never again raise my voice against the violence of the oppressed in the ghettos without having first spoken clearly to the greatest purveyor of violence in the world today—my own government. For the sake of those boys, for the sake of this government, for the sake of the hundreds of thousands trembling under our violence, I cannot be silent.

For those who ask the question, "Aren't you a Civil Rights leader?" and thereby mean to exclude me from the movement for peace, I have this further answer. In 1957 when a group of us formed the Southern Christian Leadership Conference, we chose as our motto: "To save the soul of America." We were convinced that we could not limit our vision to certain rights for black people, but instead affirmed the conviction that America would never be free or saved from itself unless the descendants of its slaves were loosed completely from the shackles they still wear. In a way we were agreeing with Langston Hughes, that black bard of Harlem, who had written earlier:

O, *yes,*
I say it plain,
America never was America to me,
And yet I swear this oath —
America will be!

Now, it should be incandescently clear that no one who has any concern for the integrity and life of America today can ignore the present war. If America's soul becomes totally poisoned, part of the autopsy must read Vietnam. It can never be saved so long as it destroys the deepest hopes of men the world over. So it is that those of us who are yet determined that America *will* be are led down the path of protest and dissent, working for the health of our land.

As if the weight of such a commitment to the life and health of America were not enough, another burden of responsibility was placed upon me in 1964; and I cannot forget that the Nobel Prize for Peace was also a commission—a commission to work harder than I had ever worked before for "the brotherhood of man." This is a calling that takes me beyond national allegiances, but even if it were not present I would yet have to live with the meaning of my commitment to the ministry of Jesus Christ. To me the relationship of this ministry to the making of peace is so obvious that I sometimes marvel at those who ask me why I am speaking against the war. Could it be that they do not know that the good news was meant for all men—for communist and capitalist, for their children and ours, for black and for white, for revolutionary and conservative? Have they forgotten that my ministry is in obedience to the one who loved his enemies so fully that he died for them? What then can I say to the Vietcong or to Castro or to Mao as a faithful minister of this one? Can I threaten them with death or must I not share with them my life?

Finally, as I try to delineate for you and for myself the road that leads from Montgomery to this place I would have offered all that was most valid if I simply said that I must be true to my conviction that I share with all men the calling to be a son of the Living God. Beyond the calling of race or nation or creed is this vocation of sonship and brotherhood, and because I believe that the Father is deeply concerned especially for his suffering and helpless and outcast children, I come tonight to speak for them.

This I believe to be the privilege and the burden of all of us who deem ourselves bound by allegiances and loyalties which are broader and deeper than nationalism and which go beyond our nation's self-defined goals and positions. We are called to speak for the weak, for the voiceless, for victims of our nation and for those it calls enemy, for no document from human hands can make these humans any less our brothers.

And as I ponder the madness of Vietnam and search within myself for ways to understand and respond in compassion my mind goes constantly to the people of that peninsula. I speak now not of the soldiers of each side, not of the junta in Saigon, but simply of the people who have been living under the curse of war for almost three continuous decades now. I think of them too because it is clear to me that there will be no meaningful solution there until some attempt is made to know them and hear their broken cries.

They must see Americans as strange liberators. The Vietnamese people proclaimed their own independence in 1945 after a combined French and Japanese occupation, and before the communist revolution in China. They were led by Ho Chi Minh. Even though they quoted the American Declaration of Independence in their own document of freedom, we refused to recognize them. Instead, we decided to support France in its re-conquest of her former colony.

Our government felt then that the Vietnamese people were not "ready" for independence, and we again fell victim to the deadly western arrogance that has poisoned the international atmosphere for so long. With that tragic decision we rejected a revolutionary government seeking self-determination, and a government that had been established not by China (for whom the Vietnamese have no great love) but by clearly indigenous forces that included some communists. For the peasants this new government meant real land reform, one of the most important needs in their lives.

For nine years following 1945 we denied the people of Vietnam the right of independence. For nine years we vigorously supported the French in their abortive effort to re-colonize Vietnam.

Before the end of the war we were meeting 80% of the French war costs. Even before the French were defeated at Dien Bien Phu, they began to despair of the reckless action, but we did not. We encouraged them with our huge financial and military supplies to continue the war even after they had lost the will. Soon we would be paying almost the full costs of this tragic attempt at re-colonization.

After the French were defeated it looked as if independence and land reform would come again through the Geneva agreements. But instead there came the United States, determined that Ho should not unify the temporarily divided nation, and the peasants watched again as we supported one of the most vicious modern dictators—our chosen man, Premier Diem. The peasants watched and cringed as Diem ruthlessly routed out all opposition, supported their extortionist landlords and refused even to discuss re-unification with the North. The peasants watched as all this was presided over by U.S. influence and then by increasing numbers of U.S. troops who came to help quell the insurgency that Diem's methods had aroused. When Diem was overthrown they may have been happy, but the long line of military dictatorships seemed to offer no real change—especially in terms of their need for land and peace.

The only change came from America as we increased our troop commitments in support of governments which were singularly corrupt, inept and without popular support. All the while the people read our leaflets and received regular promises of peace and democracy—and land reform. Now they languish under our bombs and consider us—not their fellow Vietnamese—the real enemy. They move sadly and apathetically as we herd them off the land of their fathers into concentration camps where minimal social needs are rarely met. They know they must move or be destroyed by our bombs. So they go—primarily women and children and the aged.

They watch as we poison their water, as we kill a million acres of their crops. They must weep as the bulldozers roar through their areas preparing to destroy the precious trees. They wander into the hospitals, with at least 20 casualties from American firepower for one Vietcong-inflicted injury. They wander into the towns and see thousands of the children, homeless, without clothes, running in packs on the streets like animals. They see the children degraded by our soldiers as they beg for food. They see the children selling their sisters to our soldiers, soliciting for their mothers.

What do the peasants think as we ally ourselves with the landlords and as we refuse to put any action into our many words concerning land reform? What do they think as we test out our latest weapons on them, just as the Germans tested out new medicine and new tortures in the concentration camps of Europe? Where are the roots of the independent Vietnam we claim to be building? Is it among these voiceless ones?

We have destroyed their two most cherished institutions: the family and the village. We have destroyed their land and their crops. We have cooperated in the crushing of the nation's only non-communist revolutionary political force—the unified Buddhist Church. We have supported the enemies of the peasants of Saigon. We have corrupted their women and children and killed their men. What liberators!

Now there is little left to build on—save bitterness. Soon the only solid physical foundations remaining will be found at our military bases and in the concrete of the concentration camps we call fortified hamlets. The peasants may well wonder if we plan to build our new Vietnam on such grounds as these? Could we blame them for such thoughts? We must speak for them and raise the questions they cannot raise. These too are our brothers.

Perhaps the more difficult but no less necessary task is to speak for those who have been designated as our enemies. What of the National Liberation Front—that strangely anonymous group we call VC or Communists? What must they think of us in America when they realize that we permitted the repression and cruelty of Diem which helped to bring them into being as a resistance group in the south? What do they think of our condoning the violence which led to their own taking up of arms? How can they believe in our integrity when now we speak of "aggression from the North" as if there were nothing more essential to the war? How can they trust us when now we charge them with violence after the murderous reign of Diem, and charge them with violence while we pour every new weapon of death into their land? Surely we must understand their feelings even if we do not condone their actions. Surely we must see that the men we supported pressed them to their violence. Surely we must see that our own computerized plans of destruction simply dwarf their greatest acts.

How do they judge us when our officials know that their membership is less than 25 percent communist and yet insist on giving them the blanket name? What must they be thinking when they know that we are aware of their control of major sections of Vietnam and yet we appear ready to allow national elections in which this highly organized political parallel government will have no part? They ask how we can speak of free elections when the Saigon press is censored and controlled by the military junta. And they are surely right to wonder what kind of new government we plan to help form without them—the only party in real touch with the peasants. They question our political goals and they deny the reality of a peace settlement from which they will be excluded. Their questions are frighteningly relevant. Is our nation planning to build on political myth again and then shore it up with the power of new violence?

Here is the true meaning and value of compassion and non-violence when it helps us to see the enemy's point of view, to hear his questions, to know his assessment of ourselves. For from his view we may indeed see the basic weaknesses of our own condition, and if we are mature, we may learn and grow and profit from the wisdom of the brothers who are called the opposition.

So, too, with Hanoi. In the North, where our bombs now pummel the land, and our mines endanger the waterways, we are met by a deep but understandable mistrust. To speak for them is to explain this lack of confidence in western words, and especially their distrust of American intentions now. In Hanoi are the men who led the nation to independence against the Japanese and the French, the men who sought membership in the French commonwealth and were betrayed by the weakness of Paris and the willfulness of the colonial armies. It was they who led a second struggle against French domination at tremendous costs, and then were persuaded to give up the land they controlled between the 13th and 17th parallel as a temporary measure at Geneva. After 1954 they watched us conspire with Diem to prevent elections which would have surely brought Ho Chi Minh to power over a united Vietnam, and they realized they had been betrayed again.

When we ask why they do not leap to negotiate, these things must be remembered. Also it must be clear that the leaders of Hanoi considered the presence of American troops in support of the Diem regime to have been the initial military breach of the Geneva Agreements concerning foreign troops, and they remind us that they did not begin to send in any large number of supplies or men until American forces had moved into the tens of thousands.

Hanoi remembers how our leaders refused to tell us the truth about the earlier North Vietnamese overtures for peace, how we claimed that none existed when they had clearly been made. Ho Chi Minh has watched as America has spoken of peace and built up its forces, and now he has surely heard the increasing international rumors of American plans for an invasion of the North. Perhaps only his sense of humor and irony can save him when he hears the most powerful nation of the world speaking of *his* aggression as it drops thousands of bombs on a poor weak nation more than 8,000 miles away from its shores.

At this point I should make it clear that while I have tried in these last few minutes to give a voice to the voiceless on Vietnam and to understand the arguments of those who are called enemy, I am as deeply concerned about our own troops there as anything else. For it occurs to me that what we are submitting them to in Vietnam is not simply the brutalizing process that goes on in any war where armies face each other and seek to destroy. We are adding cynicism to the process of death, for they must know after a short period there that none of the things we claim to be fighting for are really involved. Before long they must know that their government has sent them into a struggle among Vietnamese, and the more sophisticated surely realize that we are on the side of the wealthy and the secure while we create a hell for the poor.

Somehow this madness must cease. We must stop now. I speak as a child of God and brother to the suffering poor of Vietnam. I speak for those whose land is being laid waste, whose homes are being destroyed, whose culture is being subverted. I speak for the poor of America who are paying the double price of smashed hopes at home and death and corruption in Vietnam. I speak as a citizen of the world, for the world as it stands aghast at the path we have taken. I speak as an American to the leaders of my own nation. The great initiative in this war is ours. The initiative to stop it must be ours.

This is the message of the great Buddhist leaders of Vietnam. Recently one of them wrote these words: "Each day the war goes on, the hatred increases in the heart of the Vietnamese and in the hearts of those of humanitarian instinct. The Americans are forcing even their friends into becoming their enemies. It is curious that the Americans, who calculate so carefully on the possibilities of military victory, do not realize that in the process they are incurring deep psychological and political defeat. The image of America will never again be the image of revolution, freedom and democracy, but the image of violence and militarism."

If we continue there will be no doubt in my mind and in the mind of the world that we have no honorable intentions in Vietnam. It will become clear that our minimal expectation is to occupy it as an American colony and men will not refrain from thinking that our maximum hope is to goad China into a war so that we may bomb her nuclear installations. If we do not stop our war against the people of Vietnam immediately the world will be left with no other alternative than to see this as some horribly clumsy and deadly game we have decided to play.

The world now demands a maturity of America that we may not be able to achieve. It demands that we admit that we have been wrong from the beginning of our adventure in Vietnam, that we have been detrimental to the life of the Vietnamese people.

In order to atone for our sins and errors in Vietnam, we should take the initiative in bringing a halt to this tragic war. I would like to suggest five concrete things that our government should do immediately to begin the long and difficult process of extricating ourselves from this nightmarish conflict:

1. End all bombing in North and South Vietnam.

2. Declare a unilateral cease-fire in the hope that such action will create the atmosphere for negotiation.

3. Take immediate steps to prevent other battlegrounds in Southeast Asia by curtailing our military build-up in Thailand and our interference in Laos.

4. Realistically accept the fact that the National Liberation Front has substantial support in South Vietnam and must thereby play a role in any meaningful negotiations and in any future Vietnam government.

5. Set a date that we will remove all foreign troops from Vietnam in accordance with the 1954 Geneva Agreement.

Part of our ongoing commitment might well express itself in an offer to grant asylum to any Vietnamese who fears for his life under a new regime which included the Liberation Front. Then we must make what reparations we can for the damage we have done. We must provide the medical aid that is badly needed, making it available in this country if necessary.

Meanwhile we in the churches and synagogues have a continuing task while we urge our government to disengage itself from a disgraceful commitment. We must continue to raise our voices if our nation persists in its perverse ways in Vietnam. We must be prepared to match actions with words by seeking out every creative means of protest possible.

As we counsel young men concerning military service we must clarify for them our nation's role in Vietnam and challenge them with the alternative of conscientious objection. I am pleased to say that this is the path now being chosen by more than seventy students at my own Alma Mater, Morehouse College, and I recommend it to all who find the American course in Vietnam a dishonorable and unjust one. Moreover I would encourage all ministers of draft age to give up their ministerial exemptions and seek status as conscientious objectors. These are the times for real choices and not false ones. We are at the moment when our lives must be placed on the line if our nation is to survive its own folly. Every man of humane convictions must decide on the protest that best suits his convictions, but we must all protest.

There is something seductively tempting about stopping there and sending us all off on what in some circles has become a popular crusade against the war in Vietnam. I say we must enter that struggle, but I wish to go on now to say something even more disturbing. The war in Vietnam is but a symptom of a far deeper malady within the American spirit, and if we ignore this sobering reality we will find ourselves organizing clergy and laymen-concerned committees for the next generation. They will be concerned about Guatemala and Peru. They will be concerned about Thailand and Cambodia. They will be concerned about Mozambique and South Africa. We will be marching for these and a dozen other names and attending rallies without end unless there is a significant and profound change in American life and policy. Such thoughts take us beyond Vietnam, but not beyond our calling as sons of the living God.

In 1957 a sensitive American official overseas said that it seemed to him that our nation was on the wrong side of a world revolution. During the past 10 years we have seen emerge a pattern of suppression which now has justified the presence of U.S. military "advisors" in Venezuela. This need to maintain social stability for our investments accounts for the counter-revolutionary action of American forces in Guatemala. It tells why American helicopters are being used against guerrillas in Colombia and why American napalm and green beret forces have already been active against rebels in Peru. It is with such activity in mind that the words of the late John F. Kennedy come back to haunt us. Five years ago he said, "Those who make peaceful revolution impossible will make violent revolution inevitable."

Increasingly, by choice or by accident, this is the role our nation has taken—the role of those who make peaceful revolution impossible by refusing to give up the privileges and the pleasures that come from the immense profits of overseas investment.

I am convinced that if we are to get on the right side of the world revolution, we as a nation must undergo a radical revolution of values. We must rapidly begin the shift from a "thing-oriented" society to a "person-oriented" society. When machines and computers, profit motives and property rights are considered more important than people, the giant triplets of racism, materialism, and militarism are incapable of being conquered.

A true revolution of values will soon cause us to question the fairness and justice of many of our past and present policies. On the one hand we are called to play the Good Samaritan on life's roadside; but that will be only an initial act. One day we must come to see that the whole Jericho Road must be transformed so that men and women will not be constantly beaten and robbed as they make their journey on Life's highway. True compassion is more than flinging a coin to a beggar; it is not haphazard and superficial. It comes to see that an edifice which produces beggars needs re-structuring. A true revolution of values will soon look uneasily on the glaring contrast of poverty and wealth. With righteous indignation, it will look across the seas and see individual capitalists of the West investing huge sums of money in Asia, Africa and South America, only to take the profits out with no concern for the social betterment of the countries, and say: "This is not just." It will look at our alliance with the landed gentry of Latin America and say: "This is not just." The Western arrogance of feeling that it has everything to teach others and nothing to learn from them is not just. A true revolution of values will lay hands on the world order and say of war: "This way of settling differences is not just." This business of burning human beings with napalm, of filling our nation's homes with orphans and widows, of injecting poisonous drugs of hate into the veins of peoples normally humane, of sending men home from dark and bloody battlefields physically handicapped and psychologically deranged, cannot be reconciled with wisdom, justice, and love. A nation that continues year after year to spend more money on military defense than on programs of social uplift is approaching spiritual death.

America, the richest and most powerful nation in the world, can well lead the way in this revolution of values. There is nothing, except a tragic death wish, to prevent us from re-ordering our priorities, so that the pursuit of peace will take precedence over the pursuit of war. There is nothing to keep us from molding a recalcitrant status-quo with bruised hands until we have fashioned it into a brotherhood.

This kind of positive revolution of values is our best defense against Communism. War is not the answer. Communism will never be defeated by the use of atomic bombs or nuclear weapons. Let us not join those who shout war and through their misguided passions urge the United States to relinquish its participation in the United Nations. These are days which demand wise restraint and calm reasonableness. We must not call everyone a Communist or an appeaser who advocates the seating of Red China in the United Nations and who recognizes that hate and hysteria are not the final answers to the problem of these turbulent days. We must not engage in a negative anti-Communism, but rather in a positive thrust for democracy, realizing that our greatest defense against Communism is to take offensive action in behalf of justice. We must with positive action seek to remove those conditions of poverty, insecurity and injustice which are the fertile soil in which the seed of Communism grows and develops.

These are revolutionary times. All over the globe men are revolting against old systems of exploitation and oppression and out of the wombs of a frail world new systems of justice and equality are being born. The shirtless and barefoot people of the land are rising up as never before. "The people who sat in darkness have seen a great light." We in the West must support these revolutions. It is a sad fact that, because of comfort, complacency, a morbid fear of Communism, and our proneness to adjust to injustice, the Western nations that initiated so much of the revolutionary spirit of the modern world have now become the arch anti-revolutionaries. This has driven many to feel that only Marxism has the revolutionary spirit. Therefore, Communism is a judgment against our failure to make democracy real and follow through on the revolutions that we initiated. Our only hope today lies in our ability to recapture the revolutionary spirit and go out into a sometimes hostile world declaring eternal hostility to poverty, racism, and militarism. With this powerful commitment we shall boldly challenge the status-quo and unjust mores and thereby speed the day when "every valley shall be exalted, and every mountain and hill shall be made low, and the crooked shall be made straight and the rough places plain."

A genuine revolution of values means in the final analysis that our loyalties must become ecumenical rather than sectional. Every nation must now develop an overriding loyalty to mankind as a whole in order to preserve the best in their individual societies.

This call for a world-wide fellowship that lifts neighborly concern beyond one's tribe, race, class and nation is in reality a call for an all-embracing and unconditional love for all men. This oft misunderstood and misinterpreted concept—so readily dismissed by the Nietzsches of the world as a weak and cowardly force—has now become an absolute necessity for the survival of man. When I speak of love I am not speaking of some sentimental and weak response. I am speaking of that force which all of the great religions have seen as the supreme unifying principle of life. Love is somehow the key that unlocks the door which leads to ultimate reality. This Hindu-Moslem-Christian-Jewish-Buddhist belief about ultimate reality is beautifully summed up in the first epistle of Saint John:

> Let us love one another: for love is of God; and everyone that loveth is born of God, and knoweth God. He that loveth not knoweth not God; for God is love. . . . If we love one another, God dwelleth in us, and his love is perfected in us.

Let us hope that this spirit will become the order of the day. We can no longer afford to worship the God of hate or bow before the altar of retaliation. The oceans of history are made turbulent by the ever-rising tides of hate. History is cluttered with the wreckage of nations and individuals that pursued this self-defeating path of hate. As

Arnold Toynbee says: "Love is the ultimate force that makes for the saving choice of life and good against the damning choice of death and evil. Therefore the first hope in our inventory must be the hope that love is going to have the last word."

We are now faced with the fact that tomorrow is today. We are confronted with the fierce urgency of now. In this unfolding conundrum of life and history there is such a thing as being too late. Procrastination is still the thief of time. Life often leaves us standing bare, naked and dejected with a lost opportunity. The "tide in the affairs of men" does not remain at the flood; it ebbs. We may cry out desperately for time to pause in her passage, but time is deaf to every plea and rushes on. Over the bleached bones and jumbled residue of numerous civilizations are written the pathetic words: "Too late." There is an invisible book of life that faithfully records our vigilance or our neglect. "The moving finger writes, and having written moves on." We still have a choice today: non-violent co-existence or violent co-annihilation.

We must move past indecision to action. We must find new ways to speak for peace in Vietnam and justice throughout the developing world—a world that borders on our doors. If we do not act we shall surely be dragged down the long dark and shameful corridors of time reserved for those who possess power without compassion, might without morality, and strength without sight.

Now let us begin. Now let us re-dedicate ourselves to the long and bitter—but beautiful—struggle for a new world. This is the calling of the sons of God, and our brothers wait eagerly for our response. Shall we say the odds are too great? Shall we tell them the struggle is too hard? Will our message be that the forces of American life militate against their arrival as full men, and we send our deepest regrets? Or will there be another message, of longing, of hope, of solidarity with their yearnings, of commitment to their cause, whatever the cost? The choice is ours, and though we might prefer it otherwise we *must* choose in this crucial moment of human history.

Delivered at Riverside Church, New York, New York, April 4, 1967.

PART FOUR

OVERCOMING THE TYRANNY OF POVERTY AND HATRED

Dr. Martin Luther King, Jr., and his wife, Coretta, lead a five-day march to the Alabama State Capitol in Montgomery, March 25, 1965.

TWO DECADES AGO, I was blessed to speak with the legendary Coretta Scott King. Her brilliant intellect, wise counsel, and spiritual fortitude had always inspired me. When I asked about the young Martin Luther King, Jr., she said something that startled me: "On my first date with Martin I was surprised because I had never met a black socialist before." Was the young King already the radical King? We know that Professor Walter R. Chivers taught Marxism in his famous sociology courses at Morehouse College from 1925 to 1968. And King learned much from him. We also know that the great Howard Thurman looked favorably on forms of libertarian socialism and that King carried Thurman's *Jesus and the Disinherited* with him on his road trips. When King was asked about his Nobel Peace Prize, he said Norman Thomas should receive one. Who was this Norman Thomas? For the radical King, Norman Thomas was "The Bravest Man I Ever Met," the title of his revealing essay included herein. Spiritual giants like Dorothy Day, Myles Horton, A. J. Muste, Gardner Taylor, Pete Seeger, Fannie Lou Hamer, Vincent Harding, Abraham Joshua Heschel, Mahalia Jackson, and Norman Thomas were soul mates of the radical King. They were conductors on the love train that the "gentle genius" Curtis Mayfield sang about. King's reflections on the radical love of Norman Thomas should be read by all who dare to know the radical King. The crucial role of Michael Harrington—who inherited the democratic socialist leadership mantle from Norman Thomas—in King's Poor People's Campaign is more well known.

King's fundamental commitment to progressive trade unionism is integral to his calling. He not only died in Memphis supporting sanitation workers, but his plea for a multiracial coalition to shut down Washington in order to get action targeting poor people's needs—jobs, education, housing, and health care—was supported by many progressive trade unionists. For King, radical love produced a seething in his soul, a holy anger and righteous indignation because of priceless persons living in poverty. His crusade to eradicate poverty, in America and abroad, was like Frederick Douglass's crusade to abolish slavery or Ida B. Wells-Barnett's crusade to eliminate lynching. For King, poverty was a barbaric form of tyranny to be banished from the earth.

The greatness of nations or civilizations is measured not by military might, architectural prowess, or the number of billionaire citizens. Rather, the greatness of who and what we are consists of how we treat the least of these—the weak, the vulnerable, orphan, widow, stranger, poor, marginal, and prisoner. In this sense, America has many great persons, but it is not a great nation. When more than 20 percent of American children live in poverty and nearly 40 percent of American children of color live in poverty,[1] we fail King's litmus test of national greatness. When he implicitly gave his own powerful eulogy and said he wanted to be remembered as a drum major for justice "who tried to love somebody,"[2] we as a nation and a world are still not able to hear and bear all his words.

This is especially true of King's last monumental speech, given at Mason Temple that rainy Thursday night in Memphis. He didn't want to go; his feet and his soul were weary. But he was always pulled by the sacred needs of God's people. As he said in Montgomery twelve years earlier, "Well, if you think I can render some service, I will."[3] And so he went to Mason Temple.

The last speech of Martin Luther King, Jr., is his greatest oratorical expression of his radical love. It is the sublime culmination of his commitment in his kitchen back during the Montgomery bus boycott—the majestic expression of his courage to think, love, and die for a despised people. Yet in the face of an institutional and individual hatred, the radical King refused to hate and, hence, he would not allow hatred to have the last word in his witness.

In his panoramic tour through history, King's prophetic vision connects global analysis to local praxis. His rhetorical genius dramatizes the revolution of nonviolent resistance against empire and white supremacy. His witty counterfactual claim "I'm so happy that I didn't sneeze"[4]—after his near-death experience in Harlem—on the eve of his physical death in Memphis is prescient. There was intense FBI pressure, including attempts to make him commit suicide. The black civil rights leadership was trashing him. The white establishment had rejected him. The young black revolutionaries were dismissing him. Yet deep down they knew his radical love for them was unconditional. Deep down they knew his radical witness was sincere, shot through with a depth of radical humility and radical integrity they could not deny.

I felt this radical sincerity as a ten-year-old when my parents, Clifton and Irene West, took me to hear King speak in Sacramento, California. So when he was killed, love overflowed and rage overwhelmed us. We knew something had died in us because he had loved us so. He had reminded us in Reidsville State Prison in Tattnall County, Georgia, after a four-hour ride in the pitch-blackness of a paddy wagon alone with a German shepherd threatening him: "This is the cross that we must bear for the freedom of our people."[5]

Yet the questions linger: What Promised Land did the radical King see? What made him so sure that we, as a people, would get there? Since his horrible death, too many Americans of all colors have cast life as a gold rush and, hence, worship the golden calf. I think King was well aware of this gold rush and spiritual blackout, especially among the wealthy and professional classes. Yet he joyfully cast his lot with the least of these, the wretched of the earth, because they are forever worthy of the radical love that Martin Luther King, Jr., embodied and enacted for thirty-nine years in this seemingly God-forsaken world. His life beckons us to stay strong, be not afraid, and not sell our souls for a market price!

NINETEEN

THE BRAVEST MAN I EVER MET

This article about Norman Thomas was originally published in *Pageant* magazine, June 1965.

Last December 2000 Americans gathered at New York's Hotel Astor to celebrate the 80th birthday of Norman Thomas. I could not be present because I had to go to Oslo to accept the Nobel Peace Prize. But before I enplaned for Norway, I taped the following message to be sent to America's foremost Socialist:

> I can think of no man who has done more than you to inspire the vision of a society free of injustice and exploitation. While some would adjust to the status quo, you urged struggle. While some would corrupt struggle with violence or undemocratic perversions, you have stood firmly for the integrity of ends and means. Your example has ennobled and dignified the fight for freedom, and all that we hear of the Great Society seems only an echo of your prophetic eloquence. Your pursuit of racial and economic democracy at home, and of sanity and peace in the world, has been awesome in scope. It is with deep admiration and indebtedness that I carry the inspiration of your life to Oslo.

■　■　■

Truly, the life of Norman Thomas has been one of deep commitment to the betterment of all humanity. In 1928, the year before I was born, he waged the first of six campaigns as the Socialist Party's candidate for President of the United States. A decade earlier, as a preacher, he fought gallantly, if unsuccessfully, against American involvement in World War I. Both then and now he has raised aloft the banner of civil liberties, civil rights, labor's right to organize, and has played a significant role in so many diverse areas of activity that newspapers all over the land have termed him "America's conscience."

There are those who call Norman Thomas a failure because he has never been elected to office. One of his severest critics is Thomas himself. When asked what he had accomplished in his life, the white-haired Socialist leader replied:

> I suppose it is an achievement to live to my age and feel that one has kept the faith, or tried to. It is an achievement to have had a part, even if it was a minor part, in some of the things that have been accomplished in the field of civil liberty, in the field of better race relations, and the rest of it. It is something of an achievement, I think, to keep the idea of socialism before a rather indifferent or even hostile public. That's the kind of achievement that I have to my credit, if any. As the world counts achievement, I have not got much.

But the world disagrees. The Washington *Post,* echoed by scores of other newspapers, called Thomas "among the most influential individuals in 20th century politics" and added: "We join great numbers of his fellow Americans in congratulating the country on having him as a leader at large."

During our historic March on Washington in the summer of 1963, when 250,000 Negro and white Americans joined together in an out-pouring of fellowship and brotherly cooperation for a world of freedom and equality, a little Negro boy listened at the Washington Monument to an eloquent orator.

Turning to his father, he asked: "Who is that man?"

Came the inevitable answer: "That's Norman Thomas. He was for us before any other white folks were."

His concern for racial equality flows naturally from his heritage. His father and both grandparents were Presbyterian ministers. His maternal grandfather Stephen Mattoon was not only an abolitionist but went south to Charlotte, North Carolina, after the Civil War and became the founder and first president of a college for Negroes, then named Biddle College but now called Johnson C. Smith University. Emma Mattoon, Norman's mother, was a girl of about 12 when the family moved to Charlotte. She remembered vividly how the other white girls in the area ostracized her and her sister because their father, a Northerner, taught "niggers."

Thomas, of course, was actively opposed to racial discrimination. In 1921, when he edited a pacifist magazine, *The World Tomorrow*, he wrote (and this perhaps indicates how far we are from those days):

> Northern industrial centers may seem by comparison desirable to the southern Negroes who emigrate to them. But they are a very poor sort of earthly paradise, as *The World Tomorrow* can testify. This thought has been brought home to the magazine from an experience of its own. We are obliged to move to new offices at 108 Lexington Avenue, New York City, and the reason is this—the owners of the building demanded of us signature of a lease forbidding the employment of any Negro. We should have refused such a demand on principle, but in addition we are proud of the fact that one of the most faithful of our office staff is a Negro woman. That her race should be discriminated against in more than one office building in New York City is a practical denial of the fundamental principles of brotherhood and Christianity.

And in 1933, when labor, farm, unemployed, Socialist and liberal groups joined together in a New Continental Congress in Washington, D.C., to lobby for a decent deal for America's depressed millions, Thomas was instrumental in dealing a blow to Jim Crow. Most of the New York delegates were originally housed in the Cairo Hotel. In his book *Norman Thomas: A Biography* (Norton), Harry Fleischman relates that when the hotel barred Floria Pinkney, a Negro delegate, hundreds of the delegates marched to the hotel in a body, canceled their reservations, and demanded return of the money they had paid in advance: Thomas was their spokesman. When the hotel refused to return the money, Thomas arranged with lawyers to bring suit, whereupon the hotel agreed to return the money.

Thomas also worked hand in hand with our most illustrious Negro labor leader, A. Philip Randolph, in speaking at organizing meetings of the Brotherhood of Sleeping Car Porters, in fighting for permanent Federal Fair Employment Practices executive orders and laws, and in helping to abolish discrimination in the nation's armed forces.

But his concern for civil rights is only one facet of Thomas's life that has aroused my admiration and that of many of his fellow Americans, black and white. Describing the Socialist leader's career, Dr. John Haynes Holmes recalled the words of the Prophet Isaiah:

> *For Zion's sake will I not hold my peace,*
> *And for Jerusalem's sake I will not rest,*
> *Until the righteousness thereof go forth as brightness,*
> *And the salvation thereof as a lamp that burneth.*
> *Upon thy walls, O Jerusalem, have I set watchmen,*
> *Who shall never hold their peace, day and night.*
> *Go through, go through the gates;*
> *Prepare ye the way of the people.*

The role of watchman on the tower has never been an easy calling. Who stands upon the wall stands alone. And a man's arms can weary of lifting a standard for the people. There is no rest in it, nor worldly success, nor choice. Yet his courageous championship of exhausted sharecroppers in the South, of persecuted Japanese Americans in World War II, of conscientious objectors in federal prisons, of exploited hospital workers in northern cities, of Mississippi Negroes fighting for the right to vote, his lifelong campaign for economic and social democracy, and his unceasing drive for the maximum international cooperation for peace with justice have endeared him to millions around the globe. He has proved that there is something truly glorious in being forever engaged in the pursuit of justice and equality. He is one of the bravest men I ever met.

"So long as Norman Thomas is alive and capable of standing before a public forum," stated dramatist Morton Wishengrad, "those who are alienated and excluded are not entirely mute. One man articulate in the service of so many. It is beyond socialism, beyond political system, and beyond economic doctrine."

The overriding passion of Thomas's life has been the pursuit of peace—not the deadly apathy of appeasement or submission to tyranny but the insistence that the resolution of differences must be transferred from the dreadful realm of military force to economic and ideological conflict and, ultimately, international law and cooperation. He has put that philosophy practically—maximum isolation from war, maximum cooperation for peace.

His quest for peace started during World War I when he came to the conviction that Christianity and war were in complete opposition, that "you cannot conquer war by war, cast out Satan by Satan, or do the enormous evil of war that good may come." Thomas was so passionate a speaker even then that his intense convictions drew forth strong responses from his audiences.

After a talk in February 1917 at Wesleyan University's Y.M.C.A., its president, Fred Stevens, who had been in the U.S. Army for six years, was much impressed by Thomas's remarks. He was scheduled to address the entire student body at a University preparedness rally. The chairman arose and said: "Wesleyan is fortunate in having an Army officer in its midst who has agreed to drill our volunteers and teach them military tactics. I give you Fred Stevens." Stevens got up and told his startled audience: "I'm sorry, fellows. I can't do it. I heard Norman Thomas last night. I'm a pacifist now."

Through that war, and between wars, and into the next war, Thomas proclaimed that ethical imperative: Thou shalt not kill. When it was popular to do so and when it was dangerous to do so, he kept insisting that war is an evil that men make—and that only men can cure.

This message the dynamic Socialist leader has taken to his country and to the world in every form that human energy and eloquence allow. A score of books that have reached people all over the world reveals some of their content in their titles: *Is Conscience a Crime?*;

War—No Profit, No Glory, No Need; Appeal to The Nations; The Prerequisites For Peace. It has been the basis for rallying the American people in times of crisis in organizations from the American Union Against Militarism at the time of World War I to the National Committee For a Sane Nuclear Policy and Turn Toward Peace today (two organizations in which I am happy to work with him).

Peace has been the theme of countless hundreds of broadcasts over radio and, later, TV networks over a period of 40 years. Peace has been included in conferences on the economic and other practical aspects of universal disarmament under effective international inspection, which have drawn Senators and scholars as well as representatives of voluntary agencies. The search for peace has taken Thomas across the American continent year after year, speaking to small groups and large. And peace has taken him across the world to conferences with leaders of nations and with the prototype of that international fellowship of free men whose vision he has helped to create.

Thomas, a Presbyterian minister, found his interest in socialism stimulated by the antiwar declaration of the Socialist Party in 1917. He wrote Morris Hillquit, one of the declaration's authors, to offer help in Hillquit's New York mayoralty campaign: "The hope for the future lies in a new social and economic order which demands the abolition of the capitalist system. War itself is only the most horrible and dramatic of the many evil fruits of our present organized system of exploitation and the philosophy of life which exalts competition instead of cooperation." When Thomas joined the Socialist Party in 1918, it was with certain reservations: "Perhaps to certain members of the Party my socialism would not be of the most orthodox variety. As you know I have a profound fear of the undue exaltation of the State and a profound faith that the new world we desire must depend upon freedom and fellowship rather than upon any sort of coercion whatsoever. I am interested in political parties only to the extent in which they may be serviceable in advancing certain ideals and in winning liberty for men and women."

Even before becoming a Socialist, Thomas displayed a lack of orthodoxy in nonconformity when he coupled his support of women's suffrage with an expressed doubt that women would vote any more wisely than men. While maintaining that women had just as much right to be wrong as men, Thomas annoyed those suffragettes who argued passionately, "When women get the vote, war will be ended for all time."

In the dark days before the New Deal, when the open shop prevailed and unions were weak and poor, the Socialist leader was a familiar figure to workers in scores of strikes. Thomas could be found, noted David Dubinsky, president of the Ladies International Garment Workers' Union, "In each and every strike on the picket lines and in the hall meetings. We found him when we could not raise money to supply food, sandwiches, or literature for our strikers. We found him championing every battle for free speech, for free assemblage."

Before I was in kindergarten, America was in the throes of a desperate depression, with the Wall Street crash followed by the grim misery of rapidly growing mass unemployment. In the 1932 Presidential campaign Thomas, as the Socialist Presidential nominee, called for socialization of the nation's major industries and natural resources, but his major stress was on immediate programs to ameliorate the tragic effects of the depression and to lead to economic recovery. The platform called for a $10 billion federal program of public works and unemployment relief plus laws to acquire land, buildings, and equipment to put the unemployed to work producing food, fuel, clothing, and homes for their own use. The platform also urged:

- Compulsory insurance against unemployment.
- Employment agencies free to the public.
- Old-age pensions for men and women 60 years old.
- Abolition of child labor.
- The six-hour day, five-day week with no wage reductions.
- Aid to farmers and homeowners against foreclosures of their mortgages.
- Health insurance and maternity insurance.
- Adequate minimum wage laws.

■ ■ ■

Neither the Republican nor Democratic platforms showed any comparable understanding of the nation's needs in that time of crisis. It is to Franklin D. Roosevelt's credit that, when elected, he did not hesitate to use many of Thomas's planks to build his New Deal.

I have remarked upon Thomas's suspicion of orthodoxy, but in one respect he accepted orthodox Socialist views on race. The Socialist Party had no special plank on the problem of the Negro. It assumed that abolishing capitalism would automatically mean equality for the Negro. Thomas did not find out how inadequate this approach was until the W.P.A. (Works Progress Administration) came on the scene. While in Birmingham, Alabama, on a speaking tour, Thomas was told by a white Socialist who was on W.P.A. that he had asked his fellow white workers if they would prefer getting $5 a day if Negroes were paid the same wage, or only $4 a day, with Negroes getting only $3.50. Overwhelmingly, he told Thomas, they preferred less money so long as it was more than Negroes were given! This failure to understand the deeply rooted psychological bases of racism contributed to the Socialist failure to win massive Negro support.

It has been my good fortune to work with Norman Thomas not only for world peace and for racial equality but for fair treatment of all the world's minorities and for social justice everywhere. Several years ago, when the Soviet Union sentenced more than 120 persons—most of them Jews—to death for "economic" crimes, we joined with Dr. Linus Pauling, Dr. Henry Steele Commager, and Dr. William Ernest Hocking in initiating a petition signed by more than 200 prominent Americans urging the Soviet Union to abandon such a practice.

When the U.S.S.R. formally abolished the death penalty some years ago, it boasted that it "was leaving the capitalistic countries behind and was moving toward a more liberal, enlightened Communist society." When the death penalty was invoked in the United States, particularly in the case of convicted Soviet spies, many anti-Communists, running the gamut from Pope Pius XII to Norman Thomas and myself, inveighed against such death sentences.

By reverting to capital punishment, the Khrushchev regime abandoned any propaganda advantages it had boasted. Boris Nikiforov, head of the Criminal Law Department of the U.S.S.R. Institute of Jurisprudence, attempted to whitewash the Soviet death penalty by claiming that state property "is sacred and inviolable" and whoever appropriates state property "encroaches on the basic principle of life of Soviet society." To that argument, we joined former Sen. Herbert Lehman when he aptly replied: "Property rights are no less important in a private economy than in a Communist economy. But one of the chief glories of a sane society is that it places human rights and human life on a higher and more sacred plane than property rights." Incidentally, the "economic" crimes for which the Russians imposed the death penalty included currency speculation and black marketing. One man was doomed for running a private cosmetics business. Three others were condemned to death for selling low-grade apples at top prices.

One of Norman Thomas's most endearing qualities has been his ability to hate the sin but love the sinner. While recognizing that people are influenced by their economic and social backgrounds, he knows that they are often capable of rising above narrow self- or class-interest. He has often been critical of leaders in high places, but he has been scrupulous in giving credit where credit is due, a circumstance that has appealed to Presidents and hosts of other public officials. And, in a time when apathy and indifference have characterized much of mankind, one of his outstanding attributes has been his capacity for indignation at any injustice, which led Roger Baldwin to call Thomas "a civil liberties agency all by himself, with an acute sense of timing and publicity."

Nor is Thomas a dissenter just for the sake of dissent. "The secret of a good life," he once wrote, "is to have the right loyalties and to hold them in the right scale of values. The value of dissent and dissenters is to make us reappraise those values with supreme concern for the truth. . . . Rebellion per se is not a virtue. If it were, we would have some heroes on very low levels."

At Thomas's 80th birthday party, one of the greetings read:

> I understand the moment of truth has arrived and you are confessing
> another birthday. In your instance this should be easy because you re-
> main eternally young of heart and young of spirit. As one of your older
> friends, I wish to join in wishing you not only a happy birthday but
> continued good health. Your life has been dedicated to the practice
> and ideals of democracy. It has also been a life of courage in the battle
> against all forms of totalitarianism. With equal vigor and determina-
> tion you have challenged the evil forces both of fascism and commu-
> nism—never flinching or retreating, always advocating the cause of
> freedom and social justice. America is a better land because of you,
> your life, your work, your deeds.

Signing that greeting was Vice President Hubert H. Humphrey.
Other greetings came from present or former prime ministers, Su-
preme Court judges, Senators, Congressmen, and leaders of all of
America's political parties.

Yet America has never fully utilized Thomas's great abilities. He
has been a marvelous unofficial ambassador-at-large to our friends in
Europe, Asia, Africa, and Latin America. Would it not make sense to
make him our *official* representative to the United Nations?

Originally published in *Pageant* magazine, June 1965.

TWENTY
THE OTHER AMERICA

As he traveled across the country on behalf of his Poor People's Campaign, Dr. King approached possible allies—such as the National Welfare Rights Association, through which black women organized; Native American nations; farmworkers led by Cesar Chavez; and poor whites in Appalachia—in an effort to mobilize a multiracial movement of the poor. On March 10, 1968, King spoke to supporters participating in a celebratory "Salute to Freedom," organized by the Local 1199 in New York City, a union consisting largely of African Americans, Puerto Ricans, and other people of color.

There are times, and I must confess it very honestly as many of us have to confess it as we look at contemporary developments, that I'm often disenchanted with some segments of the power structure of the labor movement. But in these moments of disenchantment, I begin to think of unions like Local 1199 and it gives me renewed courage and vigor to carry on . . . and the feeling that there are *some* unions left that will always maintain the radiant and vibrant idealism that brought the labor movement into being. And I would suggest that if all of labor would emulate what you have been doing over the years, our nation would be closer to victory in the fight to eliminate poverty and injustice.

I also believe that if all of labor were to follow your example of mobilizing and involving working people in the campaign to end the war in Vietnam, our nation would be much closer to a swift settlement of that immoral, unjust, and ill-considered war.

I know that Leon Davis and Moe Foner have played a decisive role in organizing the Labor Leadership Assembly for Peace, a development that has been a source of great encouragement to all of us engaged in the fight to end the war. I note with pride that your union is sponsoring an all-day fast for peace on March 24 at the Community Church. I sincerely hope that each and every one of you here tonight will personally participate and get others to join you in demonstrating to the nation and the world that Local 1199 represents the authentic conscience of the labor movement.

And so for many reasons I'm happy to be here, because of your fight for justice, your fight for peace, your fight for human decency, and for dignity for every working person.

I don't consider myself a stranger. I've been with 1199 so many times in the past that I consider myself a fellow 1199er.

. . . I'm going to really try to be brief, and say a few things about what is happening in our nation and try to say some things about our campaign, our Poor People's Campaign, our campaign for jobs or income which will take place in a few weeks . . . and I want to deal with all of this by using as my subject tonight "The Other America."

And I use this subject because there are literally two Americas. One America is flowing with the milk of prosperity and the honey of equality. That America is the habitat of millions of people who have food and material necessities for their bodies, culture and education for their minds, freedom and human dignity for their spirits. That America is made up of millions of young people who grow up in the sunlight of opportunity.

But as we assemble here tonight, I'm sure that each of us is painfully aware of the fact that there is another America, and that other America has a daily ugliness about it that transforms the buoyancy of hope into the fatigue of despair. In that other America, millions of people find themselves forced to live in inadequate, substandard, and often dilapidated housing conditions. In these conditions they don't have wall-to-wall carpets, but all too often they find themselves living with wall-to-wall rats and roaches. In this other America, thousands, yea, even millions, of young people are forced to attend inadequate, substandard, inferior, quality-less schools, and year after year thousands of young people in this other America finish our high schools reading at an eighth- and a ninth-grade level sometimes. Not because they are dumb, not because they don't have innate intelligence, but because the schools are so inadequate, so overcrowded, so devoid of quality, so segregated, if you will, that the best in these minds can never come out.

And probably the most critical problem in the other America is the economic problem. By the millions, people in the other America find themselves perishing on a lonely island of poverty in the midst of a vast ocean of material prosperity. We only need look at the facts, and they tell us something tragic. . . . The fact is that the black man in the United States of America is facing a literal depression. Now you know they don't call it that. When there is massive unemployment in the black community, it's called a social problem. But when there is massive unemployment in the white community, it's called a depression. With the black man, it's "welfare," with the whites it's "subsidies." This country has socialism for the rich, rugged individualism for the poor.

Now the fact is that there is a literal depression in the black community. Labor statistics would say that. I mean statistics from the Department of Labor would say that the unemployment rate among Negroes is about 8.8 percent. . . . This does not take under consideration what we would refer to as the discouraged thousands and thousands of people who have lost hope; who have lost motivation; who have had so many doors closed in their faces that they feel defeated; who've come to feel that life is a long and desolate corridor with no exit sign and they've given up. And when you add this, the unemployment rate in the black community would probably be nearer 16 or 18 percent, and when you get to Negro youth, in some cities, the unemployment rate goes as high as 40 percent. Now that's a major depression.

But the problem is not only unemployment. It's under- or subemployment. People who work full-time jobs for part-time wages. Most of the poor people in our country are working every day, but they're making wages so inadequate that they cannot even begin to function in the mainstream of the economic life of the nation. You know where they are working. So often they're working in our hospitals, and all over this country. And I thank God for what your union has done and what you continue to do. I can remember just a few years ago, right here in this city, that hospital workers made wages so inadequate that it was a shame to say to anybody that these people were being paid.

But I've been over the country and I know about it. I've been on the picket lines. Hospital workers, whether it's in St. Louis or Cleveland or somewhere else, in Chicago—and I think of the fact that in most instances, in all too many instances, hospital workers are not yet organized. And just think of the low wages in Atlanta, Georgia. I move around as a minister and . . . visit members in the hospitals and . . . they're working every day, working hard, and yet, they are not making enough money to even have adequate food to eat.

Somewhere in life, people of justice and goodwill come to see the dignity of labor. . . . Somewhere they will come to see that person working in the hospital—even if he happens to be a janitor in the hospital—he is in the final analysis as significant as the physician, because if he doesn't do his job, germs can develop, which can be as injurious to the patient as anybody else.

We look around and we see thousands and millions of people making inadequate wages every day. Not only do they work in our hospitals, they work in our hotels, they work in our laundries, they work in domestic service, and they find themselves underemployed. You see, no labor is really menial unless you're not getting adequate wages. People are always talking about menial labor. But if you're getting a good wage . . . that isn't menial labor. What makes it menial is the income, the wages.

Now, what we've got to do . . . is to attack the problem of poverty and really mobilize the forces of our country to have an all-out war against poverty, because what we have now is not even a good skirmish against poverty. I need not remind you that poverty, the gaps in our society, the gulfs between inordinate superfluous wealth and abject deadening poverty have brought about a great deal of despair, a great deal of tension, a great deal of bitterness. We've seen this bitterness expressed over the last few summers in the violent explosions in our cities.

And the great tragedy is that the nation continues in its national policy to ignore the conditions that brought the riots or the rebellions into being. For in the final analysis, the riot is the language of the unheard. And what is it that America's failed to hear? It's failed to hear that the plight of the Negro poor has worsened over the last few years. It has failed to hear that the promises of justice and freedom have not been met. It has failed to hear that large segments of white society are more concerned about tranquility and the status quo than about justice, humanity, and equality, and it is still true. It is still true that these things are being ignored.

Now, every year here about this time our newspapers and our television, and people generally . . . begin to talk about the long hot summer ahead. And what always bothers me about this is that the long hot summer has always been preceded by a long cold winter. And the tragedy is that the nation has failed to use its winters creatively, compassionately . . . and our nation's summers of riots are still caused by our nation's winters of delay. And as long as justice is postponed, as long as there are those in power who fail to address themselves to the problem, we're going to find ourselves sinking into darker nights of social disruption.

Now, I'm concerned about trying to get the nation to use the winter and autumn and the spring and all of this creatively. And this is why we're going to Washington. I wish I had time to talk to you about it in detail tonight. I've been through the ghettos of our nation, been in the Delta of Mississippi. I've been all over and people are frustrated. They're confused, they're bewildered, and they've said that they want a way out of their dilemma. They are angry and many are on the verge, on the brink of despair.

Now, I know that something has to be done. I can't advise them to riot. I don't need to make a long speech tonight. You know my views on nonviolence. And I'm still absolutely convinced that nonviolence, massively organized, powerfully executed, militantly developed, is still the most potent weapon available to the black man in his struggle in the United States of America.

The problem with a riot is that it can always be halted by superior force, so I couldn't advise that. On the other hand, I couldn't advise following a path of Martin Luther King just sitting around signing statements, and writing articles condemning the rioters, or engaging in a process of timid supplications for justice. The fact is that freedom is never voluntarily given by the oppressor. It must be demanded by the oppressed—that's the long, sometimes tragic and turbulent story of history. And if people who are enslaved sit around and feel that freedom is some kind of lavish dish that will be passed out on a silver platter by the federal government or by the white man while the Negro merely furnishes the appetite, he will never get his freedom.

So, I had to sit down with my friends and my associates and think about the people with whom I live and work all over the ghettos of our nation, and I had to try to think up an alternative to riots on the one hand, and to timid supplications for justice on the other hand. And I have come to see that it must be a massive movement organizing poor people in this country, to demand their rights at the seat of government in Washington, D.C.

Now, I said poor people, too, and by that I mean all poor people. When we go to Washington, we're going to have black people because black people are poor, but we're going to also have Puerto Ricans because Puerto Ricans are poor in the United States of America. We're going to have Mexican Americans because they are mistreated. We're going to have Indian Americans because they are mistreated. And for those who will not allow their prejudice to cause them to blindly support their oppressor, we're going to have Appalachian whites with us in Washington.

We're going there to engage in powerful nonviolent direct action to demand, to bring into being an attention-getting dramatic movement, which will make it impossible for the nation to overlook these demands. Now, they may not do anything about it. People ask me, "Suppose you go to Washington and you don't get anything?" You ask people and you mobilize and you organize, and you don't get anything. You've been an absolute failure. My only answer is that when you stand up for justice, you can never fail.

The forces that have the power to make a concession to the forces of justice and truth and right, but who refuse to do it and they follow the path of darkness still, are the forces that fail. We, as poor people, going to struggle for justice, can't fail. If there is no response from the federal government, from the Congress, that's the failure, not those who are struggling for justice.

Now, I'm going to rush on and take my seat, but I want to say that we're going to Washington to demand what is justly ours. Some years ago, almost two hundred now, our nation signed a huge promissory note, "We hold these truths to be self-evident, that all men are created equal, that they are endowed by their creator with certain unalienable rights, that among these are life, liberty, and the pursuit of happiness." Oh, what a marvelous creed. Just think about what it says. It didn't say some men; it said all men. It didn't say all white men; it said all men, which includes black men. It didn't say all Gentiles. It said all men, which includes Jews. It didn't say all Protestants, it said all men, which includes Catholics. And I can go right down the line. And then it said something else. That every man has certain basic rights that are neither derived from nor conferred by the state. . . . They are God given.

Now this is what the creed says. Now the problem is America has had a high blood pressure of creeds and an anemia of deeds on the question of justice. We're going to Washington to say that if a man does not have a job or an income at that moment, you deprive him of life. You deprive him of liberty. And you deprive him of the pursuit of happiness. We're going to demand that America live up to her promise. We're organizing all over, and as I said, we aren't going begging. We are going to demand justice.

Just let me say to you that I have experiences . . . that leave me a little despondent. I get disturbed sometimes that some of our white brothers and sisters don't understand. A man was on a plane with me the other day and I just didn't feel like arguing. He said, "Now the thing you all need to do is something for yourself." He said all other ethnic groups have come to this country and they had problems, too, just like you all have, but they lifted themselves by their own bootstraps. Then he started telling me about his ethnic background, his parents coming from a country in Europe and how they had lifted themselves by their own bootstraps.

Then he said, "Why don't you Nigras do that?" He couldn't pronounce the word *Negro*, and he meant well, really . . . And I was listening and I didn't mean any harm. As I said I wasn't in an arguing mood. But I said, "Sir, it doesn't help the Negro for unfeeling, insensitive white people to say [this] to the Negro that has been here three hundred, almost three hundred and sixty years now, brought here in chains involuntarily, [while] other people who have been here one hundred or one hundred and fifty years came voluntarily." They've gotten ahead of him [and] I said that doesn't help him to just tell him that. It only deepens his frustration and his sense of nobodyness. And I, then, I looked at him and I said, "Sir, do you recognize that no other ethnic group has been a slave on American soil?"

And then I went on to say to him, "But, sir, I've got another thing I want to mention to you. The nation made my color a stigma." And Ossie Davis has said it well. I quoted it in the last book that I wrote. Open *Roget's Thesaurus*. That's a book that gives you all of the synonyms of words. And if you look there for the synonyms for black, they all represent something evil and degrading—smut, dirt, you know, everything. And all of the synonyms for white—pure, chaste . . . So, in our society, you know, a white lie is a little better than a black lie. That's the way, and if somebody goes wrong in a family, you don't call him a white sheep, he's a black sheep, you see. You do something wrong, they don't call it whitemail, [they] call it blackmail. I could go right down the line.

Now, this is a bit of semantics and humorous. But what I'm trying to get over to us is that linguistics, semantics conspired against us to make the black man feel that he was nobody, that he didn't count, made him feel that he was on another level of humanity. That man didn't realize that there was nothing the black man could change because of his disability. He couldn't change his actions. It didn't matter about that. It was a problem growing out of the fact that the nation made his color a stigma.

It is a cruel jest to say to a bootless man that he should lift himself up by his own bootstraps. It is even worse to tell a man to lift himself up by his own bootstraps when somebody is standing on the boot. . . . I had to tell him finally that nobody else in this country has lifted themselves by their own bootstraps alone, so why expect the black man to do it? Nobody else. Now, let me illustrate this. And I believe in lifting yourself by your own bootstraps to the extent that that's possible. I think black people and poor people must organize themselves. I think we must mobilize our political and economic power. I really believe in these programs to get your legitimate goals, so don't think I'm not saying that one must not do anything for himself.

But I'm getting at something deeper. I never will forget, and you cannot forget, that in 1863 the black man was freed from the bondages of physical slavery, but he wasn't given any land to make that freedom meaningful. Frederick Douglass had talked about forty acres and a mule and then nothing was done. He was just told, "you're free," and you know it was something like keeping a man in prison for many, many years, and suddenly discovering that he is not guilty of the crime for which he was imprisoned. And then you just go up to him and say, "Now, you're free." But you don't give him any bus fare to get to town. You don't give him any money to get some clothes to put on his back. You don't give him anything to get started in life again. Every code of jurisprudence would rise up against that, but this is what happened.

This is what America did to the black man. We were left illiterate, penniless, just told, "you're free." But . . . the basic thing to be seen is this: at that very moment America, through an act of Congress, was giving away millions of acres of land in the West and the Midwest. Not only did it give the land, which meant that it was willing to undergird its white peasants from Europe with a walk through the economic floor, but it built land-grant colleges to teach them how to farm, provided county agents to further their expertise in farming, and then later provided low interest rates so that they could mechanize their farms. And now, many of these people are being paid millions of dollars in federal subsidies not to farm, and these are the people who are often telling the Negro that he should lift himself by his own bootstraps.

What I'm simply saying is that in this movement in Washington, we are going to demand what is ours and, my friends, the resources are here in America. The question is whether the will is here. And this is the question I'm raising—a question more and more as I move around—something is wrong with the ship of state. It is not moving toward new and more secure shores, but toward old destructive rocks. There's something wrong with the policies, the priorities, and the purposes of our nation now, and we've got to say it in no uncertain terms.

And I simply say to you that I'm afraid that our government is more concerned about winning an unjust war in Vietnam than about winning the war against poverty right here at home.

And I close by saying that let all of us assembled here continue to struggle for peace and justice. And, you know, they go together. I know there are those who still think they can be separated. They mention to me all the time, there are those who sincerely feel that. But I answered a man the other day who told me I should stick to civil rights, and not deal with the war thing and the war question in Vietnam. I told him that I had been fighting too long and too hard now against segregated public accommodations to end up segregating my moral concerns. And the fact is that justice is indivisible; injustice anywhere is a threat to justice everywhere.

And the other thing is we've got to come to see that however much we're misunderstood or criticized for taking a stand for justice or for peace, we must do it anyway. The arc of the moral universe is long, but it bends toward justice. . . .

And I say that if we will stand and work together, we will bring into being that day when justice will roll down like waters and righteousness like a mighty stream. We will bring into being that day when America will no longer be two nations, but when it will be one nation, indivisible, with liberty and justice for all. Thank you.

Delivered at the Local 1199's "Salute to Freedom,"
New York, New York, March 10, 1968.

TWENTY-ONE

ALL LABOR HAS DIGNITY

On February 12, 1968—President Lincoln's birthday—as Dr. King traveled from state to state, garnering rousing support for the Poor People's Campaign, more than a thousand sanitation workers in Memphis walked off the job. A month into the strike, on March 18, strikers and their supporters packed Bishop Charles Mason Temple of the Church of God in Christ in what the Reverend James Lawson would describe as a "sardine atmosphere." With few notes, King addressed the overflowing church by connecting the localized strike to the plight of all workers, especially those in the service economy.

My dear friend James Lawson and to all of these dedicated and distinguished ministers of the gospel assembled here tonight, and to all of the sanitation workers and their families and to all of my brothers and sisters—I need not pause to say how very delighted I am to be in Memphis tonight, and to see you here in such large and enthusiastic numbers.

As I came in tonight, I turned around and said to Ralph Abernathy, "They really have a great movement here in Memphis." You are demonstrating something here that needs to be demonstrated all over our country. You are demonstrating that we can stick together and you are demonstrating that we are all tied in a single garment of destiny, and that if one black person suffers, if one black person is down, we are all down. I've always said that if we are to solve the tremendous problems that we face we are going to have to unite beyond the religious line, and I'm so happy to know that you have done that in this movement in a supportive role. We have Baptists, Methodists, Presbyterians, Episcopalians, members of the Church of God in Christ, and members of the Church of Christ in God, we are all together, and all of the other denominations and religious bodies that I have not mentioned.

But there is another great need, and that is to unite beyond class lines. The Negro "haves" must join hands with the Negro "have-nots." And armed with compassionate traveler checks, they must journey into that other country of their brother's denial and hurt and exploitation. This is what you have done. You've revealed here that you recognize that the no D is as significant as the PhD, and the man who has been to no-house is as significant as the man who has been to Morehouse. And I just want to commend you.

It's been a long time since I've been in a situation like this and this lets me know that we are ready for action. So I come to commend you and I come also to say to you that in this struggle you have the absolute support, and that means financial support also, of the Southern Christian Leadership Conference.

You are doing many things here in this struggle. You are demanding that this city will respect the dignity of labor. So often we overlook the work and the significance of those who are not in professional jobs, of those who are not in the so-called big jobs. But let me say to you tonight, that whenever you are engaged in work that serves humanity and is for the building of humanity, it has dignity, and it has worth. One day our society must come to see this. One day our society will come to respect the sanitation worker if it is to survive, for the person who picks up our garbage, in the final analysis, is as significant as the physician, for if he doesn't do his job, diseases are rampant. All labor has dignity.

But you are doing another thing. You are reminding, not only Memphis, but you are reminding the nation that it is a crime for people to live in this rich nation and receive starvation wages. And I need not remind you that this is our plight as a people all over America. The vast majority of Negroes in our country are still perishing on a lonely island of poverty in the midst of a vast ocean of material prosperity. My friends, we are living as a people in a literal depression. Now you know when there is mass unemployment and underemployment in the black community they call it a social problem. When there is mass unemployment and underemployment in the white community they call it a depression. But we find ourselves living in a literal depression, all over this country as a people.

Now the problem is not only unemployment. Do you know that most of the poor people in our country are working every day? And they are making wages so low that they cannot begin to function in the mainstream of the economic life of our nation. These are facts which must be seen, and it is criminal to have people working on a full-time basis and a full-time job getting part-time income. You are here tonight to demand that Memphis will do something about the conditions that our brothers face as they work day in and day out for the well-being of the total community. You are here to demand that Memphis will see the poor.

You know Jesus reminded us in a magnificent parable one day that a man went to hell because he didn't see the poor. His name was Dives. And there was a man by the name of Lazarus who came daily to his gate in need of the basic necessities of life, and Dives didn't do anything about it. And he ended up going to hell. There is nothing in that parable which says that Dives went to hell because he was rich. Jesus never made a universal indictment against all wealth. It is true that one day a rich young ruler came to Him talking about eternal life, and He advised him to sell all, but in that instance Jesus was prescribing individual surgery, not setting forth a universal diagnosis.

If you will go on and read that parable in all of its dimensions and its symbolism you will remember that a conversation took place between heaven and hell. And on the other end of that long-distance call between heaven and hell was Abraham in heaven talking to Dives in hell. It wasn't a millionaire in hell talking with a poor man in heaven, it was a little millionaire in hell talking with a multimillionaire in heaven. Dives didn't go to hell because he was rich. His wealth was his opportunity to bridge the gulf that separated him from his brother Lazarus. Dives went to hell because he passed by Lazarus every day, but he never really saw him. Dives went to hell because he allowed Lazarus to become invisible. Dives went to hell because he allowed the means by which he lived to outdistance the ends for which he lived. Dives went to hell because he maximized the minimum and minimized the maximum. Dives finally went to hell because he sought to be a conscientious objector in the war against poverty.

And I come by here to say that America, too, is going to hell if she doesn't use her wealth. If America does not use her vast resources of wealth to end poverty and make it possible for all of God's children to have the basic necessities of life, she, too, will go to hell. And I will hear America through her historians, years and generations to come, saying, "We built gigantic buildings to kiss the skies. We built gargantuan bridges to span the seas. Through our spaceships we were able to carve highways through the stratosphere. Through our airplanes we are able to dwarf distance and place time in chains. Through our submarines we were able to penetrate oceanic depths."

It seems that I can hear the God of the universe saying, "Even though you have done all of that, I was hungry and you fed me not, I was naked and you clothed me not. The children of my sons and daughters were in need of economic security and you didn't provide it for them. And so you cannot enter the kingdom of greatness." This may well be the indictment on America. And that same voice says in Memphis to the mayor, to the power structure, "If you do it unto the least of these of my children you do it unto me."

Now you are doing something else here. You are highlighting the economic issue. You are going beyond purely civil rights to questions of human rights. That is a distinction.

We've fought the civil rights battle over the years. We've done many electrifying things. Montgomery, Alabama, in 1956, fifty thousand black men and women decided that it was ultimately more honorable to walk the streets in dignity than to ride segregated buses in humiliation. Fifty thousand strong, we substituted tired feet for tired souls. We walked the streets of that city for 381 days until the sagging walls of bus segregation were finally crushed by the battering rams of the forces of justice. In 1960, by the thousands in this city and practically every city across the South, students and even adults started sitting in at segregated lunch counters. As they sat there, they were not only sitting down, but they were in reality standing up for the best in the American dream and carrying the whole nation back to those great wells of democracy, which were dug deep by the founding fathers in the formulation of the Constitution and the Declaration of Independence.

In 1961, we took a ride for freedom and brought an end to segregation in interstate travel. In 1963, we went to Birmingham, said, "We don't have a right, we don't have access to public accommodations." Bull Connor came with his dogs and he did use them. Bull Connor came with his fire hoses and he did use them. What he didn't realize was that the black people of Birmingham at that time had a fire that no water could put out. We stayed there and worked until we literally subpoenaed the conscience of a large segment of the nation, to appear before the judgment seat of morality on the whole question of civil rights. And then in 1965 we went to Selma. We said, "We don't have the right to vote." And we stayed there, we walked the highways of Alabama until the nation was aroused, and we finally got a voting rights bill.

Now all of these were great movements. They did a great deal to end legal segregation and guarantee the right to vote. With Selma and the voting rights bill one era of our struggle came to a close and a new era came into being. Now our struggle is for genuine equality, which means economic equality. For we know now that it isn't enough to integrate lunch counters. What does it profit a man to be able to eat at an integrated lunch counter if he doesn't earn enough money to buy a hamburger and a cup of coffee? What does it profit a man to be able to eat at the swankiest integrated restaurant when he doesn't earn enough money to take his wife out to dine? What does it profit one to have access to the hotels of our city and the motels of our highway when we don't earn enough money to take our family on a vacation? What does it profit one to be able to attend an integrated school when he doesn't earn enough money to buy his children school clothes?

And so we assemble here tonight, and you have assembled for more than thirty days now to say, "We are tired. We are tired of being at the bottom. We are tired of being trampled over by the iron feet of oppression. We are tired of our children having to attend overcrowded, inferior, quality-less schools. We are tired of having to live in dilapidated substandard housing conditions where we don't have wall-to-wall carpets but so often we end up with wall-to-wall rats and roaches. We are tired of smothering in an airtight cage of poverty in the midst of an affluent society. We are tired of walking the streets in search for jobs that do not exist. We are tired of working our hands off and laboring every day and not even making a wage adequate to get the basic necessities of life. We are tired of our men being emasculated so that our wives and our daughters have to go out and work in the white lady's kitchen, leaving us unable to be with our children and give them the time and the attention that they need. We are tired."

And so in Memphis we have begun. We are saying, *"Now is the time."* Get the word across to everybody in power in this time in this town that now is the time to make real the promises of democracy. Now is the time to make an adequate income a reality for all of God's children. Now is the time for city hall to take a position for that which is just and honest. Now is the time for justice to roll down like water and righteousness like a mighty stream. *Now is the time.*

Now let me say a word to those of you who are on strike. You have been out now for a number of days, but don't despair. Nothing worthwhile is gained without sacrifice. The thing for you to do is stay together, and say to everybody in this community that you are going to stick it out to the end until every demand is met, and that you are gonna say, "We ain't gonna let nobody turn us around." Let it be known everywhere that along with wages and all of the other securities that you are struggling for, you are also struggling for the right to organize and be recognized.

We can all get more together than we can apart; we can get more organized together than we can apart. And this is the way we gain power. Power is the ability to achieve purpose, power is the ability to affect change, and we need power. What is power? Walter Reuther said once that "power is the ability of a labor union like UAW to make the most powerful corporation in the world—General Motors—say yes when it wants to say no." That's power. And I want you to stick it out so that you will be able to make Mayor Loeb and others say yes, even when they want to say no.

Now the other thing is that nothing is gained without pressure. Don't let anybody tell you to go back on the job and paternalistically say, "Now, you are my men and I'm going to do the right thing for you. Just come on back on the job." Don't go back on the job until the demands are met. Never forget that freedom is not something that is voluntarily given by the oppressor. It is something that must be demanded by the oppressed. Freedom is not some lavish dish that the power structure and the white forces in policy-making positions will voluntarily hand out on a silver platter while the Negro merely furnishes the appetite. If we are going to get equality, if we are going to get adequate wages, we are going to have to struggle for it.

Now you know what? You may have to escalate the struggle a bit. If they keep refusing, and they will not recognize the union, and will not agree for the check-off for the collection of dues, I tell you what you ought to do, and you are together here enough to do it: in a few days you ought to get together and just have a *general work stoppage* in the city of Memphis.

And you let that day come, and not a Negro in this city will go to any job downtown. When no Negro in domestic service will go to anybody's house or anybody's kitchen. When black students will not go to anybody's school and black teachers . . .

[After conferring with his aides, King returned to the microphone briefly to say he would return to Memphis to lead a mass march within a few days.]

Delivered at the American Federation of State, County, and Municipal Employees mass meeting, Bishop Charles Mason Temple, Church of God in Christ, Memphis, Tennessee, March 18, 1968.

TWENTY-TWO

THE DRUM MAJOR INSTINCT

Dr. King delivered the following sermon—one of his most famous—at Atlanta's Ebenezer Baptist Church on February 4, 1968, just two months before he was assassinated. Excerpts from the sermon were played at King's funeral service, held at Ebenezer Baptist Church, five days after his assassination.

This morning I would like to use as a subject from which to preach: "The Drum Major Instinct." And our text for [this] morning is taken from a very familiar passage in the tenth chapter as recorded by Saint Mark. Beginning with the thirty-fifth verse of that chapter, we read these words: "And James and John, the sons of Zebedee, came unto him saying, 'Master, we would that thou shouldest do for us whatsoever we shall desire.' And he said unto them, 'What would ye that I should do for you?' And they said unto him, 'Grant unto us that we may sit, one on thy right hand, and the other on thy left hand, in thy glory.' But Jesus said unto them, 'Ye know not what ye ask: Can ye drink of the cup that I drink of? And be baptized with the baptism that I am baptized with?' And they said unto him, 'We can.' And Jesus said unto them, 'Ye shall indeed drink of the cup that I drink of, and with the baptism that I am baptized withal shall ye be baptized: but to sit on my right hand and on my left hand is not mine to give; but it shall be given to them for whom it is prepared.'" And then Jesus goes on toward the end of that passage to say, "But so shall it not be among you: but whosoever will be great among you, shall be your servant: and whosoever of you will be the chiefest, shall be servant of all."

The setting is clear. James and John are making a specific request of the master. They had dreamed, as most of the Hebrews dreamed, of a coming king of Israel who would set Jerusalem free and establish his kingdom on Mount Zion, and in righteousness rule the world. And they thought of Jesus as this kind of king. And they were thinking of that day when Jesus would reign supreme as this new king of Israel. And they were saying, "Now when you establish your kingdom, let one of us sit on the right hand and the other on the left hand of your throne."

Now very quickly, we would automatically condemn James and John, and we would say they were selfish. Why would they make such a selfish request? But before we condemn them too quickly, let us look calmly and honestly at ourselves, and we will discover that we too have those same basic desires for recognition, for importance. That same desire for attention, that same desire to be first. Of course, the other disciples got mad with James and John, and you could understand why, but we must understand that we have some of the same James and John qualities. And there is deep down within all of us an instinct. It's a kind of drum major instinct—a desire to be out front, a desire to lead the parade, a desire to be first. And it is something that runs the whole gamut of life.

And so before we condemn them, let us see that we all have the drum major instinct. We all want to be important, to surpass others, to achieve distinction, to lead the parade. Alfred Adler, the great psychoanalyst, contends that this is the dominant impulse. Sigmund Freud used to contend that sex was the dominant impulse, and Adler came with a new argument saying that this quest for recognition, this desire for attention, this desire for distinction is the basic impulse, the basic drive of human life, this drum major instinct.

And you know, we begin early to ask life to put us first. Our first cry as a baby was a bid for attention. And all through childhood the drum major impulse or instinct is a major obsession. Children ask life to grant them first place. They are a little bundle of ego. And they have innately the drum major impulse or the drum major instinct.

Now, in adult life, we still have it, and we really never get by it. We like to do something good. And you know, we like to be praised for it. Now if you don't believe that, you just go on living life, and you will discover very soon that you like to be praised. Everybody likes it, as a matter of fact. And somehow this warm glow we feel when we are praised or when our name is in print is something of the vitamin A to our ego. Nobody is unhappy when they are praised, even if they know they don't deserve it and even if they don't believe it. The only unhappy people about praise is when that praise is going too much toward somebody else. But everybody likes to be praised because of this real drum major instinct.

Now the presence of the drum major instinct is why so many people are "joiners." You know, there are some people who just join everything. And it's really a quest for attention and recognition and importance. And they get names that give them that impression. So you get your groups, and they become the "Grand Patron," and the little fellow who is henpecked at home needs a chance to be the "Most Worthy of the Most Worthy" of something. It is the drum major impulse and longing that runs the gamut of human life. And so we see it everywhere, this quest for recognition. And we join things, over-join really, that we think that we will find that recognition in.

Now the presence of this instinct explains why we are so often taken by advertisers. You know, those gentlemen of massive verbal persuasion. And they have a way of saying things to you that kind of gets you into buying. In order to be a man of distinction, you must drink this whiskey. In order to make your neighbors envious, you must drive this type of car. In order to be lovely to love you must wear this kind of lipstick or this kind of perfume. And you know, before you know it, you're just buying that stuff. That's the way the advertisers do it.

I got a letter the other day, and it was a new magazine coming out. And it opened up, "Dear Dr. King: As you know, you are on many mailing lists. And you are categorized as highly intelligent, progressive, a lover of the arts and the sciences, and I know you will want to read what I have to say." Of course I did. After you said all of that and explained me so exactly, of course I wanted to read it.

But very seriously, it goes through life; the drum major instinct is real. And you know what else it causes to happen? It often causes us to live above our means. It's nothing but the drum major instinct. Do you ever see people buy cars that they can't even begin to buy in terms of their income? You've seen people riding around in Cadillacs and Chryslers who don't earn enough to have a good Model-T Ford. But it feeds a repressed ego.

You know, economists tell us that your automobile should not cost more than half of your annual income. So if you make an income of five thousand dollars, your car shouldn't cost more than about twenty-five hundred. That's just good economics. And if it's a family of two, and both members of the family make ten thousand dollars, they would have to make out with one car. That would be good economics, although it's often inconvenient. But so often, haven't you seen people making five thousand dollars a year and driving a car that costs six thousand? And they wonder why their ends never meet. That's a fact.

Now the economists also say that your house shouldn't cost—if you're buying a house, it shouldn't cost more than twice your income. That's based on the economy and how you would make ends meet. So, if you have an income of five thousand dollars, it's kind of difficult in this society. But say it's a family with an income of ten thousand dollars, the house shouldn't cost much more than twenty thousand. Well, I've seen folk making ten thousand dollars, living in a forty- and fifty-thousand-dollar house. And you know they just barely make it. They get a check every month somewhere, and they owe all of that out before it comes in. Never have anything to put away for rainy days.

But now the problem is, it is the drum major instinct. And you know, you see people over and over again with the drum major instinct taking them over. And they just live their lives trying to outdo the Joneses. They got to get this coat because this particular coat is a little better and a little better-looking than Mary's coat. And I got to drive this car because it's something about this car that makes my car a little better than my neighbor's car. I know a man who used to live in a thirty-five-thousand-dollar house. And other people started building thirty-five-thousand-dollar houses, so he built a seventy-five-thousand-dollar house. And then somebody else built a seventy-five-thousand-dollar house, and he built a hundred-thousand-dollar house. And I don't know where he's going to end up if he's going to live his life trying to keep up with the Joneses.

There comes a time that the drum major instinct can become destructive. And that's where I want to move now. I want to move to the point of saying that if this instinct is not harnessed, it becomes a very dangerous, pernicious instinct. For instance, if it isn't harnessed, it causes one's personality to become distorted. I guess that's the most damaging aspect of it: what it does to the personality. If it isn't harnessed, you will end up day in and day out trying to deal with your ego problem by boasting. Have you ever heard people that—you know, and I'm sure you've met them—that really become sickening because they just sit up all the time talking about themselves? And they just boast and boast and boast, and that's the person who has not harnessed the drum major instinct.

And then it does other things to the personality. It causes you to lie about who you know sometimes. There are some people who are influence peddlers. And in their attempt to deal with the drum major instinct, they have to try to identify with the so-called big-name people. And if you're not careful, they will make you think they know somebody that they don't really know. They know them well, they sip tea with them, and they this-and-that. That happens to people.

And the other thing is that it causes one to engage ultimately in activities that are merely used to get attention. Criminologists tell us that some people are driven to crime because of this drum major instinct. They don't feel that they are getting enough attention through the normal channels of social behavior, and so they turn to anti-social behavior in order to get attention, in order to feel important. And so they get that gun, and before they know it they robbed a bank in a quest for recognition, in a quest for importance.

And then the final great tragedy of the distorted personality is the fact that when one fails to harness this instinct, he ends up trying to push others down in order to push himself up. And whenever you do that, you engage in some of the most vicious activities. You will spread evil, vicious, lying gossip on people, because you are trying to pull them down in order to push yourself up. And the great issue of life is to harness the drum major instinct.

Now the other problem is, when you don't harness the drum major instinct—this uncontrolled aspect of it—is that it leads to snobbish exclusivism. It leads to snobbish exclusivism. And you know, this is the danger of social clubs and fraternities—I'm in a fraternity; I'm in two or three—for sororities and all of these, I'm not talking against them. I'm saying it's the danger. The danger is that they can become forces of classism and exclusivism where somehow you get a degree of satisfaction because you are in something exclusive. And that's fulfilling something, you know—that I'm in this fraternity, and it's the best fraternity in the world, and everybody can't get in this fraternity. So it ends up, you know, a very exclusive kind of thing.

And you know, that can happen with the church; I know churches get in that bind sometimes. I've been to churches, you know, and they say, "We have so many doctors, and so many school teachers, and so many lawyers, and so many businessmen in our church." And that's fine, because doctors need to go to church, and lawyers, and businessmen, teachers—they ought to be in church. But they say that—even the preacher sometimes will go all through that—they say that as if the other people don't count.

And the church is the one place where a doctor ought to forget that he's a doctor. The church is the one place where a PhD ought to forget that he's a PhD. The church is the one place that the school teacher ought to forget the degree she has behind her name. The church is the one place where the lawyer ought to forget that he's a lawyer. And any church that violates the "whosoever will, let him come" doctrine is a dead, cold church, and nothing but a little social club with a thin veneer of religiosity.

When the church is true to its nature, it says, "Whosoever will, let him come." And it [is] not supposed to satisfy the perverted uses of the drum major instinct. It's the one place where everybody should be the same, standing before a common master and savior. And a recognition grows out of this—that all men are brothers because they are children of a common father.

The drum major instinct can lead to exclusivism in one's thinking and can lead one to feel that because he has some training, he's a little better than that person who doesn't have it. Or because he has some economic security, that he's a little better than that person who doesn't have it. And that's the uncontrolled, perverted use of the drum major instinct.

Now the other thing is, that it leads to tragic—and we've seen it happen so often—tragic race prejudice. Many who have written about this problem—Lillian Smith used to say it beautifully in some of her books. And she would say it to the point of getting men and women to see the source of the problem. Do you know that a lot of the race problem grows out of the drum major instinct? A need that some people have to feel superior. A need that some people have to feel that they are first, and to feel that their white skin ordained them to be first. And they have said it over and over again in ways that we see with our own eyes. In fact, not too long ago, a man down in Mississippi said that God was a charter member of the White Citizens Council. And so God being the charter member means that everybody who's in that has a kind of divinity, a kind of superiority. And think of what has happened in history as a result of this perverted use of the drum major instinct. It has led to the most tragic prejudice, the most tragic expressions of man's inhumanity to man.

The other day I was saying—I always try to do a little converting when I'm in jail. And when we were in jail in Birmingham the other day, the white wardens and all enjoyed coming around the cell to talk about the race problem. And they were showing us where we were so wrong demonstrating. And they were showing us where segregation was so right. And they were showing us where intermarriage was so wrong. So I would get to preaching, and we would get to talking—calmly, because they wanted to talk about it. And then we got down one day to the point—that was the second or third day—to talk about where they lived, and how much they were earning. And when those brothers told me what they were earning, I said, "Now, you know what? You ought to be marching with us. You're just as poor as Negroes." And I said, "You are put in the position of supporting your oppressor, because through prejudice and blindness, you fail to see that the same forces that oppress Negroes in American society oppress poor white people. And all you are living on is the satisfaction of your skin being white, and the drum major instinct of thinking that you are somebody big because you are white. And you're so poor you can't send your children to school. You ought to be out here marching with every one of us every time we have a march."

Now that's a fact. That the poor white has been put into this position, where through blindness and prejudice, he is forced to support his oppressors. And the only thing he has going for him is the false feeling that he's superior because his skin is white—and can't hardly eat and make his ends meet week in and week out.

And not only does this thing go into the racial struggle, it goes into the struggle between nations. And I would submit to you this morning that what is wrong in the world today is that the nations of the world are engaged in a bitter, colossal contest for supremacy. And if something doesn't happen to stop this trend, I'm sorely afraid that we won't be here to talk about Jesus Christ and about God and about brotherhood too many more years. If somebody doesn't bring an end to this suicidal thrust that we see in the world today, none of us are going to be around, because somebody's going to make the mistake through our senseless blunderings of dropping a nuclear bomb somewhere. And then another one is going to drop. And don't let anybody fool you, this can happen within a matter of seconds. They have twenty-megaton bombs in Russia right now that can destroy a city as big as New York in three seconds, with everybody wiped away, and every building. And we can do the same thing to Russia and China.

But this is why we are drifting. And we are drifting there because nations are caught up with the drum major instinct. "I must be first." "I must be supreme." "Our nation must rule the world." And I am sad to say that the nation in which we live is the supreme culprit. And I'm going to continue to say it to America, because I love this country too much to see the drift that it has taken.

God didn't call America to do what she's doing in the world now. God didn't call America to engage in a senseless, unjust war as the war in Vietnam. And we are criminals in that war. We've committed more war crimes almost than any nation in the world, and I'm going to continue to say it. And we won't stop it because of our pride and our arrogance as a nation.

But God has a way of even putting nations in their place. The God that I worship has a way of saying, "Don't play with me." He has a way of saying, as the God of the Old Testament used to say to the Hebrews, "Don't play with me, Israel. Don't play with me, Babylon. Be still and know that I'm God. And if you don't stop your reckless course, I'll rise up and break the backbone of your power." And that can happen to America. Every now and then I go back and read Gibbon's *Decline and Fall of the Roman Empire.* And when I come and look at America, I say to myself, "The parallels are frightening. And we have perverted the drum major instinct."

But let me rush on to my conclusion, because I want you to see what Jesus was really saying. What was the answer that Jesus gave these men? It's very interesting. One would have thought that Jesus would have condemned them. One would have thought that Jesus would have said, "You are out of your place. You are selfish. Why would you raise such a question?"

But that isn't what Jesus did; he did something altogether different. He said in substance, "Oh, I see, you want to be first. You want to be great. You want to be important. You want to be significant. Well, you ought to be. If you're going to be my disciple, you must be." But he reordered priorities. And he said, "Yes, don't give up this instinct. It's a good instinct if you use it right. It's a good instinct if you don't distort it and pervert it. Don't give it up. Keep feeling the need for being important. Keep feeling the need for being first. But I want you to be first in love. I want you to be first in moral excellence. I want you to be first in generosity. That is what I want you to do."

And he transformed the situation by giving a new definition of greatness. And you know how he said it? He said, "Now brethren, I can't give you greatness. And really, I can't make you first." This is what Jesus said to James and John. "You must earn it. True greatness comes not by favoritism, but by fitness. And the right hand and the left are not mine to give, they belong to those who are prepared."

And so Jesus gave us a new norm of greatness. If you want to be important—wonderful. If you want to be recognized—wonderful. If you want to be great—wonderful. But recognize that he who is greatest among you shall be your servant. That's a new definition of greatness.

And this morning, the thing that I like about it: By giving that definition of greatness, it means that everybody can be great, because everybody can serve. You don't have to have a college degree to serve. You don't have to make your subject and your verb agree to serve. You don't have to know about Plato and Aristotle to serve. You don't have to know Einstein's theory of relativity to serve. You don't have to know the second theory of thermodynamics in physics to serve. You only need a heart full of grace, a soul generated by love. And you can be that servant.

I know a man—and I just want to talk about him a minute, and maybe you will discover who I'm talking about as I go down the way because he was a great one. And he just went about serving. He was born in an obscure village, the child of a poor peasant woman. And then he grew up in still another obscure village, where he worked as a carpenter until he was thirty years old. Then for three years, he just got on his feet, and he was an itinerant preacher. And he went about doing some things. He didn't have much. He never wrote a book. He never held an office. He never had a family. He never owned a house. He never went to college. He never visited a big city. He never went two hundred miles from where he was born. He did none of the usual things that the world would associate with greatness. He had no credentials but himself.

He was only thirty-three when the tide of public opinion turned against him. They called him a rabble-rouser. They called him a troublemaker. They said he was an agitator. He practiced civil disobedience; he broke injunctions. And so he was turned over to his enemies and went through the mockery of a trial. And the irony of it all is that his friends turned him over to them. One of his closest friends denied him. Another of his friends turned him over to his enemies. And while he was dying, the people who killed him gambled for his clothing, the only possession that he had in the world. When he was dead he was buried in a borrowed tomb, through the pity of a friend.

Nineteen centuries have come and gone and today he stands as the most influential figure that ever entered human history. All of the armies that ever marched, all the navies that ever sailed, all the parliaments that ever sat, and all the kings that ever reigned put together have not affected the life of man on this earth as much as that one solitary life. His name may be a familiar one. But today I can hear them talking about him. Every now and then somebody says, "He's King of Kings." And again I can hear somebody saying, "He's Lord of Lords." Somewhere else I can hear somebody saying, "In Christ there is no East nor West." And then they go on and talk about, "In Him there's no North and South, but one great Fellowship of Love throughout the whole wide world." He didn't have anything. He just went around serving and doing good.

This morning, you can be on his right hand and his left hand if you serve. It's the only way in.

Every now and then I guess we all think realistically about that day when we will be victimized with what is life's final common denominator—that something that we call death. We all think about it. And every now and then I think about my own death and I think about my own funeral. And I don't think of it in a morbid sense. And every now and then I ask myself, "What is it that I would want said?" And I leave the word to you this morning.

If any of you are around when I have to meet my day, I don't want a long funeral. And if you get somebody to deliver the eulogy, tell them not to talk too long. And every now and then I wonder what I want them to say. Tell them not to mention that I have a Nobel Peace Prize—that isn't important. Tell them not to mention that I have three or four hundred other awards—that's not important. Tell them not to mention where I went to school.

I'd like somebody to mention that day that Martin Luther King, Jr., tried to give his life serving others.

I'd like for somebody to say that day that Martin Luther King, Jr., tried to love somebody.

I want you to say that day that I tried to be right on the war question.

I want you to be able to say that day that I did try to feed the hungry.

And I want you to be able to say that day that I did try in my life to clothe those who were naked.

I want you to say on that day that I did try in my life to visit those who were in prison.

I want you to say that I tried to love and serve humanity.

Yes, if you want to say that I was a drum major, say that I was a drum major for justice. Say that I was a drum major for peace. I was a drum major for righteousness. And all of the other shallow things will not matter. I won't have any money to leave behind. I won't have the fine and luxurious things of life to leave behind. But I just want to leave a committed life behind. And that's all I want to say.

If I can help somebody as I pass along,
If I can cheer somebody with a word or song,
If I can show somebody he's traveling wrong,
Then my living will not be in vain.
If I can do my duty as a Christian ought,
If I can bring salvation to a world once wrought,
If I can spread the message as the master taught,
Then my living will not be in vain.

Yes, Jesus, I want to be on your right or your left side, not for any selfish reason. I want to be on your right or your left side, not in terms of some political kingdom or ambition. But I just want to be there in love and in justice and in truth and in commitment to others, so that we can make of this old world a new world.

Delivered at Ebenezer Baptist Church,
Atlanta, Georgia, February 4, 1968.

TWENTY-THREE

I'VE BEEN
TO THE
MOUNTAINTOP

Dr. King arrived in Memphis feeling exhausted. Less than a month prior, he
had addressed striking sanitation workers and their allies, and soon after led
a march that erupted in violence and was immediately called off. Against the
advice of his colleagues, King returned to Memphis to restore nonviolence back
to the movement. On April 3, 1968, on what turned out to be the eve of his
assassination, King delivered one of his most prophetic and lasting sermons
extemporaneously to an overflowing crowd at Bishop Charles Mason Temple.

Thank you very kindly, my friends. As I listened to Ralph Abernathy
in his eloquent and generous introduction and then thought about
myself, I wondered who he was talking about. It's always good to have
your closest friend and associate say something good about you. And
Ralph is the best friend that I have in the world.

I'm delighted to see each of you here tonight in spite of a storm
warning. You reveal that you are determined to go on anyhow. Something is happening in Memphis, something is happening in our world.

As you know, if I were standing at the beginning of time, with
the possibility of taking a kind of general and panoramic view of
the whole human history up to now, and the Almighty said to me,
"Martin Luther King, which age would you like to live in?" I would

take my mental flight by Egypt through, or rather across the Red Sea, through the wilderness on toward the promised land. And in spite of its magnificence, I wouldn't stop there. I would move on by Greece, and take my mind to Mount Olympus. And I would see Plato, Aristotle, Socrates, Euripides and Aristophanes assembled around the Parthenon as they discussed the great and eternal issues of reality.

But I wouldn't stop there. I would go on, even to the great hey-day of the Roman Empire. And I would see developments around there, through various emperors and leaders. But I wouldn't stop there. I would even come up to the day of the Renaissance, and get a quick picture of all that the Renaissance did for the cultural and esthetic life of man. But I wouldn't stop there. I would even go by the way that the man for whom I'm named had his habitat. And I would watch Martin Luther as he tacked his ninety-five theses on the door at the church in Wittenberg.

But I wouldn't stop there. I would come on up even to 1863, and watch a vacillating president by the name of Abraham Lincoln finally come to the conclusion that he had to sign the Emancipation Proclamation. But I wouldn't stop there, I would even come up to the early thirties, and see a man grappling with the problems of the bankruptcy of his nation. And come with an eloquent cry that we have nothing to fear but fear itself.

But I wouldn't stop there. Strangely enough, I would turn to the Almighty, and say, "If you allow me to live just a few years in the second half of the twentieth century, I will be happy." Now that's a strange statement to make, because the world is all messed up. The nation is sick. Trouble is in the land. Confusion all around. That's a strange statement. But I know, somehow, that only when it is dark enough, can you see the stars. And I see God working in this period of the twentieth century in a way that men, in some strange way, are responding—something is happening in our world. The masses of people are rising up. And wherever they are assembled today, whether they are in Johannesburg, South Africa; Nairobi, Kenya; Accra, Ghana; New York City; Atlanta, Georgia; Jackson, Mississippi; or Memphis, Tennessee—the cry is always the same—"We want to be free."

And another reason that I'm happy to live in this period is that we have been forced to a point where we're going to have to grapple with the problems that men have been trying to grapple with through history, but the demands didn't force them to do it. Survival demands that we grapple with them. Men, for years now, have been talking about war and peace. But now, no longer can they just talk about it. It is no longer a choice between violence and nonviolence in this world; it's nonviolence or nonexistence.

That is where we are today. And also in the human rights revolution, if something isn't done, and in a hurry, to bring the colored peoples of the world out of their long years of poverty, their long years of hurt and neglect, the whole world is doomed. Now, I'm just happy that God has allowed me to live in this period, to see what is unfolding. And I'm happy that he's allowed me to be in Memphis.

I can remember, I can remember when Negroes were just going around as Ralph has said, so often, scratching where they didn't itch, and laughing when they were not tickled. But that day is all over. We mean business now, and we are determined to gain our rightful place in God's world.

And that's all this whole thing is about. We aren't engaged in any negative protest and in any negative arguments with anybody. We are saying that we are determined to be men. We are determined to be people. We are saying that we are God's children. And that we don't have to live like we are forced to live.

Now, what does all of this mean in this great period of history? It means that we've got to stay together. We've got to stay together and maintain unity. You know, whenever Pharaoh wanted to prolong the period of slavery in Egypt, he had a favorite, favorite formula for doing it. What was that? He kept the slaves fighting among themselves. But whenever the slaves get together, something happens in Pharaoh's court, and he cannot hold the slaves in slavery. When the slaves get together, that's the beginning of getting out of slavery. Now let us maintain unity.

Secondly, let us keep the issues where they are. The issue is injustice. The issue is the refusal of Memphis to be fair and honest in its dealings with its public servants, who happen to be sanitation workers. Now, we've got to keep attention on that. That's always the problem with a little violence. You know what happened the other day, and the press dealt only with the window-breaking. I read the articles. They very seldom got around to mentioning the fact that one thousand, three hundred sanitation workers were on strike, and that Memphis is not being fair to them, and that Mayor Loeb is in dire need of a doctor. They didn't get around to that.

Now we're going to march again, and we've got to march again, in order to put the issue where it is supposed to be. And force everybody to see that there are thirteen hundred of God's children here suffering; sometimes going hungry, going through dark and dreary nights wondering how this thing is going to come out. That's the issue. And we've got to say to the nation: we know it's coming out. For when people get caught up with that which is right and they are willing to sacrifice for it, there is no stopping point short of victory.

We aren't going to let any mace stop us. We are masters in our non-violent movement in disarming police forces; they don't know what to do. I've seen them so often. I remember in Birmingham, Alabama, when we were in that majestic struggle there we would move out of the 16th Street Baptist Church day after day; by the hundreds we would move out. And Bull Connor would tell them to send the dogs forth and they did come; but we just went before the dogs singing, "Ain't gonna let nobody turn me round." Bull Connor next would say, "Turn the fire hoses on." And as I said to you the other night, Bull Connor didn't know history. He knew a kind of physics that somehow didn't relate to the transphysics that we knew about. And that was the fact that there was a certain kind of fire that no water could put out. And we went before the fire hoses; we had known water. If we were Baptist or some other denomination, we had been immersed. If we were Methodist, and some others, we had been sprinkled, but we knew water.

That couldn't stop us. And we just went on before the dogs and we would look at them; and we'd go on before the water hoses and we would look at it, and we'd just go on singing "Over my head I see freedom in the air." And then we would be thrown in the paddy wagons, and sometimes we were stacked in there like sardines in a can. And they would throw us in, and old Bull would say, "Take them off," and they did; and we would just go in the paddy wagon singing, "We Shall Overcome." And every now and then we'd get in the jail, and we'd see the jailers looking through the windows being moved by our prayers, and being moved by our words and our songs. And there was a power there which Bull Connor couldn't adjust to; and so we ended up transforming Bull into a steer, and we won our struggle in Birmingham.

Now we've got to go on to Memphis just like that. I call upon you to be with us Monday. Now about injunctions: We have an injunction and we're going into court tomorrow morning to fight this illegal, unconstitutional injunction. All we say to America is, "Be true to what you said on paper." If I lived in China or even Russia, or any totalitarian country, maybe I could understand the denial of certain basic First Amendment privileges, because they hadn't committed themselves to that over there. But somewhere I read of the freedom of assembly. Somewhere I read of the freedom of speech. Somewhere I read of the freedom of the press. Somewhere I read that the greatness of America is the right to protest for right. And so just as I say, we aren't going to let any injunction turn us around. We are going on.

We need all of you. And you know what's beautiful to me, is to see all of these ministers of the Gospel. It's a marvelous picture. Who is it that is supposed to articulate the longings and aspirations of the people more than the preacher? Somehow the preacher must be an Amos, and say, "Let justice roll down like waters and righteousness like a mighty stream." Somehow, the preacher must say with Jesus, "The spirit of the Lord is upon me, because he hath anointed me to deal with the problems of the poor."

And I want to commend the preachers, under the leadership of these noble men: James Lawson, one who has been in this struggle for many years; he's been to jail for struggling; but he's still going on, fighting for the rights of his people. Rev. Ralph Jackson, Billy Kiles; I could just go right on down the list, but time will not permit. But I want to thank them all. And I want you to thank them, because so often, preachers aren't concerned about anything but themselves. And I'm always happy to see a relevant ministry.

It's all right to talk about "long white robes over yonder," in all of its symbolism. But ultimately people want some suits and dresses and shoes to wear down here. It's all right to talk about "streets flowing with milk and honey," but God has commanded us to be concerned about the slums down here, and his children who can't eat three square meals a day. It's all right to talk about the new Jerusalem, but one day, God's preacher must talk about the New York, the new Atlanta, the new Philadelphia, the new Los Angeles, the new Memphis, Tennessee. This is what we have to do.

Now the other thing we'll have to do is this: Always anchor our external direct action with the power of economic withdrawal. Now, we are poor people, individually, we are poor when you compare us with white society in America. We are poor. Never stop and forget that collectively, that means all of us together, collectively we are richer than all the nations in the world, with the exception of nine. Did you ever think about that? After you leave the United States, Soviet Russia, Great Britain, West Germany, France, and I could name the others, the Negro collectively is richer than most nations of the world. We have an annual income of more than thirty billion dollars a year, which is more than all of the exports of the United States, and more than the national budget of Canada. Did you know that? That's power right there, if we know how to pool it.

We don't have to argue with anybody. We don't have to curse and go around acting bad with our words. We don't need any bricks and bottles, we don't need any Molotov cocktails, we just need to go around to these stores, and to these massive industries in our country, and say, "God sent us by here, to say to you that you're not treating his children right. And we've come by here to ask you to make the first item on your agenda—fair treatment, where God's children are concerned. Now, if you are not prepared to do that, we do have an agenda that we must follow. And our agenda calls for withdrawing economic support from you."

And so, as a result of this, we are asking you tonight, to go out and tell your neighbors not to buy Coca-Cola in Memphis. Go by and tell them not to buy Sealtest milk. Tell them not to buy—what is the other bread?—Wonder Bread. And what is the other bread company, Jesse? Tell them not to buy Hart's bread. As Jesse Jackson has said, up to now, only the garbage men have been feeling pain; now we must kind of redistribute the pain. We are choosing these companies because they haven't been fair in their hiring policies; and we are choosing them because they can begin the process of saying, they are going to support the needs and the rights of these men who are on strike. And then they can move on downtown and tell Mayor Loeb to do what is right.

But not only that, we've got to strengthen black institutions. I call upon you to take your money out of the banks downtown and deposit your money in Tri-State Bank—we want a "bank-in" movement in Memphis. So go by the savings and loan association. I'm not asking you something that we don't do ourselves at SCLC. Judge [Benjamin] Hooks and others will tell you that we have an account here in the savings and loan association from the Southern Christian Leadership Conference. We're just telling you to follow what we're doing. Put your money there. You have six or seven black insurance companies in Memphis. Take out your insurance there. We want to have an "insurance-in."

Now these are some practical things we can do. We begin the process of building a greater economic base. And at the same time, we are putting pressure where it really hurts. I ask you to follow through here.

Now, let me say as I move to my conclusion that we've got to give ourselves to this struggle until the end. Nothing would be more tragic than to stop at this point, in Memphis. We've got to see it through. And when we have our march, you need to be there. Be concerned about your brother. You may not be on strike. But either we go up together, or we go down together.

Let us develop a kind of dangerous unselfishness. One day a man came to Jesus; and he wanted to raise some questions about some vital matters in life. At points, he wanted to trick Jesus, and show him that he knew a little more than Jesus knew, and through this, throw him off base. Now that question could have easily ended up in a philosophical and theological debate. But Jesus immediately pulled that question from mid-air, and placed it on a dangerous curve between Jerusalem and Jericho. And he talked about a certain man, who fell among thieves. You remember that a Levite and a priest passed by on the other side. They didn't stop to help him. And finally a man of another race came by. He got down from his beast, decided not to be compassionate by proxy. But with him, administered first aid, and helped the man in need. Jesus ended up saying, this was the good man, this was the great man, because he had the capacity to project the "I" into the "thou"; and to be concerned about his brother. Now you know, we use our imagination a great deal to try to determine why the priest and the Levite didn't stop. At times we say they were busy going to church meetings—an ecclesiastical gathering—and they had to get on down to Jerusalem so they wouldn't be late for their meeting. At other times we would speculate that there was a religious law that "One who was engaged in religious ceremonials was not to touch a human body twenty-four hours before the ceremony." And every now and then we begin to wonder whether maybe they were not going down to Jerusalem, or down to Jericho, rather to organize a "Jericho Road Improvement Association." That's a possibility. Maybe they felt that it was better to deal with the problem from the causal root, rather than to get bogged down with an individual effort.

But I'm going to tell you what my imagination tells me. It's possible that these men were afraid. You see, the Jericho road is a dangerous road. I remember when Mrs. King and I were first in Jerusalem. We rented a car and drove from Jerusalem down to Jericho. And as soon as we got on that road, I said to my wife, "I can see why Jesus used this as a setting for his parable." It's a winding, meandering road. It's really conducive for ambushing. You start out in Jerusalem, which is about 1200 miles, or rather 1200 feet above sea level. And by the time you get down to Jericho, fifteen or twenty minutes later, you're about 2200 feet below sea level. That's a dangerous road. In the days of Jesus it came to be known as the "Bloody pass." And you know, it's possible that the priest and the Levite looked over that man on the ground and wondered if the robbers were still around. Or it's possible that they felt that the man on the ground was merely faking. And he was acting like he had been robbed and hurt, in order to seize them over there, lure them there for quick and easy seizure. And so the first question that the Levite asked was, "If I stop to help this man, what will happen to me?" But then the Good Samaritan came by. And he reversed the question: "If I do not stop to help this man, what will happen to him?"

That's the question before you tonight. Not, "If I stop to help the sanitation workers, what will happen to all of the hours that I usually spend in my office every day and every week as a pastor?" The question is not, "If I stop to help this man in need, what will happen to me?" "If I do not stop to help the sanitation workers, what will happen to them?" That's the question.

Let us rise up tonight with a greater readiness. Let us stand with a greater determination. And let us move on in these powerful days, these days of challenge to make America what it ought to be. We have an opportunity to make America a better nation. And I want to thank God, once more, for allowing me to be here with you.

You know, several years ago, I was in New York City autographing the first book that I had written. And while sitting there autographing books, a demented black woman came up. The only question I heard from her was, "Are you Martin Luther King?"

And I was looking down writing, and I said yes. And the next minute I felt something beating on my chest. Before I knew it I had been stabbed by this demented woman. I was rushed to Harlem Hospital. It was a dark Saturday afternoon. And that blade had gone through, and the X-rays revealed that the tip of the blade was on the edge of my aorta, the main artery. And once that's punctured, you drown in your own blood—that's the end of you.

It came out in the *New York Times* the next morning, that if I had sneezed, I would have died. Well, about four days later, they allowed me, after the operation, after my chest had been opened, and the blade had been taken out, to move around in the wheel chair in the hospital. They allowed me to read some of the mail that came in, and from all over the states, and the world, kind letters came in. I read a few, but one of them I will never forget. I had received one from the President and the Vice-President. I've forgotten what those telegrams said. I'd received a visit and a letter from the Governor of New York, but I've forgotten what the letter said. But there was another letter that came from a little girl, a young girl who was a student at the White Plains High School. And I looked at that letter, and I'll never forget it. It said simply, "Dear Dr. King: I am a ninth-grade student at the White Plains High School." She said, "While it should not matter, I would like to mention that I am a white girl. I read in the paper of your misfortune, and of your suffering. And I read that if you had sneezed, you would have died. And I'm simply writing you to say that I'm so happy that you didn't sneeze."

And I want to say tonight, I want to say that I am happy that I didn't sneeze. Because if I had sneezed, I wouldn't have been around here in 1960, when students all over the South started sitting-in at lunch counters. And I knew that as they were sitting in, they were really standing up for the best in the American dream. And taking the whole nation back to those great wells of democracy which were dug deep by the Founding Fathers in the Declaration of Independence and the Constitution. If I had sneezed, I wouldn't have been around in 1962, when Negroes in Albany, Georgia, decided to straighten their backs up. And whenever men and women straighten their backs up, they are going somewhere, because a man can't ride your back unless it is bent. If I had sneezed, I wouldn't have been here in 1963, when the black people of Birmingham, Alabama, aroused the conscience of this nation, and brought into being the Civil Rights Bill. If I had sneezed, I wouldn't have had a chance later that year, in August, to try to tell America about a dream that I had had. If I had sneezed, I wouldn't have been down in Selma, Alabama, to see the great movement there. If I had sneezed, I wouldn't have been in Memphis to see the community rally around those brothers and sisters who are suffering. I'm so happy that I didn't sneeze.

And they were telling me, now it doesn't matter now. It really doesn't matter what happens now. I left Atlanta this morning, and as we got started on the plane, there were six of us, the pilot said over the public address system, "We are sorry for the delay, but we have Dr. Martin Luther King on the plane. And to be sure that all of the bags were checked, and to be sure that nothing would be wrong with the plane, we had to check out everything carefully. And we've had the plane protected and guarded all night."

And then I got into Memphis. And some began to say the threats, or talk about the threats that were out. What would happen to me from some of our sick white brothers?

Well, I don't know what will happen now. We've got some difficult days ahead. But it doesn't matter with me now. Because I've been to the mountaintop. And I don't mind. Like anybody, I would like to live a long life. Longevity has its place. But I'm not concerned about that now. I just want to do God's will. And He's allowed me to go up to the mountain. And I've looked over. And I've seen the promised land. I may not get there with you. But I want you to know tonight, that we, as a people, will get to the promised land. And I'm happy, tonight. I'm not worried about anything. I'm not fearing any man. Mine eyes have seen the glory of the coming of the Lord.

> Delivered at the Bishop Charles Mason Temple, Church
> of God in Christ, Memphis, Tennessee, April 3, 1968.

ACKNOWLEDGMENTS

The fundamental aim of this book is to keep alive the memory of the radical love and prophetic legacy of Martin Luther King, Jr. I first encountered this love and legacy in my precious family: Clifton and Irene West (parents), Clifton, Cynthia, and Cheryl (siblings), and, later, my wonderful children, Clifton and Dilan Zeytun; grandson Kalen West; and great-granddaughter Kennedy Courtney West. My home church, Shiloh Baptist Church in Sacramento, California, led by the legendary Rev. Willie P. Cooke, extended my deep family love into the community. Great teachers at Harvard and Princeton—such as Martin Kilson and Preston Williams, Hilary Putnam and Stanley Cavell, John Rawls and Israel Scheffler, Sheldon Wolin and Richard Rorty—deepened this love and legacy. Magnificent students and colleagues at Union Theological Seminary, Yale Divinity School, Princeton University, and Harvard University helped sustain this love and legacy. And brilliant students in prisons in Ossining and Stormville, New York, as well as in Rahway, Bordentown, and Trenton, New Jersey—such as Dr. Anthony Edwards, Russell Owen, Anton Henshaw, and Dameon Stackhouse—enacted this love and legacy. The towering scholar of Martin Luther King, Jr., and the Black Church—James Melvin Washington (the best friend I've ever had)—exemplified this great help and support for me.

The idea of this book came from my dear sisters at Beacon Press, especially executive editor Gayatri Patnaik, encouraged by the visionary director, Helene Atwan. They conceived this text as a second work in a trilogy—preceded by *Black Prophetic Fire* and to be followed by *Justice Matters*. I'm additionally grateful to others at Beacon Press, including Tom Hallock, Pamela MacColl, Joanna Green, Caitlin Meyer, and Rachael Marks. The wise counsel and professional support of Maria Cole greatly aided this work. And the miraculous experience of knowing Christine Passarella—immersed in the radical love and prophetic legacy of John Coltrane—enables and empowers me.

I dedicate this book—the most important in my corpus—to the most King-like, Coltrane-like, and Christ-like person I know: my blood brother Clifton West.

NOTES

Where indicated, we have included the original notes from Dr. King's writings.

INTRODUCTION: THE RADICAL KING WE DON'T KNOW

1. Quoted in Michael Eric Dyson, *I May Not Get There with You: The True Martin Luther King, Jr.* (New York: Simon & Schuster, 2000), 88.
2. Martin Luther King, Jr., "Beyond Vietnam," delivered at Riverside Church, New York, April 4, 1967.
3. Per a May 22, 1967, Harris poll.
4. Quoted in James H. Cone, *Martin & Malcolm & America: A Dream or a Nightmare* (Maryknoll, NY: Orbis Books, 1991), 239.
5. Quoted in David J. Garrow, *Bearing the Cross* (New York: HarperCollins, 1986), 622.
6. "Conversation with Martin Luther King," *Conservative Judaism* XXII, no. 3 (Spring 1968).
7. Quoted in Garrow, *Bearing the Cross*, 580.
8. Based on author's conversations with Harry Belafonte.
9. King, "Beyond Vietnam."
10. Quoted in Garrow, *Bearing the Cross*, 559.
11. US Bureau of the Census, *Income, Poverty, and Health Insurance Coverage in the United States: 2010*, table B-2.

PART ONE: RADICAL LOVE

1. Martin Luther King, Jr., "Pilgrimage to Nonviolence," in *Christian Century* 77 (April 13, 1960).

CHAPTER FIVE: WHAT IS YOUR LIFE'S BLUEPRINT?

1. The first part of the poem Dr. King reads is from William Cowper's "The Negro's Complaint" (1788); the second is from Isaac Watts's "False Greatness" (1706), from *Horae Lyricae*, book II.

CHAPTER SIX: THE WORLD HOUSE

[Endnotes from the original]

1. [From] Abraham Mitrie Rihbany, *Wise Men from the East and from the West,* Houghton Mifflin, 1922, 137.
2. Harper, 1944.

PART THREE: THE REVOLUTION OF NONVIOLENT RESISTANCE

1. Martin Luther King, Jr., "Conscience and the Vietnam War," *The Trumpet of Conscience* (1967; Boston: Beacon Press, 2010), 34.
2. Martin Luther King, Jr., from his speech to the Southern Christian Leadership Conference, Penn Community Center, Frogmore, SC, May 22, 1967.
3. Martin Luther King, Jr., from his closing address to the National Conference on Religion and Race, Chicago, January 17, 1963.

CHAPTER TWELVE: LETTER FROM BIRMINGHAM JAIL

1. The following from Dr. King appeared with this essay: "Author's Note: This response to a published statement by eight fellow clergymen from Alabama (Bishop C. C. J. Carpenter, Bishop Joseph A. Durick, Rabbi Hilton L. Grafman, Bishop Paul Hardin, Bishop Holan B. Harmon, the Reverend George M. Murray, the Reverend Edward V. Ramage and the Reverend Earl Stallings) was composed under somewhat constricting circumstances. Begun on the margins of the newspaper in which the statement appeared while I was in jail, the letter was continued on scraps of writing paper supplied by a friendly Negro trusty, and concluded on a pad my attorneys were eventually permitted to leave me. Although the text remains in substance unaltered, I have indulged in the author's prerogative of polishing it for publication."

CHAPTER SEVENTEEN: BLACK POWER

[Endnotes from the original]

1. Southern Regional Council, 1966.
2. Harper, 1964, 162ff.
3. Knopf, 1956.

PART FOUR: OVERCOMING THE TYRANNY OF POVERTY AND HATRED

1. US Bureau of the Census, *Income, Poverty, and Health Insurance Coverage in the United States: 2010*, table B-2.
2. Martin Luther King, Jr., "The Drum Major Instinct," sermon at the Ebenezer Baptist Church, Atlanta, February 4, 1968, text at Martin Luther King, Jr., Research and Education Institute website, Stanford University, http://mlk-kpp01 .stanford.edu/.
3. Quoted in David J. Garrow, *Bearing the Cross* (New York: HarperCollins, 1986), 22.
4. Martin Luther King, Jr., "I've Been to the Mountaintop," speech delivered at Bishop Charles Mason Temple, Memphis, April 3, 1968; text at Martin Luther King, Jr., Research and Education Institute website, Stanford University, http://mlk-kpp01.stanford.edu/.
5. Martin Luther King, Jr., letter to Coretta Scott King, from Reidsville State Prison, Tattnall County, GA, October 26, 1960, in *The Autobiography of Martin Luther King, Jr.*, Clayborne Carson, ed. (New York: IPM/Warner Books, 2001).

INDEX

296   INDEX

predominantly black colleges, 115
Price, Leontyne, 67
prison-industrial complex, xi
Progress and Poverty (George), 173
Protestant liberalism, 47

racism: cultural tradition supporting, 11–12, 52, 137, 161–62, 259;
"drum major instinct" as source
of racial prejudice, 259–60;
impact of hate on the hater and,
59–60; impact on America's
international standing, 156; as
internal threat to civilization,
83; King's call for international
alliance against, 110; moral
catastrophe of, xi; organized and
institutionalized racism in the
world, 80–82; race relations in
America and (*see* black power);
responsibilities of global institutions (*see* global institutions
and social justice); socialism
and, 232; in South Africa (*see*
South Africa); US and Britain's
complicity in world-wide racism, 81–82
Randolph, A. Philip, 194, 228
Rauschenbusch, Walter, 40
Reeb, James, 190–91
religions of the world: promotion of
peace by, 97–99; responsibilities
of Christians (*see* Christianity)
Reuther, Walter, 171, 250–51
Rhodesia, 81, 110
Ricks, Willie, 186
Rillieux, Norbert, 197
Riverside Church, New York City,
126, 201

Robinson, Jackie, 68
Robinson, James, 168
Roosevelt, Franklin D., 232

Sabarmati ashram, 29, 30
Salt March, 29–30, 44
sanitation workers strike: example
of successful nonviolence in
Birmingham, 268–69; Good Samaritan parable's relevance to,
272–73; history of the civil rights
movement and, 248–49; King on
power and, 250–51; King's advice
for the strikers, 250–51; King's
advocacy of a nonviolent approach, 268, 269; King's prediction of a judgment on America
over materialism, 248; King's
support of higher wages for
service workers, 246–47; King's
view of need to unite beyond
class lines, 246; King's view of
the dignity inherent in sanitation work, 246; opening remarks
of King's speech to, 245–46;
parable about wealth in King's
speech, 247–48; potential of
economic power against oppression and, 270–71; preachers role
in the strikers' struggle, 269–70;
struggle for economic equality
and, 249–50
Satyagraha, 44, 158–59
SCLC. *See* Southern Christian
Leadership Conference
Scott, C. A., 16
Scott, Obie, 12
Sealtest, 166–67
Seay, S. S., 8

—THE—
KING
LEGACY

THE KING LEGACY SERIES

In partnership with the Estate of Dr. Martin Luther King, Jr., Beacon Press is proud to share the great privilege and responsibility of furthering Dr. King's powerful message of peace, nonviolence, and social justice with a historic publishing program—the King Legacy.

The series encompasses Dr. King's most important writings, including sermons, orations, lectures, prayers, and all of his previously published books that were out of print. Beacon Press has worked with leading scholars and civil rights activists, delving into archives and transcribing audio, to create entirely new books. Published accessibly and in multiple formats, each volume includes new material from acclaimed scholars, activists, and religious leaders underscoring Dr. King's continued relevance for the twenty-first century and bringing his message to a new generation of readers.

Clayborne Carson is general editorial advisor to the King Legacy and is director of the Martin Luther King, Jr. Research and Education Institute at Stanford University.

thekinglegacy.org

Library of Congress Cataloging-in-Publication Data

King, Martin Luther, Jr., 1929–1968.
 [Works. Selections]
 The radical King / Martin Luther King, Jr. ; edited and introduced by
Cornel West.
     pages cm. — (King legacy series)
 Includes bibliographical references and index.
 ISBN 978-0-8070-1282-6 (hardcover : alk. paper) — ISBN 978-0-8070-1283-3
(ebook) 1. King, Martin Luther, Jr., 1929–1968—Political and social views.
2. King, Martin Luther, Jr., 1929–1968—Philosophy. I. West, Cornel, editor.
II. Title.
 E185.97.K5A5 2014
 323.092—dc23   2014022515